Managing an Age Diverse Workforce

# Managing an Age Diverse Workforce

Edited by

Emma Parry

and

Shaun Tyson

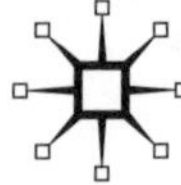



First published 2011 by
PALGRAVE MACMILLAN

Palgrave Macmillan in the UK is an imprint of Macmillan Publishers Limited, registered in England, company number 785998, of Houndmills, Basingstoke, Hampshire RG21 6XS.

Palgrave Macmillan in the US is a division of St Martin's Press LLC, 175 Fifth Avenue, New York, NY 10010.

Palgrave Macmillan is the global academic imprint of the above companies and has companies and representatives throughout the world.

Palgrave® and Macmillan® are registered trademarks in the United States, the United Kingdom, Europe and other countries.

ISBN 978–0–230–24093–3 hardback

This book is printed on paper suitable for recycling and made from fully managed and sustained forest sources. Logging, pulping and manufacturing processes are expected to conform to the environmental regulations of the country of origin.

A catalogue record for this book is available from the British Library.

Library of Congress Cataloging-in-Publication Data

Managing an age diverse workforce / edited by Emma Parry and Shaun Tyson.
p. cm.
Includes bibliographical references.
ISBN 978–0–230–24093–3 (alk. paper)
1. Diversity in the workplace—Management. 2. Conflict of generations in the workplace—Management. 3. Intergenerational relations. 4. Older people—Employment. 5. Youth—Employment.
I. Parry, Emma. II. Tyson, Shaun
HF5549.5.C75M36 2010
658.30084—dc22 2010034189

10 9 8 7 6 5 4 3 2 1
20 19 18 17 16 15 14 13 12 11

Printed and bound in Great Britain by
CPI Antony Rowe, Chippenham and Eastbourne

# Contents

# List of Figures

# List of Tables

# About the Editors

Dr **Emma Parry** is a Principal Research Fellow at Cranfield School of Management. Her research interests include managing an ageing workforce, generational diversity, e-HRM and HRM in the voluntary sector. Emma earned her BSc (Hons) in Psychology from London Guildhall University in 1993 and her MSc and Ph.D. in Applied (Occupational) Psychology from Cranfield University in 1996 and 2001 respectively. Emma has conducted a considerable amount of research looking at the ageing workforce including a number of CIPD-commissioned projects regarding 'Age and Recruitment', 'Total Rewards for an Ageing Workforce' and 'The Impact of Generational Diversity on People Management'. Emma is a member of the '5C' global academic collaboration examining career success and career transitions across cultures and generations, and a member of the global team for the Center of Aging and Work at Boston College, USA. Emma is the author of numerous publications and conference papers in the field of HRM, including several in the area of managing an ageing workforce.

**Shaun Tyson** is Emeritus Professor of Human Resource Management, Cranfield University. He was awarded a Ph.D. from London School of Economics, and is a Fellow of the Chartered Institute of Personnel and Development. He is also a member of the Association Française de Gestion des Ressources Humaines, and was a Visiting Professor at the University of Paris for five years. He is currently a visiting professor at the University of Westminster. He spent 11 years working as a senior HR practitioner in retail and manufacturing industries, and five years in the public sector. For 20 years he was the Director of the Human Resource Research Centre at Cranfield School of Management. He has written 20 books on human resource management, industrial relations and organisational behaviour, and has published extensively on human resource strategy and policies. He has carried out consultancy assignments and research with a wide range of public sector and private sector organisations in the UK and abroad, including a number of research projects concerned with age discrimination and diversity. He currently chairs the Remuneration Committee of the Law Society.

# Notes on Contributors

**Vanessa Beck** is a Lecturer in Employment Studies at the Centre for Labour Market Studies, University of Leicester.

**Dianne Bown-Wilson** is a consultant in age management and a Doctoral Researcher at Cranfield School of Management.

**Melissa Brown** is a Research Assistant at the Sloan Center on Aging & Work and a doctoral candidate in the School of Social Work at Boston College.

**Donna Buttigieg** an Associate Professor in the Department of Management at Monash University.

**Fiona Carmichael** is Reader in Industrial and Labour Economics at the University of Birmingham.

**Alan Felstead** is Research Professor at the School of Social Sciences, Cardiff University.

**Matt Flynn** is a Senior Lecturer in Human Resource Management at Middlesex University Business School.

**Sarah Harper** is Professor of Gerontology at the University of Oxford and Director of the Oxford Institute of Ageing.

**Jonathan Herring** is a Fellow in Law at Exeter College, University of Oxford.

**Masa Higo** a Research Associate at Sloan Center on Aging & Work at Boston College.

**Claire Hulme** is a Lecturer in Health Economics at the Academic Unit of Health Economics, Leeds Institute of Health Sciences, University of Leeds.

**Barbara Ingham** is Reader in Economics at the University of Salford.

**Jungui Lee** a research associate at Sloan Center on Aging & Work at Boston College.

**Wendy Loretto** is Senior Lecturer in Organisation Studies at the University of Edinburgh Business School.

**Christina Matz-Costa**, MSW, is the Associate Director of Research at the Sloan Center on Aging & Work at Boston College and a Ph.D. candidate in the Boston College Graduate School of Social Work.

**Wolfgang Mayrhofer** is Professor of Management at Vienna University of Economics and Business.

**Michael Müller-Camen** is a Professor of International Human Resource Management at Middlesex University Business School.

**Odd Nordhaug** is a Professor in Administrative Science at the Norwegian School of Economics and Business Administration.

**Carlos Obeso** is a Professor in Personnel Management at ESADE-Barcelona.

**Emma Parry** is a Principal Research Fellow in Human Resource Management at Cranfield School of Management, and a co-editor of the present collection.

**Marcie Pitt-Catsouphes** directs the Sloan Center on Aging & Work at Boston College, where she is Associate Professor at the Graduate School of Social Work, with an appointment at the Carroll School of Management. She is a visiting professor at Middlesex University in the UK.

**Lorna Porcellato** is a Senior Lecturer in Public Health, Faculty of Health and Applied Social Sciences at Liverpool John Moore's University.

**Arvin Prashar** is a Research Fellow at the University of Salford.

**Kat Riach** is a lecturer in Management at Essex Business School, University of Essex.

**Heike Schroeder** is a Ph.D. candidate in Human Resource Management at Middlesex University Business School.

**Shaun Tyson** is Emeritus Professor in Human Resource Management at Cranfield School of Management, and a co-editor of the present collection.

**Peter Urwin** is Professor of Applied Economics at the University of Westminster and Director of the Centre for Employment Research at the Westminster Business School.

**Sarah Vickerstaff** is Professor of Work and Employment at the School of Social Policy, Sociology and Social Research at the University of Kent.

# Acknowledgements

The editors would like to thank our contributors for providing such insightful and thought-provoking chapters. Without them, this volume would have been impossible. In addition, we would like to thank Jean Hutton, Alison Cain and Jayne Ashley for their practical, and at times psychological, support in putting this book together; and also our publisher, Palgrave Macmillan, for helping us to bring this project to the market place.

# 1
# Introduction

*Emma Parry and Shaun Tyson*

A majority of the population being over 50 years of age is a new prospect for organisations around the world, where there will be greater diversity in ages, lifestyles and personal circumstances among employees than at any time in the past. We see this as a timely moment, perhaps even a strategic inflection point, when all those interested in the management of people might take new bearings and consider what this kind of major social change means.

The challenge for our society is how to reconceptualise age and work and to change attitudes that are embedded in our relationships. This comes at a time when the impact of a world recession, the worst in the United Kingdom and the USA since the Second World War, has put even more pressure on the need to manage organisations effectively, with consequential cost reductions, redundancies, pay cuts and restructuring in the public and the private sectors. Often it is the most vulnerable people who suffer most from the recession. There are in many countries already lower employment participation rates, and there is substantial unemployment among the young and the older members of the workforce, yet at this time managers have to rethink management processes and to keep cost criteria at the centre of their attention. Age discrimination legislation has now entered the statutes of all European Community Member States, having already become a part of employment law in many other countries, including the USA, Canada, Australia and New Zealand.

As a shorthand for the human condition of having lived for a particular number of years, age carries with it the important symbols by which the stages of life are often measured, famously described by Shakespeare in *As You Like It* as the seven ages of man. Although age symbolises the temporal aspect of our lives, the stages we move through are extremely varied, and life chances are not equal. However, age is only one ingredient in the establishment of a sense of self. For example, Søren Kierkegaard, a nineteenth-century Danish philosopher, saw existence as the meeting point of time and eternity (Grimsley 1973). His philosophy suggests our existence is to be constantly striving, a dynamic process which continues over time, a kind of moral career alongside our actual career, an inner, individual debate which continues while physical temporal changes occur, in which we have to resolve the issue of coming to terms with eternity by making individual choices. From this perspective, life is not predetermined by our age; rather, we are free to make decisions at any physical stage of our existence, although there are constant tensions between the aesthetic and the moral. This reminds us that people are always striving for some new equilibrium, and that our work lives are only one aspect of our identity. The young and the old alike are engaged on a wider journey through life.

Our sense of self is, however, not just a matter for the individual. We are also given a sense of identity by our relationships, in which our age plays an important part (Mead 1934). It is hardly surprising, therefore, that there are strong common perceptions of what values, attitudes and behaviours are appropriate for different ages. Some of these stereotypes can be found in the literature on generational differences. Stereotyping is shorthand for discounting all other aspects of an individual's existence and presenting the person as a single, undifferentiated set of commonly believed attributes. For example: 'The old believe everything; the middle-aged suspect everything; the young know everything' (Oscar Wilde 1894) in his witty satire of the tendency to generalise about age).

The belief grows in these generalisations, so that these preconceptions become gradually institutionalised in the formal ways in which the state provides rules for the different ages (for example, ages for schooling, marriage and pensions). This then creates a sense in which it is normal to treat people differently according to their age, irrespective of the reality of their capabilities, health, experience, knowledge and values, and their own stage of personal development or maturity. Age discrimination is similar to other forms of discrimination in this regard.

Another aspect of discrimination is that it tends to be directed against the seemingly vulnerable and powerless. Young people often feel discriminated against in employment, housing, mortgages and status. Older people have long experienced exclusion, with lower incomes, housing inequalities and a poor quality of life for many, as well as the burdens of illness and loneliness. Many of these problems, like those of younger people, can be related to unemployment, low incomes or the low quality of working life (Cann and Dean 2009).

However, the demographic changes and economic pressures are already shifting the balance of power. Recession aside, the need for talented people even in this period is such that selection is becoming related more to candidates' ability to meet job demands than to age, for young and old alike. Older people have more power to influence parliamentary elections and therefore the promises in the party manifestos. The importance of training is now more emphasised as a route out of unemployment as a result of the recession; and senior managers, professional journals and the press pay more attention to ideas about developing human capital. Anti-age discrimination legislation has no doubt also encouraged more rational selection and training policies.

The management of age-diverse organisations poses many challenges and possibilities, which we explore in this book. The subject is necessarily eclectic, and we are not purely concerned with the formal legislative requirements. Rather, we are interested in exploring all those institutionalised organisational processes that relate to age, including attitudes towards employing people of different age groups and the experiences of the workers themselves. We also believe that there is a strong case to be made that an age-diverse workforce brings economic benefits to organisations. These include the capacity to market products to society as a whole, to strengthen the brand and the brand values through inclusivity, and to bring in talent from across the age spectrum. There are other implications for all the human resources policy areas, including recruitment, selection, development and reward, as well as those relating to the broader business strategy.

Age diversity is related to other forms of diversity. This collection therefore includes contributions that examine the relationship of age diversity to other areas of diversity, such as gender, and the cross-cutting issues this raises. Age discrimination is a topic of international relevance; the demographic profiles of countries such as Japan, the USA and Germany provide interesting examples for comparison.

Only a group of authors would do justice to this range of topics; hence our decision to produce an edited collection. All the contributors have taken as their starting point the questions about managing an age-diverse workforce which relate to the topics in which they engage as significant scholars in the field, and which we have alluded to here.

We have put together this book with a range of readers in mind: academics with an interest in age diversity from the fields of human resource management or employee relations, postgraduate students, and also the thinking practitioner: human resource, diversity or general managers looking for insights into the issues involved in managing an age-diverse workforce. The book will also have international appeal as we have taken care to provide comparisons between countries and to include contributions from authors from the USA, Australia and across Europe, as well as from the United Kingdom.

In order to ensure that the book is coherent and easy to follow, we have grouped the chapters into five parts. Part I examines the reasons why managing age diversity may be important to employers and individuals, through an analysis of the business case for creating an age-diverse workforce and the legislation on age discrimination. Part II looks at the concept of age diversity and age itself in more detail, by focusing on the nature of diversity and age diversity in particular, and its relationship to another area of diversity – gender. We then examine the concept of age as a multifaceted construct before focusing on an interpretation of age as a categorical variable, that of generations. Part III adopts the perspective of the employees themselves, through an analysis of employees' experiences of ageism, the motivation of older workers and then the preferences of younger workers. Part IV takes an employer perspective, focusing more on the practices that may be used to manage older workers in particular, through a discussion of the extension of working life, training and learning in older workers and the management of potential health issues that affect them. Finally, Part V adopts an international comparative perspective, looking at the impact of national context on age diversity. In this part we compare first the United Kingdom and Germany and then the USA and Japan.

Our goals are to provide a relatively comprehensive overview of the issues inherent in managing an age-diverse workforce, and, we hope, to encourage thereby academics and practitioners to develop their understanding of, and to give further thought to, research and practice in this varied and interesting field.

# Part I
# The Importance of Age Diversity

Before we discuss the nature of an ageing workforce and its impact on employees or employers, we should establish why it is important to eliminate age discrimination and to promote age diversity in the workforce. The first part of this book examines two reasons why an employer may decide to introduce policies or practices for age management. First, employers are usually encouraged to adopt age-management practices because they have developed a sound business case, so it is in their interests to do so; and second, they are forced to adopt specific policies by the introduction of legislation.

In Chapter 2 Donna Buttigieg examines the business case for age diversity from three perspectives: that of society in general, that of the employer or organisation and that of the individual or employee. This chapter seeks to establish why there are sound business reasons to consider and promote age diversity in the workplace.

In Chapter 3 Jonathan Herring examines age discrimination from a legal perspective. This chapter has a focus on the legislation introduced in 2006 against age discrimination in Great Britain and considers the efficacy of this legislation in removing age discrimination at work, citing appropriate cases. In addition, this chapter considers what we may learn from age-discrimination legislation in other countries.

# 2
# The Business Case for an Age-diverse Workforce

*Donna Buttigieg*

There is an imperative for organisations to deal with the issue of age diversity in the context of an ageing population, declining fertility rates, a decline in skilled immigration and skill shortages in a range of occupations in countries covered by the Organisation for Economic Co-operation and Development (OECD). This raises both macro issues for governments trying to support an increasingly older population through pension schemes and a micro problem for organisations where skill shortages have become a problem (Loretto and White 2006). Further, arguments have been made that age diversity is necessary for organisations for capability development, to be learning organisations, to be flexible and creative and for marketing reasons (Armstrong-Stassen and Templer 2006; Shacklock, Fulop and Hort 2007). There are also supply-side reasons for improving access to the labour market of an age-diverse workforce, particularly in relation to those older than 55 years of age. These include providing a context for healthy ageing and addressing flexibility preferences for individuals.

This chapter examines the business case for age diversity at the workplace. It is clear that there is a need for greater age diversity and that this diversity needs to be managed. This is because, in spite of the benefits at the macro and micro levels, the theoretical and empirical literature suggests that diversity at the workplace can have negative effects on organisational outcomes if not managed properly. As a consequence, diversity management (Cox and Blake 1991) as well as a coordinated approach from government regarding policy surrounding superannuation (pensions) and retirement conditions are important.

In the first section of the chapter we examine the demographic time bomb that is affecting many countries, particularly in the OECD. The second section examines the benefits of age diversity to organisations before exploring the benefits to individuals. The chapter concludes with some final thoughts on the issue of ageing workers and participation.

## 2.1 Demographic changes to populations

Older workers can be defined as individuals over the age of 55 years. This is the median retiring age for Australian workers and is a common definition across countries (Patrickson and Ranzijn 2004). OECD (2009) figures suggest that the proportion of the population over the age of 65 is increasing. Aggregate figures for the ratio of older workers to the total population have increased from 13 per cent to a projected figure of 25.7 per cent in 2050. This has created a projected crisis in terms of labour force participation with the ratio of inactive elderly to the total labour force from 27.2 per cent participation to 62.3 per cent.

Tables 2.1 and 2.2 outline the problem in more detail for OECD and some non-OECD countries. The ratio of population aged 65 and over to total population increased for most countries from 1970 to 2007. Germany and Japan have the greatest problems with ratios of 19.9 and 21.5, respectively (see Chapters 14 and 15 for more information on these countries).

In this context, raising employment rates of over-55s is an imperative. For most countries, employment rates of over-55 year olds rose between 1970 and 2007. The OECD average participation rates increased from 47.8 per cent in 1970 to 53.7 per cent in 2007. The highest rates of participation are in Iceland at 84.9 per cent and New Zealand at 72 per cent. Australia, the United States and the United Kingdom have similar rates of 56.7, 61.8 and 57.4 per cent, respectively. These data, taken in combination with the data in Tables 2.3 and 2.4, suggest a sound case for increasing the proportion of older workers in the workplace. Population growth rates in OECD countries decreased for most countries between 1970 and 2007, as did net migration and fertility rates (in 2006). The OECD average population growth rate decreased from .85 to .68 and fertility rates per 1000 inhabitants from 2.7 to 1.7.

## 2.2 Macro benefits to governments and society for age diversity

Emerging from these demographic changes are two macro problems for governments. The first relates to an increasingly older population that needs to be supported (Burtless and Quinn 2001). In 2006 public expenditure on pensions as a proportion of GDP in OECD countries

*Table 2.1* Population ratios and employment rates of older people in OECD countries, 1970–2007 %

| | Ratio of population aged 65 and over to total population 1970 | Ratio of population aged 65 and over to total population 1990 | Ratio of population aged 65 and over to total population 2007 | Percentage of population aged 55–64 in employment 1970 | Percentage of population aged 55–64 in employment 1990 | Percentage of population aged 55–64 in employment 2007 |
|---|---|---|---|---|---|---|
| Australia | 8.3 | 11.1 | 13.2 | | 41.5 | 56.7 |
| Austria | 14.1 | 14.9 | 17 | | | 38.6 |
| Belgium | 13.4 | 14.9 | 17.1 | | 21.4 | 33.8 |
| Canada | 7.9 | 11.3 | 13.4 | | 46.2 | 57.1 |
| Czech Republic | 12.1 | 12.5 | 14.5 | | | 46 |
| Denmark | 12.3 | 15.6 | 15.5 | | 53.6 | 58.7 |
| Finland | 9.2 | 13.4 | 16.5 | 56.8 | 42.8 | 55 |
| France | 12.9 | 14 | 16.5 | 55.5 | 35.6 | 38.3 |
| Germany | 13.7 | 14.9 | 19.9 | 49.6 | 36.8 | 51.3 |
| Greece | 11.1 | 13.8 | 18.6 | | 40.8 | 42.1 |
| Hungary | 11.6 | 13.3 | 16.1 | | | 33.1 |
| Iceland | 8.8 | 10.6 | 11.5 | | | 84.9 |
| Ireland | 11.1 | 11.4 | 10.8 | | 38.6 | 54.1 |
| Italy | 10.9 | 14.9 | 20 | 28.6 | 32.6 | 33.8 |
| Japan | 7.1 | 12.1 | 21.5 | 63.3 | 62.9 | 66.1 |
| Korea | 3.1 | 5.1 | 9.9 | | 61.9 | 60.6 |
| Luxembourg | 12.5 | 13.4 | 14 | | 28.2 | 34.3 |
| Mexico | 4.6 | 4.1 | 5.5 | | | 54.7 |
| Netherlands | 10.2 | 12.8 | 14.6 | | 29.7 | 50.1 |

*(continued)*

Table 2.1 Continued

| | Ratio of population aged 65 and over to total population 1970 | Ratio of population aged 65 and over to total population 1990 | Ratio of population aged 65 and over to total population 2007 | Percentage of population aged 55–64 in employment 1970 | Percentage of population aged 55–64 in employment 1990 | Percentage of population aged 55–64 in employment 2007 |
|---|---|---|---|---|---|---|
| New Zealand | 8.4 | 11.2 | 12.5 | | 41.8 | 72 |
| Norway | 12.9 | 16.3 | 14.6 | | 61.5 | 69 |
| Poland | 8.4 | 10.1 | 13.4 | | | 29.7 |
| Portugal | 9.4 | 13.4 | 17.3 | | 47 | 50.9 |
| Slovak Republic | 9.2 | 10.3 | 11.9 | | | 35.7 |
| Spain | 9.6 | 13.6 | 16.6 | | 36.9 | 44.6 |
| Sweden | 13.7 | 17.8 | 17.4 | 63.7 | 69.5 | 70.1 |
| Switzerland | 11.4 | 14.6 | 16.3 | | | 67.2 |
| Turkey | 4.4 | 4.4 | 6 | | 42.7 | 29.4 |
| United Kingdom | 12.8 | 15.7 | 16 | | 49.2 | 57.4 |
| United States | 9.8 | 12.5 | 12.6 | 60.1 | 48 | 61.8 |
| OECD Average | 9.6 | 11.7 | 14.2 | 53.9 | 47.8 | 53.7 |

*Source*: OECD (2010).

*Table 2.2* Population ratios and employment rates of older people in selected non-OECD countries, 1970–2007

| | Ratio of population aged 65 and over to total population 1970 | Ratio of population aged 65 and over to total population 1990 | Ratio of population aged 65 and over to total population 2007 | Percentage of population aged 55–64 in employment 1970 | Percentage of population aged 55–64 in employment 1990 | Percentage of population aged 55–64 in employment 2007 |
|---|---|---|---|---|---|---|
| Brazil | 3.6 | 4.4 | 6.3 | | | 53.7 |
| Chile | 5 | 6.1 | 8.5 | | | 55.6 |
| China | 4.3 | 5.4 | 7.9 | | | 66.5 |
| Estonia | 11.7 | 11.6 | 17.1 | | 60.4 | 59.5 |
| India | 3.3 | 3.9 | 5.1 | | 48.5 | |
| Israel | 6.7 | 9.1 | 10.1 | | | 57.2 |
| Russian Federation | 7.7 | 10 | 13.4 | | | 51.1 |
| Slovenia | 9.9 | 10.7 | 16 | | | 33.4 |
| South Africa | 3.4 | 3.2 | 4.5 | | | |

*Source*: OECD (2008).

*Table 2.3* Population growth rates, net migration rates and fertility rates in OECD countries, 1970–2007 (%)

| | Population growth rate 1970 | Population growth rate 1990 | Population growth rate 2007 | Net migration rate 1970 | Net migration rate 1990 | Net migration rate 2007 | Fertility rate 1970 | Fertility rate 2007 |
|---|---|---|---|---|---|---|---|---|
| Australia | 1.99 | 1.49 | 1.53 | 8.9 | 7.3 | .. | 2.9 | 1.8 |
| Austria | 0.35 | 0.76 | 0.4 | 1.5 | 7.6 | 4 | 2.3 | 1.4 |
| Belgium | 0.1 | 0.3 | 0.74 | 0.9 | 3 | .. | 2.3 | 1.8 |
| Canada | 1.43 | 1.52 | 1 | 3.1 | 6.5 | .. | 2.3 | 1.5 |
| Czech Republic | –0.92 | – | 0.55 | –0.4 | 0.1 | 8.1 | 1.9 | 1.3 |
| Denmark | 0.75 | 0.16 | 0.42 | 2.4 | 1.6 | 4.2 | 2.0 | 1.9 |
| Finland | –0.38 | 0.44 | 0.43 | –7.8 | 1.4 | 2.5 | 1.8 | 1.8 |
| France | 0.9 | 0.51 | 0.58 | 3.5 | 1.4 | 1.1 | 2.5 | 2.0 |
| Germany | 0.33 | 0.87 | –0.16 | 9.3 | 16.3 | 0.5 | 2.0 | 1.3 |
| Greece | 0.23 | 0.7 | 0.4 | –4.4 | 6.3 | .. | 2.4 | 1.4 |
| Hungary | 0.38 | –1.03 | –0.21 | –0.2 | 1.7 | 1.4 | 2.0 | 1.4 |
| Iceland | 0.58 | 0.81 | 2.32 | –7.3 | –3.9 | 12.6 | 2.8 | 2.1 |
| Ireland | 0.84 | –0.11 | 2.34 | –1 | –2.2 | .. | 3.9 | 1.9 |
| Italy | 0.53 | 0.08 | 0.69 | –0.9 | 0.2 | .. | 2.4 | 1.4 |
| Japan | 1.13 | 0.33 | – | –0.1 | – | .. | 2.1 | 1.3 |
| Korea | 2.21 | 0.99 | 0.33 | – | – | – | 4.5 | 1.1 |
| Luxembourg | 0.67 | 1.26 | 1.56 | 2.9 | 10.2 | 12.5 | 2.0 | 1.6 |
| Mexico | 0.76 | 1.96 | 0.87 | – | – | – | 6.8 | 2.2 |
| Netherlands | 1.25 | 0.69 | 0.22 | 2.5 | 4 | 1.6 | 2.6 | 1.7 |
| New Zealand | 1.42 | 0.97 | 1.04 | 0.3 | 2.7 | 1.4 | 3.2 | 2.0 |
| Norway | 0.73 | 0.34 | 1.04 | –0.3 | 0.5 | 8.5 | 2.5 | 1.9 |

| | | | | | | | | |
|---|---|---|---|---|---|---|---|---|
| Poland | 0.27 | 0.18 | –0.04 | –0.4 | –0.4 | –0.5 | 2.2 | 1.3 |
| Portugal | –0.88 | –0.22 | 0.23 | –16.5 | –3.9 | – | 2.8 | 1.4 |
| Slovak Republic | 0.21 | 0.41 | 0.12 | –1 | –0.4 | 1.3 | 2.4 | 1.2 |
| Spain | 0.93 | 0.15 | 1.83 | –0.4 | 0.9 | 16 | 2.9 | 1.4 |
| Sweden | 0.94 | 0.78 | 0.74 | 6.1 | 4.1 | 5.9 | 1.9 | 1.9 |
| Switzerland | 0.73 | 0.98 | 0.88 | –2.9 | 8.4 | 0.9 | 2.1 | 1.4 |
| Turkey | 2.54 | 2.3 | 1.24 | .. | 1.8 | – | 5 | 2.2 |
| United Kingdom | 0.32 | 0.28 | 0.64 | –0.3 | 1.2 | .. | 2.4 | 1.8 |
| United States | 1.17 | 1.14 | 0.96 | 2.1 | 3.1 | 3.4 | 2.5 | 2.1 |
| OECD Average | 0.92 | 0.85 | 0.68 | | | | 2.7 | 1.7 |

*Source*: OECD (2010).
*Notes*: Population growth rates are annual percentage growth. Net migration rates are per 1,000 inhabitants. Fertility rates are number of children born to women aged 15–49.

*Table 2.4* Population growth rates, net migration rates and fertility rates in selected non-OECD countries, 1970–2007

| | Population growth rates 1970 | Population growth rates 1990 | Population growth rates 2007 | Net migration rate 1970 | Net migration rate 1990 | Net migration rate 2007 | Fertility rates 1970 | Fertility rates 2006 |
|---|---|---|---|---|---|---|---|---|
| Brazil | 2.51 | 1.8 | 1.37 | | | | | 2.3 |
| Chile | 1.89 | 1.78 | 1.03 | | 1.3 | | 4.0 | 2.0 |
| China | 2.59 | 1.39 | 0.59 | | | | 5.8 | 1.8 |
| Estonia | 0.71 | 0.07 | –0.14 | | –2.6 | | | 1.6 |
| India | 2.19 | 2.18 | 1.5 | | | | 5.8 | 2.5 |
| Israel | 2.59 | 2.66 | 1.73 | | 40.3 | 2.1 | | 2.9 |
| Russian Federation | 0.51 | 0.5 | –0.5 | | | | | 1.3 |
| Slovenia | 0.64 | –0.07 | 0.54 | | 1.1 | 7.1 | 2.1 | 1.3 |
| South Africa | 2.63 | 2.29 | 0.61 | | | | 5.7 | 2.7 |

*Source*: OECD (2010).

*Notes*: Population growth rates are annual percentage growth. Net migration rates are per 1,000 inhabitants. Fertility rates are number of children born to women aged 15–49.

varied between 1.1 per cent in Finland and 12.1 per cent in Austria. Australia's expenditure is significantly less than the United Kingdom's at 3.6 per cent compared with 7.5 per cent of the GDP (see Table 2.5). This figure is projected to increase.

The second major problem for governments is skills shortages in various industries. Unemployment has increased as a consequence of the global economic crisis that broke in 2008, although the severity is varied (ILO 2009). Further, recent outlooks for many countries are now favourable, with the International Monetary Fund claiming that the world economy is in recovery (IMF 2009). As a consequence, the issue of labour shortages may continue in a number of sectors in the OECD. In Australia, for example, unemployment has emerged more seriously in some sectors than others. The biggest impact has been in sectors such as manufacturing and banking and finance. Stimulus packages have been introduced to expand construction and education, for example, where

*Table 2.5* Public expenditure on pensions as proportion of GDP in OECD countries, 2006

| Country | % GDP |
|---|---|
| Australia | 3.6 |
| Austria | 12.1 |
| Belgium | 8.1 |
| Canada | 3.6 |
| Czech Republic | 7.2 |
| Denmark | 4.8 |
| Finland | 1.1 |
| Germany | 11.7 |
| Hungary | 8.1 |
| Iceland | 0.4 |
| Italy | 12.0 |
| Korea | 1.3 |
| Luxembourg | 4.0 |
| Mexico | 0.7 |
| Netherlands | 5.4 |
| New Zealand | 3.7 |
| Norway | 4.4 |
| Poland | 10.4 |
| Portugal | 7.5 |
| Spain | 7.8 |
| Sweden | 7.7 |
| Switzerland | 6.7 |
| United Kingdom | 7.5 |

*Source*: OECD (2010).

skills have been in short supply (Australian Labor Party 2009). In terms of education, the Australian government has made an investment in increasing the number of training places for teachers. In this instance the net effect on the economy will be unknown (Prime Minister of Australia 2009). There has also been a reduction of the intake of skilled migrants; but this is a short-term strategy, and skills shortages may still persist in the long term in the absence of reskilling of the unemployed and an ageing population (Metcalf 2009).

Skill shortages exist in many OECD and non-OECD countries. Countries such as Australia, Canada, United Kingdom and the United States have skill shortages in various occupations. Australia has shortages of chefs, tradespersons in wood and metal, building and engineering, hairdressers, food tradespersons, health professionals, building and engineering associate professionals, automotive tradespersons and computing professionals (Clarius 2010). The UK requires civil engineers, physicists, geologists, meteorologists, chemical engineers, medical practitioners, dental practitioners, veterinarians, a range of health scientists, teachers, social workers, nurses, entertainers, welders, chefs, carers, and workers in the fishing and agricultural trades (Skillclear 2009). In the United States 90 per cent of manufacturers in a survey indicated that they had moderate to severe shortages in frontline workers and 65 per cent indicated problems filling vacancies for engineers and scientists, among other occupations. There are shortages also of nurses, auto technicians, mechanics, plumbers and correctional officers (Ohio Job and Family Services 2007; Deloitte n.d.). In Canada there are shortages of managers and professionals, particularly in education and healthcare (Armstrong-Stassen 2008). Even developing countries with high populations such as China and India are experiencing some shortages in the area of managers (China) and mechanical engineers and airline pilots (India), for example (Business Week 2005; DDI 2005).

Governments have a number of options to deal with skill shortages, including skilled migration, improving the fertility rate, training, and improving the participation rates of workers who have lower participation rates, including women and older workers. As indicated earlier, migration rates have decreased in many countries, many of which focus on policies creating incentives to attempt to retain older workers in the workforce. Various governments have attempted to address this issue in terms of policy. For example, Australian governments have put in place incentives for having a baby (baby bonus) and proposed a parental-leave scheme and changes in the retirement age. Moreover, a clear strategy in many OECD countries and organisations that operate in these countries has been to increase the participation rates of older workers. Specifically, the issue has been in relation to skill shortages in particular occupations.

A third benefit for government in retaining older workers relates to the concept of healthy ageing. This involves the full integration of older workers into society as valued members, where skills are utilised and experience is considered important. Studies show that people live longer where they have purpose to their existence and, given the centrality of work to some individuals' identity, providing an option for work at later stages of life is critical for longevity and healthy ageing (Meyer, Becker and Van Dick 2006; Oxley 2009; PMSEIC n.d).

Since the turn of the millennium various governments have introduced anti-discrimination policy, changes to retirement age and also superannuation to improve incentives for retention. Legislation that prohibits discrimination in employment on the basis of age, for example, has been introduced in the United States, Australia and, more recently, in the United Kingdom. The legislation discourages negative stereotypes often associated with older workers, such as the belief that they are slow to learn and difficult to train (Lucas 1993). Other such stereotypes maintain that, for example, older workers are resistant to change, are prone to absenteeism and are less enthusiastic about technology (Remery et al. 2003; Lucas 1993).

A number of studies demonstrate that such stereotypes result in discrimination in some organisations (Ho, Wei and Voon 2000; Ferris and King 1992; Lucas 1993). Indeed, older workers face more retrenchments and redundancies than younger workers (Lippmann 2008). Further, they receive less training and have a lower likelihood of promotion (Ho, Wei and Voon 2000). Negative stereotypes are not widely borne out by the literature, which suggests that older workers have positive attributes that contribute to the productivity of an organisation. The literature also suggests that the health of older workers is improving (Alkers 2006) and that older workers are more satisfied and more loyal than younger workers and have greater pride in their work (Lord and Farrington 2006). Age is also not related to unscheduled absences (Hackett 1990). Further, Lucas (1993) found that employing older workers results in a number of positive outcomes for the organisation, including lower recruitment and training costs, lower turnover, higher profitability, more experienced workers, and higher organisational commitment and quality of service.

A non-compulsory retirement age and amending legislation governing access to pensions are also seen to be critical to encouraging the participation of older workers. In the United States there is no compulsory retirement age, for example. A survey of 19 countries regarding policy on retirement age found that the most common statutory retirement age was 65 (Salter 2004). In countries such as Finland and Denmark, which have had some success in increasing the participation of older workers, workers have the opportunity for bridging employment during which they can receive all or part of a pension (Salter 2004). 'Bridging employment' is a term that refers to a form of phased retirement (Weckerle and Shultz 1999). Bridging employment meets important psychological needs of older workers by providing an opportunity to adapt to retirement and also serves the purpose of providing flexibility and fulfilling shortages for employers (Weckerle and Shultz 1999).

## 2.3 Micro benefits to organisations

Despite the demographic issue and the problem of skill shortages, very few managers are preparing for the future and few have strategies to attract and retain older workers (Armstrong-Stassen and Ursel 2009). The business case for increasing the participation rates of older workers involves several issues.

First, in some areas, in spite of the economic crisis, there are still skill shortages that can be addressed by employing greater numbers of older workers (Remery et al. 2003). The problem can be addressed, in part, by increasing training and development for older workers. The relative lack of training and development for older workers has been attributed to discrimination in the workplace (Ho, Wei and Voon 2000) (see Chapter 12 for an analysis of training and learning among older workers). Older workers are deemed to be less mentally agile and therefore less trainable (Ho, Wei and Voon, 2000). Further, organisations have fewer opportunities to recover the costs associated with training older workers because such workers have a shorter remaining working life (Fourage and Schils 2009). Organisations need to invest more in training older workers and ensuring that they are productive members of the organisation (Armstrong-Strassen and Ursel 2009). One study, for example, found that the provision of training opportunities for older workers resulted in higher affective commitment and reduced voluntary retirement (Herbach et al. 2009). It is also worth noting that training does not address skill shortage issues in the short term because of lag effects, and that there are also macro considerations such as apprenticeship intake, increased university intakes and training incentives that are influenced by government policy.

Second, learning organisations require the transfer of skills and knowledge. This can occur partly through documentation but it also involves the retention and transfer of knowledge through on-the-job training and mentoring by experienced workers with tenure. Older workers have greater experience and knowledge that they can transfer to other workers through mentoring programmes or supervising on-the-job training (Carstensen and Hartel 2006).

Third, in terms of marketing, organisations need to reflect the diversity that exists in the wider population (Wright et al. 1995). Organisations that are ethnically, gender-wise and demographically diverse are more reflective of wider society. It follows that there are positive reputational effects from being representative. Further, a representative workplace is able to identify the needs of its own employees and reflect on this in its organisation of employment.

Fourth, a considerable literature on creativity in organisations indicates that teams that are diverse are more likely to achieve innovative solutions to problems at work regarding product and process (Cox 1994). Encouraging an age-diverse workforce will bring in a number of factors, such as experience, that would have an impact on the creativity of solutions.

Organisations that are seeking to increase the participation of older workers need to take into account a number of factors. Supply-side factors create the need for flexibility (Sheridan and Conway 2001) because of considerations such as caring responsibilities for grandchildren and a greater demand for leisure. Increasingly, individuals are seeking bridge employment before full retirement. Flexibility should occur in relation to timing and number of hours and function. Timing and number of hours involves providing good-quality part-time employment with job security. The literature suggests that bridge employment often involves a downward move in the status of employees (Weckerle and Shultz 1999). Organisations need to address this issue by making full use of their resources and ensuring that older workers are employed in occupations that are commensurate with their qualifications and experience.

There might also be adjustments in job design in order to address specific occupational health and safety needs of older workers (Naegele and Walker 2006) (see Chapter 13). Older workers have been said to have greater occupational health and safety problems and to pose a risk for organisations (Lucas 1993), so organisations should consider job design matters such as hours of work and adjustments to physical conditions (see Chapter 13).

Finally, social identity theory and the similarity attraction hypothesis suggest that individuals formulate 'in' and 'out' groups based on identifiable characteristics such as sex, race and age (Tajfel and Turner 1986). Individuals construct their social identity based on the basis of these discernible characteristics and obtain self-esteem from identifying themselves within their group. However, the evidence suggests that divisions are created between those in the 'in' group and those in the 'out' group. As a consequence, where dominant 'in' groups are formed as the result of these discernible characteristics, the outcomes for organisations can be negative (Tsui, Egan and O'Reilly 1992). As a result, the application of diversity management techniques will also be important (Cox and Blake 1991).

Diversity management is defined as the management of differences and similarities among individuals, reflected in attributes such as sex, age, ethnic origin, language, cultural background, marital status, sexual orientation, work experience, family responsibility, educational responsibility and socio-economic status (Thomas 1996; DeCieri and Olekalns 2001). Ivancevich and Gilbert (2000, p. 75) argue that diversity management is the 'systematic and planned commitment by organisations to recruit, retain, reward and promote a heterogeneous mix of employees' to improve organisational effectiveness (for a detailed analysis of age diversity see Chapter 4). Some of the attributes outlined are immutable (for example, age and sex), whereas others are more malleable (for example, education) (Woods and Sciarini 1995). Age is an attribute that cannot be changed, which means that it is the consequences of diversity in age that need to be managed. Diversity management entails communication, education and training, career management, accountability, cultural change and employee involvement (DeCieri et al. 2008). Diversity management has been linked in the literature to improved performance, lower turnover, lower absenteeism and an improved bottom line (Cox and Blake 1991; Mollica 2003).

Human resource-management policies and practices are critical to managing a diverse workforce (D'Netto and Sohal 1999). DeCieri et al. (2008) have established that the core activities of human resource management, such as employee recruitment and retention, remuneration, training and development, performance management, workforce planning and industrial relations, need to be configured to promote diversity and to encourage positive attitudes regarding diversity within the organisation. One important component of this is, as discussed earlier, the need to provide temporal, numerical and functional flexibility and to adapt job design to suit the positions to which older workers are promoted.

## 2.4 Preferences of older workers

Aside from the advantages to government and organisations in retaining older workers at the workplace, there are also benefits to older workers themselves. As discussed earlier, work is a critical component of many individuals' identity. Healthy ageing of individuals is associated with their participating at work and continuing to feel that they are valued members of society. Further, intellectual activity promotes healthy ageing because degenerative brain diseases have been associated with a lack brain activity. Work involves intellectual exercise and is related to prolonging life expectancy and enhancing quality of life (Oxley 2009; PMSEIC n.d.).

It is a mistake to assume that all individuals are able to retire at a particular age. The literature suggests that decisions to retire are influenced by financial considerations. Many pension funds were affected by the global economic crisis, as a result of which many individuals deferred their planned retirement. Thus, there has been an increase in the supply of older workers in full-time as well as bridging employment. The impact of macro factors has been significant and will continue to affect the retirement decisions of individuals (Patrickson and Ranzijn 2004).

The type of employment that individuals choose in relation to flexibility is also relevant. Increasingly, individuals are expressing preferences for working part time in order to cater for other preferences such as leisure and also, more commonly, in order to assist with the care of grandchildren. Another section of this chapter has stressed the importance of providing good-quality part-time work to ensure that older workers' preferences are catered for, as well as to ensure maximum productivity for organisations.

## 2.5 Choosing to work or to retire

It has been argued in this chapter that there is an imperative for a more age-diverse workforce, for a range of macro and micro reasons. Often this argument is presented in an uncritical fashion: older individuals should work for the good of the nation, productivity and themselves. However, a counter-argument can be made regarding the labour-force participation of older workers. Is this another way, for example, to intensify work and extract maximum effort from individuals who should be enjoying a well-earned rest in retirement?

There are other solutions to the demographic problem, such as increasing the fertility rate, the participation of women, migration and training and development. Governments and organisations should attack the issue from a variety of angles and make the participation of older people in the workforce a matter of choice through incentives rather than compulsion. This is important for a number of reasons, as older individuals may not be in good health, may experience pressures to assist their children with childcare, or may be able to afford to realise their preferences for leisure. Patrickson and Ranzijn (2004) indicate that retirement decisions involve an assessment of three factors; health, financial position and motivation to work. Governments, through policy, can influence all three factors. Further, a study by Armstrong-Stassen (2008) found that human resources practices were important in the decision to retire; practices such as recognition and performance management were found to be particularly important.

## 2.6 Summary and conclusions

This chapter has examined the business case for employing a demographically diverse workforce. There are a number of social and economic reasons why employing older workers is important. First, there is currently a demographic problem in many OECD countries, with declining fertility and migration rates and an increase in the average age of the population that make current participation rates of older workers unsustainable. They are unsustainable largely because a smaller group of individuals are and will be supporting an increasingly larger demographic group in retirement, and because the reduction in the supply of workers has resulted in skill shortages in a range of industries and occupations.

Governments have attempted to address the problem with a range of policies such as anti-discrimination legislation, extending retirement ages and changing pension rules so as to encourage bridge employment, for example.

In addition to the social and economic advantages, there are many sound organisational reasons to employ older workers. First, the skill shortage issue is one that many organisations cannot ignore, and to address it they need to attract, retain and train their workers, particularly older workers. They can do this by providing training and flexibility and designing jobs to suit older workers. Aside from the issue of skill shortages, there are a number of other reasons why organisations need to promote higher rates of workforce participation by older people. They include the need to address marketing issues and the benefits of diversity. Diversity in itself is not going to increase productivity (although it may increase creativity). This chapter has discussed the need for organisations to manage diversity at the workplace carefully to ensure that it works in a positive manner for the organisation.

Finally, individual older people benefit from increasing participation rates. Healthy ageing requires active minds, and participation in the workforce results in individuals being proactive about reducing their vulnerability to degenerative brain disease in the future. There are also good financial reasons to increase bridge employment in particular, with macro factors currently affecting individuals' capacity to retire. And supply-side considerations point to part-time employment for many individuals because of their need to juggle other concerns such as work–family balance and preferences for leisure.

# 3
# Age Discrimination and the Law: Forging the Way Ahead

*Jonathan Herring*

This chapter focuses on age discrimination legislation in one country, Britain, as an example of how age discrimination has been combated by law. British law has been remarkably slow to respond to age discrimination. Only in recent years has legislation been enacted to address the issue. This chapter seeks to set out the current law on age discrimination and to consider the issues that are troubling (or will trouble) the courts.

Discrimination law in other countries has developed at a far faster pace than it has in the UK. In the United States, the Age Discrimination in Employment Act of 1967 prohibited discrimination in the employment context, and the Age Discrimination Act 1975 outlawed discrimination in relation to federal programmes. Notably, the 1967 Act tackles discrimination against those over the age of 40, so it is specifically aimed at old-age discrimination. This might reflect the greater political power wielded by older citizens of the United States. In Australia the federal law was consolidated in the Age Discrimination Act 2004, replacing earlier legislation from 1996. It applies to a wide range of areas as well as work, including buying goods and services and accommodation.

The forms of ageism and age discrimination are varied and have been extensively examined in the literature (Herring 2009). Ageism refers to the false assumptions and beliefs that are held about people based on their age. Age discrimination relates to behaviour in which a person is disadvantaged as a result of his or her age. Age discrimination often interacts with other sources of disadvantage such as race, class and sex discrimination.

## 3.1 The Employment Equality (Age) Regulations 2006

The Sex Discrimination Act 1975 prohibits discrimination on the grounds of sex, marital status and trans-sexualism. The Race Relations Act

1976 prohibits discrimination on the basis of colour, race, nationality or ethnic or national origins. The pressure to outlaw age discrimination came from the European Union with the Equal Treatment Framework Directive 2000/78. In 2006 the Employment Equality (Age) Regulations (SI 2006/1031) were passed, purporting to give effect to the Directive.

### 3.1.1 Extent of law

The 2006 regulations apply to all employers, vocational-training providers, trade unions, employee organisations and managers of occupational pension schemes. The regulations focus on employment issues such as: offers of employment; the terms of the employment; refusal to offer employment; promotions and transfers (reg. 7). The regulations do not apply generally to the provision of goods and services. It is not unlawful under the regulations for a hotel to refuse to house someone on the basis of age. As we shall see, the Equality Act 2010, will render such conduct unlawful.

### 3.1.2 The definition of discrimination

Regulation 3 states:

> (1) For the purposes of these Regulations, a person ('A') discriminates against another person ('B') if—
> (a) on grounds of B's age, A treats B less favourably than he treats or would treat other persons, or
> (b) A applies to B a provision, criterion or practice which he applies or would apply equally to persons not of the same age group as B, but
> (i) which puts or would put persons of the same age group as B at a particular disadvantage when compared with other persons, and
> (ii) which puts B at that disadvantage,
> and A cannot show the treatment or, as the case may be, provision, criterion or practice to be a proportionate means of achieving a legitimate aim.
> (2) A comparison of B's case with that of another person under paragraph (1) must be such that the relevant circumstances in the one case are the same, or not materially different, in the other.
> (3) In this regulation—
> (a) 'age group' means a group of persons defined by reference to age, whether by reference to a particular age or a range of ages; and
> (b) the reference in paragraph (1)(a) to B's age includes B's apparent age.

Regulation 3 deals with direct discrimination in paragraph (1)(a) and indirect discrimination in (1)(b). These two forms of discrimination will be considered separately.

### 3.1.3 Direct discrimination

Direct discrimination requires proof that B was treated less favourably on account of his or her age. This would cover the most blatant forms of discrimination where, for example, a job advertisement stated that the job was open only to those under the age of 40. Significantly the regulations cover not only age but apparent age (reg. 3. (3) (b)). In *McCoy v James McGregor and Sons* (2007) a 58-year-old unsuccessfully applied for a job advertised as requiring 'youthful enthusiasm'. The job was given to two less experienced but younger applicants. The Northern Ireland Employment Tribunal held that he was the victim of age discrimination.

The concept of direct discrimination as expressed in regulation 3(1)(a) requires proof that B was treated differently from a person of a different age. One difficulty in applying this is finding an appropriate comparator. Imagine a 55-year-old worker whose contract is not renewed and claims age discrimination. She might point to a similarly qualified worker aged 30 who had had her contract renewed. However, her employer may point to a similarly qualified 45-year-old who had not. Is the comparison to be drawn with the 45-year-old or the 30-year-old? In the case of sex discrimination, the comparator would be easy to find: a similarly qualified male worker. But with age discrimination there might be quite a number of different ages that could be used as comparators. Cases may become highly complex if each side introduces a range of possible comparators of different ages. There is evidence that this is what has happened in the US (Bamforth, Malik and O'Cinneide 2008, p. 1131). One solution is for the law to state that discrimination occurs if the claimant was treated less favourably on account of her age than any other age group. Then it would be no defence for an employer to refer to other age groups that were treated as unfairly as the claimant was. After all, it should be no defence to a charge of discrimination that other people would have been treated in just as discriminatory a way as the applicant (Hepple 2003).

Even if it is possible to point to another differently aged worker who was treated in a more favourable way, it does not follow that it has been shown that this was on account of age. In *ABN AMRO Management Services v. Hogben* (2009) the United Kingdom Employment Appeal Tribunal found it implausible that a difference in treatment between two employees whose age differed by only nine months could indicate age discrimination. Indeed, it was stated that even a difference in treatment between a 41-year-old and a 48-year-old would not be indicative of age discrimination, unless there was further evidence that age played a role in the decision.

### 3.1.4 Indirect discrimination

Indirect discrimination is covered by Regulation 1(1) (b). Indirect discrimination occurs where an apparently equal treatment in fact affects more heavily people of a particular age. Baroness Hale in *Rutherford (No.2) v. Secretary of State for Trade and Industry* (2006, para. 71) explained the concept in this way:

> The essence of indirect discrimination is that an apparently neutral ... provision, criterion or practice ... in reality has a disproportionate adverse impact upon a particular group. It looks beyond the formal equality achieved by the prohibition of direct discrimination towards the more substantive equality of results. A smaller proportion of one group can comply with the requirement, condition or criterion or a larger proportion of them are adversely affected by the rule or practice. This is meant to be a simple objective enquiry. Once disproportionate adverse impact is demonstrated by the figures, the question is whether the rule or requirement can objectively be justified.

An obvious example of indirect age discrimination would be a job advertisement which disqualifies applicants with naturally grey or white hair. Although age is not mentioned, the hair requirement is more likely to be satisfied by younger people than older people and therefore, in effect, discriminates against the latter. A less obvious example would be a requirement for a job that applicants have a degree, which may disproportionately exclude older people because older people are less likely than younger people to hold formal qualifications.

Indirect discrimination is, therefore, less obvious than direct discrimination, and can raise some tricky questions. One problematic area concerns requirements that only very slightly favour younger people – for example, where 15.4 per cent of younger potential applicants would have the requirement but only 15.2 per cent of older ones. The courts may well treat the very slight impact on older workers as relevant for the question of whether the discrimination is justified. Alternatively, they may rule that such a minor difference is simply insufficient to indicate discrimination.

Another difficulty with indirect discrimination is whether the comparison is with would-be applicants or the general population. For example, an IT job which required applicants to have a certain level of computer literacy might be said to discriminate against older people generally but not against older people who are likely to apply for the job. Baroness Hale in *Rutherford (No. 2) v. Secretary of State for Trade and Industry* (2006) addressed this issue and held that the relevant question is the impact of the requirement on the group seeking the benefit. So if a higher number of younger people than older people can meet the requirement, but few older people want the benefit in question, the requirement may not be discriminatory.

A major difficulty with indirect age discrimination is that many commonly used employment criteria are indirectly discriminatory on the basis of age: experience, knowledge, emotional maturity or qualifications, for example, are all likely to favour older candidates. This means that, although indirect age discrimination will be common, it will frequently be justified. Bamforth, Malik and O'Cinnede (2008, p. 1133) claim 'common sense application of the objective justification test should be capable of distinguishing stereotyping use of age-linked criteria from legitimate use in making rational economic decisions'. The possibility of justification is, therefore, essential to the workability of the regulations in this area.

### 3.1.5 Justification

Regulation 3, on the very definition of discrimination, states that discrimination will be justified where it is a 'proportionate means of achieving a legitimate aim'. Art. 6(1) of the EC Directive gives examples of potentially legitimate aims: 'legitimate employment policy, labour market and vocational training'. To be a legitimate aim it must link to the needs of the employer (*Rolls Royce plc v. Unite* (2008)). In other words, what may be a legitimate aim for one employer will not necessarily be so for another. Further, it is likely that an individual employer will not be able to rely on broad social policies to justify the discrimination. This is all rather vague and there is plenty of scope for the courts to fashion a clearer approach as to when age discrimination is justified.

In *Loxley v. BAE Systems* (2008, para 36) the Tribunal held:

> The principle of proportionality requires an objective balance to be struck between the discriminatory effect of the measure and the needs of the undertaking. The more serious the disparate adverse

> impact, the more cogent must be the justification for it. It is for the employment tribunal to weigh the reasonable needs of the undertaking against the discriminatory effect of the employer's measure and to make its own assessment of whether the former outweigh the latter. There is no 'range of reasonable response' test in this context.

In *Hütter v. Technische Universität Graz* (2009) it was accepted by the European Court of Justice that rewarding experience was a legitimate aim, even though it was indirectly discriminatory. Similarly, length of services in *Rolls Royce v. Unite* (2008) was found to be indirectly discriminatory, but was said to be often justifiable in redundancy selection.

The difficulties surrounding justification of age discrimination are, in part, cultural. Age discrimination is deeply embedded in our employment practices. Jonathan Swift (2006: 229) argues

> there is a conflict at the heart of the legislation not only because in the labour market conflicts of interest exist between the old and the young, but also because the characteristics of age are ones that we all possess and all use when making day to day decisions. If truthful, it is unlikely that there are many people who could honestly say that they have never allowed age to influence decisions relating to others, not merely personal decisions but also practical and professional decisions. Many occupations are dominated by notions of 'seniority' and 'experience' both of which are closely synonymous with age. Decisions are made on this basis every day.

A key question the courts will need to address is how strong the reasons for the discrimination need to be if they are to justify it. The Department of Trade and Industry (DTI) (2006) has said that the objective justification requirement is a 'tough test'. It stated (at para. 4.1.13)

> the test of objective justification will not be an easy one to satisfy. The principle remains that different treatment on grounds of age will be unlawful: treating people differently on grounds of age will be possible but only exceptionally and only for good reasons.

In *Palacios de la Villa v. Cortefiel Servicios* (2007) the European Court of Justice rejected an argument that age discrimination should be regarded as easier to justify than sex or race discrimination. The court accepted that justification may be more common, but not that it would be easier. That is a revealing comment because it is generally accepted that very strong reasons are required to justify age or sex discrimination. It indicates that marginal benefits in terms of the legitimate aims will be insufficient.

Another issue is whether it is possible to refer to the ageism of others to justify age discrimination. The DTI (2006) stated 'the legitimate aim cannot be related to age discrimination itself'. It explained what it meant by using the following example:

> A retailer of trendy fashion items wants to employ young shop assistants because it believes that this will contribute to its aim of targeting young buyers. Trying to attract a young target group will not be a legitimate aim, because this has an age discriminatory aspect.

This is a dubious way of considering the case. Attracting customers must be a legitimate aim for a business (Swift 2006). A better argument would be that the aim is, in this context, insufficient to justify age discrimination.

An important issue is whether reducing expense is a legitimate aim which can justify age discrimination. The DTI (2006) has stated that business need or considerations of efficiency may be legitimate reasons, but not expense alone. This is also problematic because the line between expense and efficiency may be hard to draw. The main aim of a business is to make money and that may be described as the ultimate business need. If saving money is not a legitimate aim for a business it is hard to see what might be. There are two responses to this. First, it may simply be denied that older workers cost more to business; and much evidence has been produced showing the benefits to employers of a diverse workforce, with claims that older workers stay in their jobs longer and are less often absent (Fredman 2003). Second, it may be argued that, even if it is accepted there is a cost to business in hiring older workers, that cost must fall somewhere. If age discrimination can be relied upon to save money for employers, the cost of doing so will fall on older workers (Fredman 2003, p. 50). So the real question is this: if there is a cost to hiring older workers, should that cost fall on business, or older employees, or the state?

The notion of proportionality is problematic, too. Weighing up the wrong in the discrimination against the legitimate aim involves comparing two very different things. How can you compare age discrimination with business efficiency? Swift (2006) suggests that proportionality requires an employer to show:

> First, that treatment that has been afforded to the claimant is rationally related to the aim he has identified. Secondly, that he has not based the specific action taken against the claimant on uninformed assumptions about the claimant which are based on the age of the claimant. Thirdly, that he has taken reasonable steps to inform himself on all material considerations prior to taking action against the claimant. Fourthly that the action taken represents a reasonable balance between the employer's pursuit of the aim actually pursued and the cost to the individual of that aim being pursued—i.e. that the action taken against the claimant is not an obviously excessive step having regard to the benefits that might reasonably be expected to accrue to the employer.

A rather different issue is the weight that should be placed on the fact that the decision objected to was in compliance with a settlement reached with unions or other representatives of the workforce. In *Pulham v. Barking LBC* (2008) it was held that such compliance did not automatically justify age discrimination. However, it was a factor that could be taken into account as evidence that the age discrimination was justifiable. Even if an agreement was negotiated, the employer would still need to be convinced that any discrimination was justified (*Loxley v. BAE Systems* (2008)).

### 3.1.6 Retirement

Under Regulation 30, if a firm has a mandatory retiring age below 65 that must be justified by the company. It must be shown that the lower retirement age is appropriate and necessary. If the retirement age is 65 or above, that can provide a justification for what would otherwise be age discrimination or unlawful retirement. However, there are certain procedural requirements. An employer is required to inform an employee in writing six months before the intended retirement date (schedule 6). The employee can request to work beyond the compulsory retirement date, and the employer must consider that request. Crucially, the employer does not need to justify the decision not to allow the employee to work beyond the retirement age. This means there is very little, if any, protection for the rights of a worker who wishes to work beyond a mandatory retiring age of 65.

Regulation 30 has proved highly controversial. It particular it has been noted that it is not consistent with government policy in relation to the 'pension crisis' where workers are encouraged to work longer to build up bigger pensions (Kilpatrick 2008). Bamforth, Malik and O'Cinnede (2008, p. 1133) summarise well the reasons why there should not be mandatory retiring age:

> The immediate transition from employment to leisure can result in damaging financial and psychological impact, and many employees experience their mandatory retirement as humiliating, degrading and denying them liberty ... by denying access to the workplace mandatory retirement can close off opportunities for individual self-realisation and constitute a paternalist intrusion in personal life that violates the principle of human dignity.

Unsurprisingly, the issue has not taken long to reach the courts. Age Concern has backed litigation to challenge the regulations in the European Court of Justice, arguing that provisions in relation to retirement in the regulations were not compatible with the prohibition on age discrimination in Directive 2000/78/EC. The judgement in *R (The Incorporated Trustees of the National Council on Ageing (Age Concern England)) v. Secretary of State for Business, Enterprise and Regulatory Reform* (2009) held that the Directive did not prohibit the use of mandatory retirement age schemes of the kind found in the Regulations. However, any such scheme had to be justified under the Directive. The court held it was a question for the national courts to determine whether the use of a mandatory scheme was justifiable.

The ball, in effect, was kicked back by the European Court to the English courts. *Age UK v. Secretary of State for Business, Innovation and Skills* (2009) is the first of what is likely to be a long line of cases where the English courts consider the issue. Blake J heard a claim that the mandatory retirement provisions amounted to unlawful age discrimination. He emphasised that in implementing the Directive 2000/78 there was a wide margin afforded to Member States in formulating social policy. He noted (at para. 72) that 'The Government's labour market objectives include encouraging the recruitment, training, retention and proper remuneration of workers, and ensuring proper pension provision for them when they retire'.

These objectives were relied upon to justify the mandatory retirement age provisions. Particular weight was placed on workforce planning. Blake (at para. 73) noted the government's view that

Workforce planning has three aspects in this context:

- a retirement age provides a target age against which employers and employees can plan work and retirement;
- prevention of 'job blocking'; and
- encouraging employees to save for retirement.

Blake J held that such concerns were legitimate ones, which justified the government's approach, and that they were a proportionate way of protecting labour market confidence. The retirement age had not been based on assumptions that those over 65 were not reasonably capable of competent performance of their duties. Had they been, they would have been discriminatory.

Legal disputes over the legality of mandatory retirement ages will continue. It was noticeable that Blake J appeared to show significant deference to the views of the government. As the government's arguments were within the margin of appreciation given by European law they could not successfully be challenged in the courts. It will be interesting to see whether later courts regard the government has having to carry a heavier burden of proof if it is to justify age discrimination. It is notable that there is evidence from the United States that removal of the retirement age has had relatively little impact on rates of retirement, and so concerns about its impact on the employment market may be exaggerated (Neumark 2009).

The Government announced on 29 July 2010 that it proposes to remove the default retiring age of 65 from 6 April 2011. The proposals are likely to receive considerable opposition. It will be interesting to see if the Government is able to get the necessary legislative changes through Parliament.

### 3.1.7 Positive action

Regulation 29 sets out the circumstances in which a company can engage in positive action in an attempt to combat the effects of ageism.

> (1) Nothing in Part 2 or 3 shall render unlawful any act done in or in connection with
> (a) affording persons of a particular age or age group access to facilities for training which would help fit them for particular work; or
> (b) encouraging persons of a particular age or age group to take advantage of opportunities for doing particular work;

> where it reasonably appears to the person doing the act that it prevents or compensates for disadvantages linked to age suffered by persons of that age or age group doing that work or likely to take up that work.

It should be noted that the scope of positive action allowed under this regulation is very limited. It is restricted to affording people training and encouraging them to take up opportunities for doing particular work. Where, therefore, a company is keen to employ more older workers, it could offer training to existing or future older workers to enable them to acquire the skills required for jobs. It could also focus advertising on older workers. However, at the selection process Regulation 29 would not authorise preferring an older candidate over a younger one purely on the basis of age. Some commentators would like to see a more robust law allowing a company to at least take age into account in preferring an older candidate over a younger candidate if in all other respects they are equally well qualified. Of course, there has been fierce debate over the extent to which affirmative action is justifiable and/or effective (McHarg and Nicolson 2006).

### 3.1.8 Remedies

The remedies available are set down in Regulation 38. These include requiring the payment of compensation; ordering the employer to respect the rights of the employee, by paying him or her a non-discriminatory wage, or not dismissing him or her in a discriminatory way.

## 3.2 The Equality Act 2010

The Equality Act is designed to consolidate the law on all areas of discrimination. However, in doing so it will greatly extend the impact of age discrimination law. The Act includes age as a 'protected characteristic' alongside, inter alia, sex, race and marital status. Section 13 will outlaw direct discrimination on the grounds of a protected characteristic:

> (1) A person (A) discriminates against another (B) if, because of a protected characteristic, A treats B less favourably than A treats or would treat others.
> (2) If the protected characteristic is age, A does not discriminate against B if A can show A's treatment of B to be a proportionate means of achieving a legitimate aim.

Section 19 prohibits indirect discrimination:

> (1) A person (A) discriminates against another (B) if A applies to B a provision, criterion or practice which is discriminatory in relation to a relevant protected characteristic of B's.
> (2) For the purposes of subsection (1), a provision, criterion or practice is discriminatory in relation to a relevant protected characteristic of B's if—
> (a) A applies, or would apply, it to persons with whom B does not share the characteristic,
> (b) it puts, or would put, persons with whom B shares the characteristic at a particular disadvantage when compared with persons with whom B does not share it,
> (c) it puts, or would put, B at that disadvantage, and
> (d) A cannot show it to be a proportionate means of achieving a legitimate aim.

These are in very similar terms to the regulations just discussed. The significance of the Act lies in the fact that the Act covers not just employment but a broad range of activities. Most significantly, Section 29 covers the provision of services:

> (1) A person (a 'service-provider') concerned with the provision of a service to the public or a section of the public (for payment or not) must not discriminate against a person requiring the service by not providing the person with the service.
> (2) A service-provider (A) must not, in providing the service, discriminate against a person (B)
> (a) as to the terms on which A provides the service to B;
> (b) by terminating the provision of the service to B;
> (c) by subjecting B to any other detriment.

Also covered are higher education, employment and membership of associations. In these areas, too, there must be no age discrimination.

The government has recognised that the Act will provide the framework for the law on age discrimination. Detailed regulations will be produced to deal with particular topics. The Government Equalities Office (2010, p. 1) has stated that age discrimination is not completely analogous to other forms of discrimination:

> the age discrimination provisions in the Equality Bill differ from all the other protected characteristics in that it is possible to justify even

> what would otherwise be direct age discrimination on the basis that it is a proportionate means of attaining a legitimate aim. This is known as 'objective justification'. Objective justification is a relatively stringent test. Establishing that particular treatment is proportionate requires demonstrating that treatment is the least discriminatory available.

It is notable that the Act applies only to those aged over 18. Under-18s will not be able to plead age discrimination. This is understandable as a matter of practicality: it will be hard enough dealing with all of the issues relating to adult age discrimination. But as a matter of principle there is no reason why unjustified discrimination on the ground of youth should be regarded as more acceptable than discrimination on the ground of old age (Herring 2003).

The Government Equalities Office (2010) has made it clear that it does not want the legislation to lead to the loss of 'beneficial age-based treatments' such as free bus passes and student and pensioner discounts. It remains to be seen whether the legislation will attempt to exempt these, or whether it will be a matter of justification, with such benefits being particularly easy to justify.

One area that is proving particularly difficult is health and social care. The government has acknowledged that age can be a relevant criterion in determining the effectiveness of treatment or health promotion programmes. The current intention is that the legislation will apply to health and social care, but special regulation will be required.

Another difficult area concerns financial service provision. There have been persistent complaints that insurance companies and others have improperly used age in determining the levels of premiums and coverage offered by policies. The current proposal is that age can be used in financial services provision, but only insofar as it can be shown to relate to risks or costs. Comparative data must be produced by the industry for travel and motor insurance.

## 3.3 Other jurisdictions

Looking at other jurisdictions is instructive. Not surprisingly, they do not offer a 'silver bullet' to solve the problems of age discrimination. However, they do provide some interesting alternative approaches to the issue. As mentioned earlier, the US age discrimination employment legislation applies only to those over the age of 40. Such an approach might be justifiable if it be thought that discrimination against older workers caused significantly more social harms than that against younger workers.

In response it might be said that prejudicing a person on account of his or her youth is as unjust as doing so on account of his or her old age.

Another issue, as we have seen, is how broad a range of areas age discrimination legislation should cover. The Australian Age Discrimination Act 2004 has a wide scope. Even so, some areas are excluded, such as some health programmes, taxation and social security. The Act also permits particular benefits to be provided to an age group, if there is an identified need.

It is noticeable that while European Union Member States are now, in theory, united behind the Equal Treatment Framework Directive 2000/78 in their approach to age discrimination, there is no consensus as to how it is to be implemented (Bokum et al. 2009). While it is clear that the Directive gives individual states a degree of discretion in its implementation, there is still a remarkable difference in approach. A survey for the Employers Forum on Age Discrimination (2010) found little agreement on major issues, such as whether age discrimination could be justified on the basis of creating an atmosphere in a bar; or for providing lower minimum wages for young workers compared to older workers; or indeed whether mandatory retirement age is lawful. On the last issue there is a wide variation: within, Belgium, mandatory retirement are always unlawful; while other countries such as Austria or Spain permit mandatory retirement only in relation to specified professions. In yet other countries, such as Denmark and France, mandatory retirement can be permitted but requires specific justification.

A final lesson from other jurisdictions is that we cannot expect dramatic changes in the fortunes of older workers. Research from the US suggests that age discrimination legislation has had some success in enabling older workers to stay in jobs longer, but less success in ensuring that older workers are hired (Hornstein 2001). Also, there are significant limits to the extent to which the law can be expected to change ingrained negative attitudes about older workers or to overcome the wider social barriers to employment they face.

## 3.4 What is wrong with age discrimination?

As the law develops, the courts will need to address in more depth the question of what is wrong with age discrimination. Discrimination law is seeking to outlaw the *improper* use of characteristics or group membership as a factor in making public decisions. It ensures that the grounds cited in making such decisions are acceptable ones and do not lead to disadvantage on the basis of the prohibited characteristics.

At the heart of discrimination is the notion of equality. At its most simple, to discriminate against a person is to treat him or her improperly as not equal to another person. However, the disagreements soon appear. Equality can be conceived in at least three ways:

1. *Equality of treatment*. This requires that the same set of rules apply to each person. As we have seen, this can lead to unequal results, but supporters of equality of treatment would argue that any differences that result from equality of treatment must be dealt with by other social changes. So if a university's admissions policies were leading to certain racial groups being under-represented, for example, the answer would not be to change the admissions requirements but to improve standards of education for the affected group.
2. *Equality of outcome*. Here the focus is on achieving an equality of result. So, using equality of outcome, the university just discussed would have lower entry requirements for disadvantaged groups to ensure a proportionate representation for each group. That would mean unfairness in one sense (different rules were applied to candidates) but the end result, supporters would say, would be fairer.
3. *Equality of opportunity*. Here the focus is on providing equal opportunities. This does not require either equality of treatment or equality of outcome. Rather, the focus is on giving everyone an equal chance to compete for particular benefits.

The arguments that may be used in favour of these different conceptions of equality are beyond the scope of this chapter (see Fredman 2003). But it will be apparent that strikingly different results will be produced depending on which conception of equality is applied.

One of the reasons for focusing on equality of outcome or equality of opportunity is that these conceptions involve accepting there are differences between groups and seeking to ensure disadvantage does not flow from these differences, rather than seeking to produce a homogeneous society. So, in the context of age discrimination, it should not be thought that the aim is necessarily to enable the old to behave in the same way as the young. Sandra Fredman (2003, p. 45) has argued that

> the central aim of equality should be to facilitate equal participation of all in society, based on equal concern and respect for the dignity of each individual.

However, others will see this as placing too heavy a burden on the notion of equality and even smuggling in a broader political agenda in the guise of equality.

A much more limited role for discrimination law would simply be to promote rationality (see the discussion in McCrudden and Kountouros 2006). This view sees discrimination law as not about equality but as promoting more rational, and therefore more effective and efficient, decision-making. The objection to discrimination, on this view, is that it is using an irrational ground to allocate a social good. Many of the debates referred to above about when age discrimination is justified reflect the issue of whether age discrimination is about ensuring rationality or whether it is dealing with deeper questions of the kind to which Fredman refers.

## 3.5 Summary and conclusions

Britain is still in the early days of finding an effective response to age discrimination. The difficulties in drafting an appropriate legislative response reflect the extent to which British society has been based on ageist assumptions and practices. The Equality Act 2010 is a welcome recognition of the need to challenge age discrimination in a variety of ways. Simply tackling the employment area, as the 2006 regulations have attempted to do, is unlikely to be successful. The Equality Act attempts also to challenge the wider social structures and forces that blight the lives of older people. Simply stopping individuals from performing acts of discrimination is unlikely on its own to effectively combat the impact of ageism on older people. Currently, the law appears to be as much about ensuring that businesses and public authorities are not overburdened as it is about protecting the rights of older people. The starting point should be agreement that to discriminate against persons on the grounds of their age is to show a lack of respect towards their humanity and is degrading to them (Hellman 2008, p. 6). Treating people with dignity may be expensive, but it is price well worth paying.

# Part II
# The Nature of Age and Age Diversity

Part I of this book discusses the reasons why an employer or individual might want to eliminate age discrimination and promote age diversity. In particular we have focused on the business case and on legislation. We now move on to consider the nature of age diversity itself, the role that it plays in the wider field of diversity and its interaction with other areas of diversity, specifically gender.

In Chapter 4 Kat Riach examines the nature and role of age diversity in detail and addresses the questions of what diversity is and how it differs from an equal opportunities approach. This chapter then examines age diversity in particular and identifies the limitations of age diversity as a concept.

In Chapter 5 Wendy Loretto and Sarah Vickerstaff examine the interaction of age with another area of diversity, gender. This chapter presents the suggestion that age and gender combine in order to affect the opportunities and discriminatory attitudes experienced by individuals in the workplace. In particular, the chapter focuses on the problems experienced by older women.

In addition to analysing age diversity, we take a closer look at age itself. We may think of age as being a simple linear variable but actually it is a multifaceted concept.

In Chapter 6 Marcie Pitt-Catsoupes, Christina Matz-Costa and Melissa Brown develop the concept of 'age' as a multifaceted construct. This chapter presents a number of interpretations of 'age' and presents the results of some empirical work that examines how the different types of age can affect an individual's attitudes and preferences. In sum, this chapter illustrates how recognising age as multifaceted is important for employers in developing age-management practices.

Finally in Part II, in Chapter 7 Emma Parry and Peter Urwin take a critical look at one concept of age that has become popular in recent years – that of generations. This chapter examines the theoretical and empirical evidence for generational differences in work values before suggesting potential impacts of generational differences within the workplace.

# 4
# Situating Age (In)equality within the Paradigm and Practices of Diversity Management

*Kat Riach*

This chapter examines how age discrimination and the older worker have been situated within the diversity approach to managing equality. After exploring the evolution of diversity management and why it became the dominant managerial approach to tackling workplace inequalities, the chapter explores its influence on the ways in which organisational age discrimination and the older worker have been treated within management practices and policies. The chapter then moves on to assess critically the concept of age diversity, exposing some of its inherent tensions that may limit managerial attempts to challenge age inequality, and illustrates these tensions through empirical studies of age discrimination. We conclude with some reflections on challenging organisational age inequality, paying particular attention to the role of broader social norms and perceptions about ageing, and how these must be considered if we are to change workplace attitudes or behaviours that perpetuate discrimination based on age.

## 4.1 What is organisational diversity?

The management of equality has long been linked to broader social norms and expectations surrounding fairness, and it is little surprise that, with the current policy and media interest in the ageing population, there has been an increased focus on the dynamics surrounding ageing at work. Age plays a key role in organisational life, and is often used consciously or unconsciously as a proxy for making personnel management decisions across a number of departments within an organisation. For example, demographic forecasts concerning the workforce are often undertaken when business strategy is being considered, while redundancy decisions can both influence and be influenced by perceptions of who is 'ready to go'. Such decision-making is increasingly contextualised within larger debates concerning the management of equality, where a growing concern has been expressed on whether the participation and advancement of those classed as 'older workers' is blighted by unfavourable treatment. These barriers or perceptions may not only prevent people from continuing to work but make it difficult for those currently outside the labour market to enter employment. In order to challenge this inherent ageism, the 'diversity' approach to equality has been heralded as providing both a philosophy and a means of practically attaining age equality in the workplace.

'Diversity management' refers to the groups of policies and practices that seek to promote equality in the workplace through valuing the individual difference and potential value each employee brings to the organisation. In many ways, the emergence of diversity management in the late 1980s was a reaction to the limitations of Equal Opportunities (EO), which had been the dominant philosophy behind discrimination legislation and management practices since the 1970s. EO was based primarily on the premise of eliminating discrimination through creating a 'level playing field of chance' (Rennie 1993) and was driven by a moral conviction that particular social groups should not be treated unfairly. Such a premise supported many of the laws within the United Kingdom that were brought in to tackle unfair treatment at work, such as the Equal Pay Act (1970), the Sex Discrimination Act (1975) and the Race Relations Act (1976). The social justice emphasis that underlined the EO approach also mirrored larger social movements of the time. Throughout the UK and North America civil rights and equality were not only abstract political issues, but increasingly promoted as an integral part of the fabric of modern, civilised society. This resulted in many grass-roots organisations emerging to fight for the rights of undermined or discriminated-against groups; an example was the 'Gray Panthers', an American movement founded by Maggie Kuhn that sought to promote civic activism and to draw attention to the challenges faced by retirees. While in the UK no such movement was concerned over age discrimination at work per se, the former National Old People's Welfare Committee began to grow into the charity Age Concern; and its document 'Manifesto on the Place of the Retired and Elderly in the Modern Economy' (1975) emphasised lack of voice of the elderly in society and the violation of their rights. Such actions may explain why EO became such a popular legislative tool and managerial approach, since it upheld social sentiments popular at the time.

However, when translated into law and subsequent practice, the EO approach can be seen to have underestimated the deep-rooted structures of prejudiced attitudes that contributed to discrimination by assuming that introducing an 'equal chance' would automatically lead to an 'equal outcome' (Liff 1999). Moreover, despite legislative intervention whereby both individuals and organisations could be found guilty of discrimination, many organisations were more concerned with avoiding litigation cases rather than ensuring there was no discrimination in the workplace. As well, a widespread critique suggests it is extremely difficult to prove a direct correlation between the presence of EO policies and a lack of discrimination in the workplace, since many cases of discrimination still went unreported even when formal procedures were in place. This has led commentators such as Hoque and Noon (2004) and Jewson and Mason (1994) to argue that many organisational EO policies are nothing more than 'empty shell' policies used to prevent litigation rather than to genuinely eradicate discrimination.

In response to these failings of EO, diversity began to emerge in the late 1980s as a way of managing organisational equality. Like EO, diversity must be situated in the social and cultural context in which it emerged. In North America, where the diversity approach originated, and in the UK governments were favouring a more individualist approach whereby responsibility and reward were situated at an individual (rather than collective) level. This emphasis on individuals fed into labour laws and contributed to a gradual change in organisational culture and perspectives on behaviour at work, as well as influencing norms and values in the culture of society as a whole.

Considering the principles upon which diversity is based can help us to differentiate between the EO and diversity approaches to equality management. First, the diversity approach places an emphasis on being relevant to everyone. Because of its close correlation with legislative obligations, the equal opportunities approach has often been accused of being relevant only to those groups or cohorts that are explicitly covered by law, such as the disabled (Disability Discrimination Act 2005) or members of ethnic minorities (Race Relations (Amendment) Act 2000) within the UK. Even in cases where the law seeks to protect everyone, such as through the Sex Discrimination Act (1975 (Amendment) Regulations 2008), in practice it is often perceived as having more relevance to one group, such as women. In contrast, the diversity approach concentrates on difference by holding that everyone is unique by virtue of their characteristics, lifestyle choices or preferences related to how they work. Under the diversity approach, such differences should be respected and celebrated, thus contributing to a harmonious (and discrimination-free) work environment.

Second, diversity is seen as an *organisation-wide* approach to equality. Because of its focus on human resource policies such as recruitment, selection and promotion, EO was often seen as mainly a concern for those involved in making key decisions surrounding career progression and development. This often meant that it became an administrative responsibility rather than a proactive approach to anticipating possible discrimination. In contrast, the promotion of diversity is often linked to external stakeholders or wider organisational messages about their practices. This is achieved in two ways. The first is the alignment of its commitments and objectives with other management practices that see employees as the key source of competitive advantage, thus requiring a workforce that is highly skilled and committed. For example, Total Quality Management and Human Resource Management share similarities with the diversity approach in promoting the view that, through recognising the individual's unique skill set and building on it, a contented workforce can become the best source of competitive advantage. The second way of ensuring that diversity remains an organisation-wide concern is by promoting the organisation's type of employment practices as evidence of a wider ethical approach to business. This can be seen in the inclusion of diversity policies and practices in statements concerning the organisational culture or ethical codes of practice. The promotion of diversity thus becomes the power tool for company branding through helping to legitimise rhetoric about being an 'ethical company'. An example of this is the 'Business Code of Conduct' adopted by organisations such as Nestle (2008) and Tate and Lyle (2008).

Finally, and most significantly, diversity offers not only a moral incentive to challenge discrimination but also an economic one. Advocates of diversity management argue that embracing diversity is not only ethically sound and the 'right thing to do' but can have economic advantages for the organisation, mainly through promoting a 'business case for equality'. This maintains that a diverse workplace will allow companies to tap into new markets and be responsive to the needs of particular groups of customers. Ensuring that the workplace is discrimination-free will also avoid costly legal discrimination cases in employment tribunals, and ensure staff retention by recognising individual needs and skill sets. For example, by considering older workers' right to request working past retirement age, organisations can ensure they are not losing valuable employees who have tacit knowledge that the company requires. Moreover, by recruiting from all age groups organisations access a wider pool of potential talent in order to improve organisational performance.

These three considerations not only influence actual day-to-day work practices but imply that diversity management invites both managers and employees to *think differently* about discrimination and equality issues through promoting particular ways of understanding age in relation to work. For example, rather than view older workers as potential victims of age discrimination, diversity encourages us to think about the unique sets of skills they may bring to the organisation, such as 'experience'. Moreover, organisations can connect their promotion of individuals with marketing campaigns, as seen in the campaigns by B&Q, the do-it-yourself chain store, which promotes the view that older shop-floor staff can draw on their past experience as tradespeople in order to help customers requests (see Figure 4.1). In this sense, we can see diversity as not simply a set of management practices but as a paradigm; in other words, a way of thinking about equality management that shapes and promotes a particular view of the world. This means that, when managers from different companies talk to each other about age diversity, they can assume that they are referring to a similar set of values and shared assumptions supporting what age diversity 'means'.

However, even though advocates of diversity management would claim it has been successful in promoting equality in the workplace, a number of critics suggest that the alleged potential of diversity management is not matched by its practice. First, while the theory of diversity suggests a distinct approach to equality that differs significantly from the EO approach, some commentators have suggested that in practice little has changed (for example, Elmuti 1993).

B&Q, a nationwide DIY store employing 40,000 people throughout the UK, has long been seen as championing the employment of older workers. As far back as 1989, it introduced a system that promoted working beyond age 60, as well as opening a store near Manchester all of whose staff were aged over 50. Since B&Q has been heralded as a benchmark for good practice by campaigning groups, the company has also enjoyed being a 'voice' in the older-worker debate, often taking part in consultations and events in the run-up to the Employment Equality Age Regulations in 2006. From the beginning of its promotion of the older worker, B&Q has used strategies that are strongly justified by a business-case rationale. The levels of high productivity and profit of its 'over 50s' store was highly publicised, and the value of its age-diverse workforce is a key part of its advertising strategy, which uses staff from its stores in television campaigns. These advertisements often show members of staff saying 'I've been a plumber for 20 years' as a means of highlighting how the past experience of workers on the shop floor can be of direct benefit to customers.

*Figure 4.1* B&Q's promotion of older workers

Consequently, diversity may suffer from the 'old wine in new bottles' problem, whereby companies change the names of policies rather than encourage a more significant change of mindset. A second criticism is the impossibility of recognising the uniqueness of individuals within larger bureaucratic systems of work. This means that often certain forms of 'difference' are seen as fixed and visible and given more attention, such as race and gender (Litvin 1997), and therefore become prioritised (Riach 2009). Finally, the claims of economic advantage made by advocates of diversity have been overplayed. While avoiding claims of discrimination may reduce costs, the correlation made between a diverse workforce and economic advantage is problematic. For example, research suggests that companies that promote the employment of older workers often limit their recruitment to customer-facing or low-skill jobs (Metcalf and Thompson 1990; Warr and Pennington 1993). This makes it unlikely that older employees occupy positions where they can influence strategic change within the company.

Notwithstanding these limitations, the impact of diversity on people management has been significant. While companies in the UK are still required by law to keep records of their employee base in relation to gender, ethnicity and disability, diversity has been used to demonstrate the extent to which companies proactively encourage equality beyond the basic legislative requirements. The beliefs and debates underpinning diversity have also served to influence policy and practice beyond immediate organisational environments. For example, a number of government publications, such as *Equality and Diversity: The Way Ahead* (Department of Trade and Industry/Department of Work and Pensions 2002), emphasise diversity as a key tenet of a civilised and forward-thinking society. In particular, the diversity paradigm has underpinned much of the increased focus on the ageing workforce and older workers' participation in the labour market, as we shall now discuss.

## 4.2 Older workers through the diversity lens

In one sense, the treatment of age in both management policy and organisational practice has been different to other forms of equality. While legislation and the framing of gender and racial inequality were mainly developed under an EO rubric, age equality, since it became a key feature of the management agenda during the 1990s, has mainly been ensconced within the diversity paradigm. As we shall illustrate, this has had particular effects on the way that age as an equality issue has been contextualised and shaped, particularly in relation to older workers.

Diversity has been one of the key resources used to promote the older worker since the early 1990s. Although they are not explicitly linked, the emergence of diversity as a management issue in the 1980s coincided with an increasing awareness of the ageing population and its effects on the labour market, especially within developed countries. The rationale of diversity comfortably supported the notion that individuals would have to work longer and organisations would need to consider this as a positive feature of the contemporary workplace. Earlier discussions of the ageing workforce were based on bio-medical assumptions in relation to exploring the abilities of older workers, with many studies focusing on the physiological decline of older workers relative to younger ones. There was an awareness that individuals were living longer, but a surge of research exploring the occupational health challenges faced by an ageing workforce reinforced the correlation between chronological age and decline in cognitive and physical capabilities. However, towards the end of the twentieth century diversity began to be used as a way of distancing or challenging medically deterministic concerns about capability and instead diverted attention to the social and economic benefits of an age-diverse workforce, with particular emphasis on older workers.

The influence of diversity as a rationale for age-management practice can be seen at a political level and may be part of the reason why, at first, the UK government preferred a voluntarist approach to age management rather than punitive sanctions through discrimination legislation. The Code of Practice on Age Diversity (1999) was the first equality-related code to be introduced voluntarily within the UK; it highlights the benefits of an 'age-diverse' population, heavily drawing on a business-case rationale. In particular, the code focused on six points in the employment cycle where age biases could creep in. Once again, its adoption was justified using a business-case approach, such as suggesting 'Employers' support for the code will also help attract potential job applicants and customers who are interested in identifying employers who deal fairly with their employees' (DfEE 1999, p. 6). However, the code met with some well-laid criticisms that claimed its voluntary status, compared with other forms of discrimination that were sanctioned by law, would have a negligible impact on practice and would fail to provide any type of guidance for tribunal cases related to age inequalities (for example, Loretto, Duncan and White 2000). It was also suggested that its focus on entry rather than exit from the labour market failed to tackle some of the wider concerns surrounding older worker participation, such as early retirement, as well as failing to acknowledge that age discrimination could be an 'organisation-wide' phenomenon that creeps into everyday interaction. Such prophecies were realised in the UK government's own assessment of the code (Department of Work and Pensions 2005), which suggested that only 29 per cent of employers were aware of the code six months after its introduction, while fewer than half of small and medium enterprises planned to change their practice as a result of the code (Employers' Forum on Age 1999).

With the introduction of the European Union legislation that required the UK to institute formal age discrimination legislation (see Chapter 3), the UK government in 2001 set up Age Positive, which fully embraced the notion of age diversity as a key way of tackling discrimination. From its launch, Age Positive was framed as a 'campaign' for 'tackling age discrimination and promoting age diversity at work' (Age Positive 2001). As well as providing examples of good practice by organisations through profiling 'age champions', such as ASDA supermarket, B&Q and Halifax Bank, it also sought to create a list of 'age positive employers', who pledged to promote age diversity within their organisations. Age Positive also brought together reports and publications related to age, as well as publishing pamphlets with advice for employers, such as guides on recruitment and retirement and on the business benefits of being 'age diverse'. The campaign also sought to debunk myths and negative stereotypes related to older-worker behaviour by drawing on statistical and qualitative studies as well as examples from a wide range of organisations. All of these carried the same message: that losing older workers was an economic challenge for organisations, and they must learn to accommodate and celebrate employees of all ages. As a result, Age Positive's website became one of the most comprehensive sources of support and up-to-date advice for organisations (in March 2009 it merged with other government online resources).

The use of the business-case approach in policy is another example of how the diversity approach can be seen as influencing the older-worker agenda in the workplace. Early UK government documents, such as 'Winning the Generation Game' (Performance Innovation Unit 2000), emphasised the £16 billion economic loss that could be attributed to age discrimination. This rhetoric appears to have filtered down into the mindset of managers when promoting age diversity, as shown in a number of empirical studies. For example, McVittie, McKinlay and Widdicombe's (2003) analysis of managers' perceptions of age diversity are strongly legitimised by a business-case rationale, while Riach's (2009) study of human resource managers' construction of age diversity demonstrates the importance of an economic rationale in upholding and promoting the value of the diversity approach.

The diversity approach to age at work can be seen as not only shaping practices and policies in the workplace, but also influencing how the 'older worker identity' is constructed. Much of the promotional literature that accompanied age-diversity campaigns, whether published by Age Positive or developed within organisations, presented older workers in a way that fully complemented the diversity message. For example, it was claimed that most older workers were able-bodied and healthy, which contradicts recent studies that highlight the overlap between occupational health conditions and the older labour market. They were also often framed as skilled in customer-facing positions, as people who had made an individual choice to continue working, and not very interested in career development (see Riach 2007). In one sense, this is unsurprising: promotional literature is often one-sided and extols the benefits of particular schemes as a win–win for employees and employers. However, in many ways this may have distorted or undermined the heterogeneity of the older-worker cohort. In order to consider these issues further, we now critically examine the meanings and sense-making processes that surround 'age diversity'.

## 4.3 Critically examining age diversity

As discussed previously, the management of age-related practices in the workplace through the diversity paradigm has had a significant impact on the political development of age management in the workplace. A number of limitations in age diversity bear out general criticisms of diversity management made by scholars such as Zanoni and Janssens (2003) or Kirkton and Greene (2005). However, the influence of diversity discourses appears to have been particularly profound in shaping 'older worker' policy and practice. In order to fully appreciate the influence of diversity discourses on age management, we must step back from the practices of age diversity and reflect on the ways in which the age-diversity paradigm has created a powerful set of beliefs that influence the way we think or talk about age and the older worker.

First, age diversity may be seen as creating an overly optimistic view of the workplace and the social dynamics that surround discrimination and inequality. In their general critique of the diversity approach, Prasad et al. (1995) refer to the 'upbeat naivety' inherent in the diversity paradigm that shrouds the more malevolent intentions behind inequality, where discrimination occurs as a result of the power dynamics at play within organisations. Marginalising groups that are disadvantaged through hierarchical, seemingly objective structures may lead to challenges or barriers, particular those facing older workers, being ignored, since it is difficult to radically change organisational systems through a diversity approach. More significantly, trying to locate diversity in particular parts of the organisational function may render obsolete larger structural or social–political disadvantages or distort the challenges older workers face. One clear example of this is the lack of space to present a more balanced view of issues surrounding ageing at work through discussing specific challenges faced by those working in later life. As discussed earlier, the diversity approach seeks to distance itself from medically determined views of age and health. However, framing older-worker participation in solely celebratory tenors often provides little room for managers to consider the larger responsibilities of supporting a body of workers who, over time, have become unhealthy *because* of their jobs rather than as a direct result of ageing, and who will subsequently require support should they remain in the labour market. Part of the reason for this may be a lack of integration of all the issues that affect 'age management', a term that is increasingly used in organisations but rarely articulated with its precise meaning. For example, rarely do discussions concerning the health of the workforce appear alongside practices promoting age diversity, since initiatives and practices are often the responsibility of different functions within the organisation (human resources and occupational health). As a result, organisational age-diversity narratives do not match the reality of the current (or even future) potential older-worker labour market.

The second challenge in using the age-diversity paradigm to prevent age discrimination is the inherent emphasis placed on economic value. An example of this is the business-case approach to older workers that (as discussed in Chapter 2) has been fundamental in shaping the older-worker agenda in the UK. One of the important elements of the business-case approach is its economic rationale and the idea that diversity is economically beneficial for everyone – individuals, organisations and the country as a whole. Such a viewpoint is strongly rooted in what may be seen as a neo-liberal approach to equality. Situated within broader political and policy narratives, a neo-liberal approach emphasises the principle of the market (and profit) as the chief rationale for policies and practices. The need to 'measure' the advantage of tacit practices has become a key issue in terms of accountability and demonstrating the 'value added' of certain management practices. Therefore, by placing some form of economic value on the promotion of age equality, an investment in diversity practices may be easier to justify to both government bodies and the boards of directors of organisations. However, using measurable economic value may disadvantage those viewed as potential 'older workers'. By privileging the idea that everything (and everyone) can be defined through some form of economic contribution or value, other contributions made outside the labour market may not be recognised. This is particularly important when considering the over-50s, many of whom make vital contributions to society beyond immediate paid employment through caring for partners or elderly parents, informal childcare or other unpaid family or social roles. For example, estimates suggest that 42 per cent of 55–64-year-olds and 41 per cent of those over 65 regularly volunteer (IVR 2007), one of the highest participation rates across age groups.

The third tension in situating age management within a diversity paradigm is the potential for the diversity paradigm to exacerbate discrimination or inadvertently oversimplify age discrimination through a conflation between age as a chronological 'fact' and the social processes through which age inequality might emerge. This is often achieved through the message that, since we all age, age diversity should be seen as relevant to everyone. For example, in the age consultation of 2003 (Department of Trade and Industry 2003, p.4), Patricia Hewitt, the then Minister for Women and Equality, wrote 'Age is a condition that we all have in common, and that we're resigned to having been younger or getting older'. However, often this creates a syllogism in assuming that since we all age, we all have an equal chance of being discriminated against. Research shows that this is not the case and it is impossible to separate age inequality from social class, profession, economic status or employment history. Exploring the intersections between age and other characteristics, such as gender (Duncan and Loretto 2004) or socio-economic status, shows that other factors have a strong bearing on the likelihood of being a victim of age discrimination and experiencing barriers to labour market entry or advancement in later life (Boyes and McCormick 2005). For this reason, it is more likely that individuals who are low-skilled and have exited the labour market a number of times throughout their working lives will be subject to discrimination (part of which may be based on age). In this sense, it is very difficult for age diversity alone to actively challenge the more complex reasons why age discrimination might occur, as it often occurs alongside other modes of inequality.

This tendency to oversimplify the social processes through which people are discriminated against is arguably the result of age diversity producing particular ways of thinking about age at work. While we know from studies (Ainsworth 2002; Riach 2007) that age discrimination is complex, insidious and widespread throughout organisations as well as in society, age diversity often focuses only on particular dimensions that serve certain managerial or organisational ends. Some scholars have argued that in this way advocates of age diversity deliberately tend to depoliticise the fight for equality by distancing it from affirmative action or social justice movements (Lorbiecki and Jack 2000) and therefore appropriate equality in a way that is palatable to managers and fully compatible with the pursuit of profit. If this is the case, it may be that age diversity becomes no more than a device used by managers to 'contain' discussions of age inequality or provide boundaries for how and when we should think about age at work.

Another consequence of age diversity is the potential for narratives and discourses of age diversity to create a mythologised 'ideal type' of older worker. Following Weber's (1904/1949) notion of ideal type, we can see that the category of 'older worker' is created as a means of comparing different ideas or beliefs, often by accentuating particular characteristics of a group. The notion of ideal types can be used to understand how the diversity paradigm promotes a particular image or archetype of an 'older worker', as well as a vision of how this older worker should act and behave. While they may be related to particular stereotypes, ideal types also carry more inherent and often subconscious assumptions about a particular group that affects how they are treated. One study of older worker recruitment strategies (Riach 2007) showed how the use of particular textual strategies and certain language created an image of the 'ideal' older worker. For example, suggesting the need to recruit older workers in bingo halls and coffee mornings implies that older workers either are different from the rest of the potential labour pool or may not be actively looking for employment. The creation of such an image is often beneficial to the organisation by positioning the company as the paternal patrons of the older workers' cause while marginalising those who do not 'fit' this projected image.

Narratives that support age diversity also create a certain image of the older worker in other ways. One tactic is to position older workers as 'suited' to particular jobs that require excellent people skills and to give them a social motivation for working. The effect of such images can be seen as implying that older workers work for social reasons and 'pin money' rather than economic necessity. Moreover, the impact of the older-worker ideal type can be seen as influencing widespread age-management tactics by making homogenised assumptions about 'what older workers want'. For example, the introduction of 'Benidorm leave' as promoted by the UK supermarket chain ASDA, where older workers can take three months unpaid leave, reinforces the notion that the 'older worker' is different in some way from the rest of the workforce (although 'Benidorm leave' is now open to all employees because the company feared restricting it to older workers might be in breach of age legislation). The impact of these older-worker ideal types not only affects age-diversity practices but also feeds into wider social perceptions of age-related stereotypes of workers that subsequently influence opinion concerning employment priority, especially when there is competition in the labour market. For example, during the UK recession of 2008–09, as has been the case in previous times of economic hardship (cf. MacNicol, 2006), younger and older workers are often positioned as directly in mutual competition for jobs, with media commentary on youth unemployment and the economic pressure on those aged under 30 implicitly framing younger workers as more 'worthy'. This has resulted in an increased priority accorded to youths who are not in employment, education or training (NEETS) rather than those aged over 50 who are in long-term unemployment, even though the coming generation of older workers may have heavier financial commitments such as large mortgages or dependent children.

Finally, the diversity paradigm can be seen to promote subtle narratives that reproduce ageist norms. Termed 'new ageism' (McVittie, McKinlay and Widdicombe 2003), diversity debates can often be used in the conscious or unconscious marginalisation of ageism as an issue. This occurs when the explicit rejection of discrimination sits alongside attempts to normalise and justify current age inequalities that exist in the workforce by appealing to rational arguments that emphasise the 'natural' differences between people of different ages. While this line of reasoning is often presented as 'common sense', often such assumptions are built upon deeply embedded age biases. As McVittie, McKinlay and Widdicombe (2003) show, this is achieved by using a language and vocabulary associated with equality together with 'common sense' factors. For example, in their study, one manager suggests that her place of work is not attractive to those who are older. This is presented as the reason for the absence of older workers, rather than the possibility that organizational cultures or practices favour the recruitment of younger workers. Narratives of new ageism can also be found through organisations or managers prioritising some forms of disadvantage over others. For example, when the diversity justification of economic incentive is used, it is often implied that tackling racial or gender inequality must be prioritised since ageism is not as socially unacceptable as other 'isms' and is less likely to attract bad publicity (see Riach 2009).

The notion of comparing ageism with other 'isms' (such as sexism or racism) raises the question whether age diversity in itself is equipped to tackle discrimination rather than simply celebrate the promotion of equality. Although diversity endorses treating individuals as unique, Litvin (1997) argues that diversity often degenerates into simply categorising particular groups when one considers who might be susceptible to unfavourable treatment. While these categories are often correlated with a discrete classification in relation to sex or colour of skin, 'being older' is often a heavily relative or contextual social construction. For example, within the IT industry workers as 'young' as 35 have been perceived as too old (EFA/Silcon 2000), while in other sectors, such as health, a surgeon may be classed as 'junior' in his or forties. In practice, therefore, the category 'older worker' can be seen not as shaped by an individual's chronological age, as espoused in policy and academia where markers such as '18–24' or '50/55–64' are used to classify older or younger workers, but as dependent on the industry, organisational context or culture of the company. 'Being' an older worker is therefore difficult to categorise since we have to take into account the influence of the individual, cultural and organisational perceptions that surround the notion of growing older at work. Individuals being discriminated against in the workplace on account of age may not be seen as 'younger' or 'older' in society in general or even consider themselves to be old or young. This makes them less sensitive to possible discriminatory attitudes or fearful of formal complaints of age discrimination. If these complexities make identifying age discrimination increasingly challenging for courts, reflected in the low number of successful UK age-discrimination cases (53 successful cases in 2008/2009, only 2 per cent of those accepted by tribunals), it may be that the ambiguities in identifying and tackling age discrimination requires more than a diversity approach to equality management.

## 4.4 Summary and conclusions

This chapter has sought to introduce the impact of diversity paradigms and practices on the management of age-related workplace issues concerning the older worker and age discrimination. As we have discussed, the diversity debate has had a particular impact on the way that issues surrounding age at work have been negotiated, particularly in relation to policies concerning the recruitment and perceptions of older workers. Some of these policies have been presented as directly benefiting the campaign for older workers, such as providing an economic incentive for employing older workers and acknowledging that they may bring valuable skill sets into business.

However, as we interrogate the relationship between age and the diversity paradigm we can see a number of limitations within the age-diversity paradigm. Age diversity may not only fail to provide an incentive for explicitly challenging discrimination beyond an economic rationale, but even exacerbate age inequality by promoting normalised homogeneous images of the older worker or ideas about how older workers should behave. This suggests that we need a broader organisational approach that allows us to consider the various intersections between age, other forms of inequality and organisational practices. One catalyst for developing this approach may be the UK Single Equalities Act 2010, which provides a legislative umbrella for all forms of discrimination. If successful, such a reform could result in organisations having to reconsider the impact of multiple forms of discrimination and how age inequality must be considered as much of a management priority as other forms of discrimination, rather than simply a concern arising from demographic pressures. More cynically, another impetus for change may be that organisations have no alternative but to consider how they might formally tackle age discrimination in order to avoid tribunal attendances. While the number of successful cases in the UK remains low, the increase in cases being taken to tribunal continues to rise, with 3801 cases during the 2008–9 period (Ministry of Justice 2009), making age discrimination a costly business for employers.

However, as with any management practice, age diversity is created not only by formal policies or legislation but by myths, narratives and social perceptions that influence how diversity principles are translated into informal cultures and everyday practices. Indeed, the promotion of age equality as a workplace concern is itself situated within historical and social patterns of labour market activity where, over the past 50 years, there has been an increase of years spent in retirement, often supported by government incentives to encourage workers to leave the labour market. As a result, such norms surrounding an extended 'third age' live on in the social memory of the UK and may prove hard to reverse.

The way ageing and older people are viewed in society can influence age diversity practices: if we hold strong opinions about what behaviours are acceptable or unacceptable based on age, then it is likely we will carry such perceptions into the workplace. As Lorbiecki and Jack (2000, S28) comment, 'The belief that diversity management is do-able rests on a fantasy that it is possible to imagine a clean slate'. In order to be effective, age-equality practices have to take into account social forces or perceptions that appear external to the immediate organisational environment but nonetheless are brought into the organisations by every employee and have an effect on how we relate to people of different ages. Such ingrained social biases will continue to influence how individuals think about age and work if they are not openly challenged or if the problem is not discussed within an organisational arena.

# 5
# The Relationship between Gender and Age

*Wendy Loretto and Sarah Vickerstaff*

There is a considerable literature on gender and work and a burgeoning research programme on age and employment, especially in relation to older workers. Yet thus far, with a few honourable exceptions, there is very little on the relationship between gender and age. As Biggs has put it:

> While age and gender are experienced by an individual as intimately and possibly inextricably connected, they are, more often than not, treated separately by academics and policymakers.
>
> (2004, p. 55)

In mainstream texts on human resource management, it is now (one is tempted to say at last!) normal to find a chapter on managing diversity, but age has only recently emerged on to the equality agenda. Moreover, there is still a tendency to treat areas of difference as relatively separate issues, notwithstanding the creation of the single equality body in the UK – the Equality and Human Rights Commission (EHRC) in 2007 – and the subsequent equality legislation, which provides a single legal framework for tackling discrimination and disadvantage (see Chapter 3 for a discussion of this legislation). It is important that the academic literature should now consider the implications of the fact that gendered subjects are also aged. This is all the more pressing for a number of reasons: there continues to be a rising proportion of women of all ages in the workforce; and older women in particular are seen as an 'untapped potential' in government's urge to extend our working lives.

This chapter seeks to bring an age perspective to gender issues, such as work–life balance and flexible working, while also bringing a gender perspective to age issues – for example, recognising that gender may be a significant differentiating factor in explaining motivations, expectations and attitudes to work in later life. The discussion is in four parts. First, using UK Labour Force Survey data we review the gendered patterns of employment, unemployment and inactivity across the life course for women and men. This part considers the sectors and occupations that women and men work in at different ages, experiences of flexible working across the life course, and the difference between female and male 'career' paths. Second, we consider the intersections of age and gender discrimination, looking at gendered ageism and its impacts. Third, we focus on the particular case of older women workers, the impact of caring responsibilities and their transitions to retirement. Finally, we conclude the chapter by considering the implications of the discussion for employers and managers.

## 5.1 Patterns of work

### 5.1.1 Participation in the labour force

Overall, in 2009 45.9 per cent of the UK workforce and 46.4 per cent of the employed workforce were female. These figures represent a long-run trend of increased participation by women in the labour market since the 1970s. Our focus here is not the increase in female employment per se, but how this relates to and intersects with participation across the age spectrum of the workforce. Table 5.1 contains full details of economic activity of men and women in five-year age bands from 16 to 70 and over. Much of the employment policy focus has been on the youth labour market (under-25s) where there have been trends towards increasing numbers of young men and women in higher and further education and rising unemployment, especially among young males. Another key focus has been on women in the child-bearing and child-rearing years, with many of the changes to employment laws since the turn of the millennium attempting to make work more 'family-friendly' in order to encourage parents (especially mothers) to remain in the workforce. At the older end of the workforce age spectrum, the main concern has been with declining employment among men in their fifties and older. In fact the groups that have received least attention have been older women. However, as Table 5.1 shows, employment rates among men and women drop sharply after state pension ages (currently 60 for women and 65 for men in the UK). The drop is especially sharp for women, as Figure 5.1 illustrates. In welfare terms, these retired women are costly; hence the UK government is raising the state pension age for women to 65 (and further raising it for both sexes to 68 by 2044). However, it is less obvious that there has been much, if

*Table 5.1* Economic activity for men and women by age group (UK), January–March 2009

| Age | Men (%) | | | Women (%) | | |
|---|---|---|---|---|---|---|
| | In employment | ILO unemployed | Economically inactive | In employment | ILO unemployed | Economically inactive |
| 16–19 | 39.2 | 13.9 | 47.0 | 41.0 | 10.7 | 48.3 |
| 20–4 | 64.4 | 13.5 | 22.1 | 61.6 | 7.6 | 30.8 |
| 25–9 | 84.9 | 8.3 | 6.8 | 71.8 | 5.3 | 22.9 |
| 30–4 | 87.9 | 5.8 | 6.4 | 72.0 | 4.1 | 23.8 |
| 35–9 | 88.8 | 4.5 | 6.7 | 73.6 | 3.7 | 22.7 |
| 40–4 | 88.1 | 4.8 | 7.1 | 76.8 | 3.7 | 19.4 |
| 45–9 | 86.6 | 4.8 | 8.6 | 78.2 | 3.8 | 17.9 |
| 50–4 | 83.2 | 4.8 | 11.9 | 75.3 | 2.7 | 22.0 |
| 55–9 | 76.4 | 4.8 | 18.7 | 64.7 | 2.0 | 33.3 |
| 60–4 | 57.6 | 3.0 | 39.4 | 34.2 | 0.7 | 65.1 |
| 65–9 | 22.2 | 0.8 | 77.0 | 13.7 | # | 85.9 |
| 70 + | 4.7 | # | 95.2 | 2.0 | # | 97.9 |
| Total 16 –70 + % | 65.0 | 5.6 | 29.4 | 53.3 | 3.4 | 43.2 |
| N (000s) | 15627 | 1349 | 7064 | 13501 | 873 | 10942 |

*Source*: LFS data, January–March 2009 (authors' own analysis).

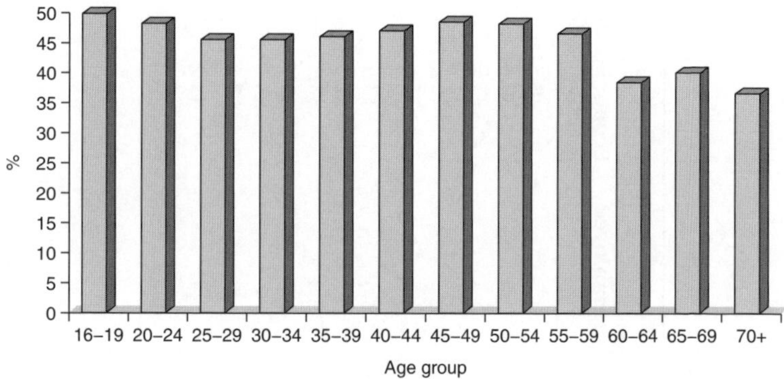


*Figure 5.1* Proportion of those in employment in each age group who are women
*Source*: LFS data, January–March 2009 (authors' own analysis).

any, recognition by government or employers that these women may represent an 'untapped potential' (Loretto, Vickerstaff and White 2005) for the UK workforce.

### 5.1.2 Part-time working

Although much employment policy is based on overall numbers of men and women in employment, these figures cannot tell us anything about the nature of the jobs being undertaken, how these might change over the age spectrum of the workforce, and how they may differ between the sexes. Female working and part-time working are often considered together as women comprise three-quarters of the 25 per cent of the workforce that works part time. To put it another way, overall, 42.4 per cent of women in employment and 11.6 per cent of men in employment work part time. Once again, the patterns of part-time working vary quite markedly over the age groups, with men and women displaying quite different patterns, as illustrated by Figure 5.2.

Part-time working among men follows a bipolar or U-shaped distribution, with part-time working being most prevalent among men at the very beginning of the work spectrum (16–19-year-olds) and those aged 60 and above. The distribution for women also peaks at the youngest and oldest age groups, but features a third peak, in the 35–44-year-old groups. The Labour Force Survey data facilitate some exploration of the reasons for part-time working, and we can examine how reasons may change according to age and gender. For this analysis we have split the workforce into three age groups: 16–19-years-old (high proportions of part-time working); 20–59 (relatively lower proportions of part-time working); and 60+ (highest proportions of part-time working).

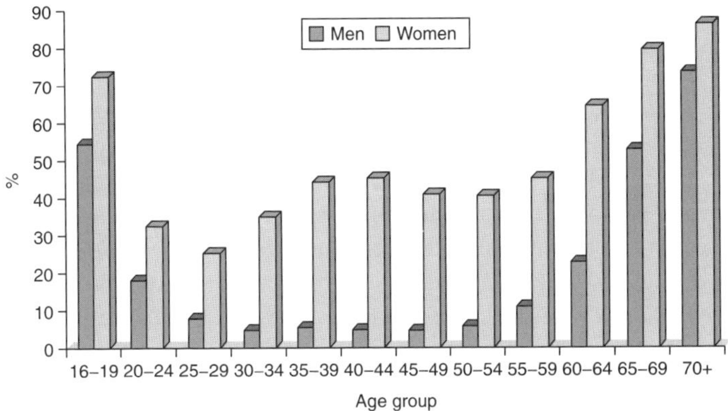


*Figure 5.2* Proportion of those in employment in each age group working part time
*Source*: LFS data, January–March 2009 (authors' own analysis).

In the 16–19–year-old age group, the predominant reason for working part-time, given by 82 per cent of men and 84 per cent of women who work part time, is that they are students or are still at school. At the other end of the working life course, there is also consensus between men and women – 91 per cent of men aged 60 + and 96.5 per cent of women age 60+ who work part time do so because they do not want a full-time job. However, in that 'middle' grouping the reasons given for working part time differ quite markedly between the sexes. Over four-fifths (83.3 per cent) of women aged 20–59 who work part time do so because they do not want a full-time job. The corresponding proportion of men is much smaller at 39.2 per cent: a third of men in these age groups working part time do so on an involuntary basis, because they could not find a full-time job. A further fifth are still studying and 6.2 per cent work part time because of a long-term illness or disability. The relevance of all this for employers and managers is that the motivations of men and women who work part time converge and differ at different ages.

### 5.1.3 Self-employment

It is not only the time spent working that may differ between men and women in different age groups; the basis of employment also varies. In total, 3.83 million or 13.2 per cent of those in employment are self-employed. Men comprise 72 per cent of the self-employed workforce, and for both sexes the proportion of self-employed rises steadily in each age group, with a steeper increase from age 55 and over. In this case, although the curves for numbers of men and women have roughly the same shape (see Figure 5.3 below), research has shown that the reasons for being self-employed may differ. A study in Australia (Walker and Webster 2007) found that older women (aged 50+) were much less likely than younger women or men of any age to say they had started their business because they wanted to be their own boss. For women of all ages, flexibility – being able to balance work and family responsibilities – was seen as a strong reason. Older women were much less likely than older men to seek self-employment as their preferred employment option. Instead they emphasised as key drivers the inability to find suitable alternative employment, as well as lack of advancement in previous careers.

### 5.1.4 Sector of employment

The location of work also varies between men and women and across age groups. First, for each age group, apart from the 16–19-year-olds, women are twice as likely as men to work in the public sector. As Figure 5.4 shows, public sector working is most prevalent for those aged 40–50, with one-fifth of men and two-fifths of women in those age groups employed by the public sector. The prevalence then declines (with a slightly sharper decrease for men). This is partly but by no means wholly accounted for by the higher proportions of the older age groups in self-employed.

### 5.1.5 Industry

This bias towards the employment of women, and older women, in the public sector is picked up in a more detailed examination of the

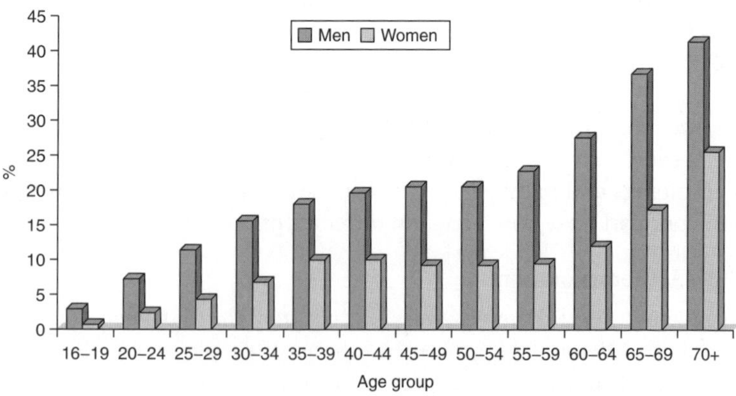


*Figure 5.3* Proportion of self-employed among those in employment, by gender and age
*Source*: LFS data, January–March 2009 (authors' own analysis)

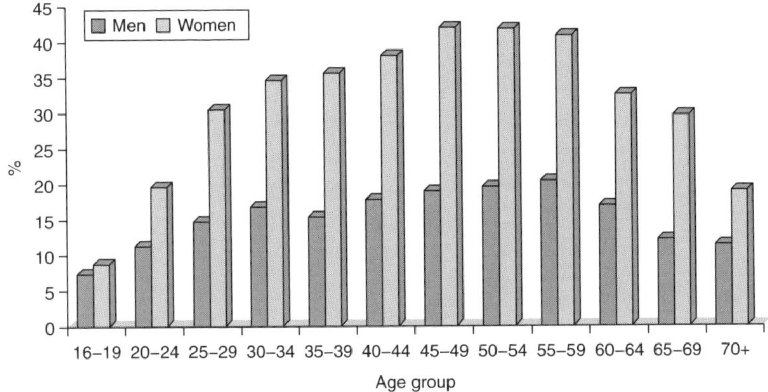


*Figure 5.4* Proportion of the employed working in the public sector, by age and gender
*Source*: LFS data, January–March 2009 (authors' own analysis).

industries people work in. Table 5.2 shows the three largest in terms of numbers employed for each age group and gender. Here the age classifications reflect the 'youth' (16–25-year-olds), 'prime' (25–49-year-olds) and 'older' (50+) labour markets.

The industries included in Table 5.2 confirm the gendered nature of employment, with construction and manufacturing featuring only in the men's top three, and health and social work featuring only in the women's. Once past the youth labour market, the three most popular industries show consistency across the age groups for both men and women. However, the table clearly shows that employment for women is more concentrated into their top three than is employment for men. It also shows that whereas for women that concentration is greater for older groups, for men the concentration is greater among younger groups. The concept of 'horizontal segregation' for women's employment, whereby women are more likely than men to work in a restricted range of industries, is a well-established one. Our current analysis suggests that there is greater horizontal segregation among older women than among younger women. Of course, as this analysis is only cross-sectional, we have no way of knowing whether it reflects a trend associated with ageing or merely reflects the patterns of employment of the present cohorts of women at the various ages.

### 5.1.6 Occupational categories

'Vertical segregation', the term used to reflect the fact that women are disproportionately represented in the higher echelons of employment, can also be examined across the age groups.

*Table 5.2* Largest industries in terms of employment, by gender and age group

| | Men | | | Women | | |
|---|---|---|---|---|---|---|
| **Age (yrs)** | **16–24** | **25–49** | **50+** | **16–24** | **25–49** | **50+** |
| 1 | Wholesale (25.7%) | Manufacturing (14.2%) | Manufacturing (15.0%) | Wholesale (27.6%) | Health and social work (22.1%) | Health and social work (24.8%) |
| 2 | Construction (15.0%) | Construction (14.2%) | Construction (13.9%) | Health and social work (14.4%) | Education (16.6%) | Education (17.8%) |
| 3 | Accommodation and food (11.0%) | Wholesale (12.0) | Wholesale (11.3%) | Accommodation and food (12.9%) | Wholesale (12.2%) | Wholesale (13.7%) |
| Total employed in Top 3 (%) | 51.7 | 40.4 | 40.2 | 54.9 | 50.9 | 56.3 |

*Source*: LFS data, January–March 2009 (authors' own analysis).

*Table 5.3* Occupational categories, by gender and age

| | Men | | | Women | | |
|---|---|---|---|---|---|---|
| Age (yrs) | 16–24 | 25–49 | 50+ | 16–24 | 25–49 | 50+ |
| Managers and senior officials (%) | 4.5 | 21.3 | 20.4 | 3.8 | 13.9 | 11.1 |
| Professional (%) | 4.8 | 15.7 | 15.4 | 4.9 | 14.1 | 13.2 |
| Associate professional and technical (%) | 11.3 | 15.3 | 11.6 | 9.5 | 18.3 | 12.5 |
| Admin and secretarial (%) | 6.5 | 4.1 | 4.8 | 16.0 | 18.3 | 22.7 |
| Skilled trades (%) | 21.9 | 17.4 | 19.4 | 1.3 | 1.6 | 2.3 |
| Personal service (%) | 3.2 | 2.4 | 2.8 | 18.9 | 15.5 | 14.4 |
| Sales and customer services (%) | 16.4 | 3.0 | 2.2 | 26.7 | 8.1 | 9.0 |
| Process, plant and machine operatives (%) | 7.4 | 11.4 | 13.4 | 0.9 | 1.7 | 2.1 |
| Elementary occupations (%) | 24.1 | 9.3 | 10.0 | 18.0 | 8.6 | 12.6 |
| Total (%) | 100 | 100 | 100 | 100 | 100 | 100 |

*Source*: LFS data, January–March 2009 (authors' own analysis).

Table 5.3 confirms vertical segregation – in all age groups women are less likely to be employed in the top occupational groups (managers, senior officials and professional occupations) and more likely to be employed in administrative and secretarial occupations. Both men and women over 50 are less likely than their counterparts of 'prime age' to be employed in these top categories. In terms of skilled work, men of all ages are markedly more likely to work in skilled trades, while women are employed in personal service jobs. A relatively greater proportion of older men and older women are employed in the elementary occupations (for example, entry-level jobs in retail, hospitality, personal services, cleaning and so on). These patterns raise issues of job quality for older workers, especially older women.

### 5.1.7 Pay

Two recent research reports conducted for the UK's Equality and Human Rights Commission have investigated how pay differs between men and women across different age groups. Analysis of LFS data from 2004–7 showed that women's pay was highest for those in the 35–9-year-old grouping as opposed to 40–4 for men (Longhi and Platt 2008). The authors noted that the gender pay gap seems to start at around age 29 and is maintained for all age groups up until the state pension age (the authors stopped their analysis at this point), with both older men and older women earning substantially less than their reference category of men aged 40–4. Metcalf's (2009) analysis of the *Annual Survey of Hours and Earnings* (2007) suggested the women's pay gap is explained partly by the rise in part-time working among those aged 30 and over. Both reports suggested these are cohort rather than age effects because of the different jobs and lower levels of qualifications among the current generation of older workers. Nevertheless, after controlling for qualifications, Longhi and Platt (2008) found that women of all ages with no qualifications earned significantly less than men aged 40–4 who had no qualifications.

Metcalf (2009, pp.75–9) reviewed research investigating possible causes of age pay gaps. The possible influences include: age differences in economic activity rates because of increasing incidence of ill-health with age; productivity changing with age; structural changes in the economy; penalties arising from periods of unemployment and from working part time; and evolution in pay systems. This overview revealed remarkably little focus on the interaction between age and gender, but did show that the part-time pay gap for older women may be greater than that for older men, again indicating that the types of job that many (older) women undertake are poorly paid compared with jobs undertaken by younger women or by men of any age.

### 5.1.8 Explaining the differences

This section has clearly illustrated that the differences between men's and women's experiences of employment change across the life course. In many respects, gender and age appear to especially disadvantage women in older age groups, as these are the least likely to be in employment and the most likely to be confined to a smaller range of jobs at the lower end of the spectrum.

One of the most vehement academic debates in relation to gender focuses on the reasons for the persistence of gender differences in the labour market. The UK has had equal pay legislation since the early 1970s, and outlawed sex discrimination in the middle of that decade. Since then the jobs landscape has altered hugely, moving to an economy where nearly three-quarters of the workforce are engaged in service-related jobs, leading to what some have termed the 'feminisation' of work. We have also seen a rise in the provision of childcare outside the home, which has enabled many mothers of young children to return to work earlier than they would have done in previous generations. The typical family structure is no longer the nuclear family – there are many more single-person households and households headed by a single parent, most often a mother. Government employment policy has moved away from the assumption of the male breadwinner model of the household towards the 'adult worker model' (Lewis 2002), which implies that men and women relate similarly to the labour market. There have also been other legal changes in relation to maternity and parental leave and a general strengthening of employee rights, for example in relation to protection against unfair dismissal. So why, despite these substantial changes, do gender differences persist? And to what extent does the interaction between age and gender contribute to these differences?

The academic debate has featured two perspectives: choice and constraints. The choice perspective, encapsulated by Hakim's (2000) preference theory, emphasises women's personal and lifestyle preferences. She argues that 'sex and gender are redundant concepts ... and are already being replaced by lifestyle preferences as the crucial differentiating characteristic in labour supply' (Hakim, 2007, pp. 124–5). While recognising the heterogeneity of women's preferences, she identifies three 'ideal types', and argues that the majority of women fit into one of three groups – family-centred, adaptive and work-centred (see Hakim 2007 for an overview of this theory and classifications). The opposing viewpoint (typified by the work of Crompton and Lyonette 2005) contests the extent to which these choices are real and instead emphasises the constraints faced by women. It is not the purpose of this chapter to enter the debate (a good overview is provided in Kan 2007); rather, we wish to point out the lack of an age perspective in the whole discussion. Kan's analysis is one of the few to explicitly consider age. It suggests that (women's) participation in the labour market alters their gender-role preference over time, but does not attempt to consider why this might be the case. Other work has focused on the balance between intrinsic and extrinsic work motivators, showing that older women may be the group most likely to value intrinsic rewards and motivators (Simpson et al. 2005), with parenthood also affecting the balance (Johnson 2005). Yet again, however, little insight has been gained into the reasons for these differences.

The remainder of this chapter aims to address this research lacuna, first, by considering the extent to which women's disadvantages in the labour market arise from a combination of gender and age, and second, by examining in some detail the position of older women in the labour market in order to assess their preferences, plans and constraints.

## 5.2 The intersections of age and gender discrimination

While gender discrimination and age discrimination in relation to work are well established and researched as discrete concepts, there has been relatively less focus on the interactions between the two – the notion of gendered ageism or the intersectionality of different forms of social division such as gender, age, race and class (on the concept of intersectionality see Moore 2009). One of the first studies to investigate the intersections between age and gender at work was Itzin and Phillipson's research in local authorities in England (1995). The authors found that women reached the high point in their careers some ten years earlier than men did. They also suggested that from the perspective of managers age was always related to how they perceived women – in the eyes of managers women may never be the 'right' age. Younger women were viewed as 'flighty' or 'preoccupied with wedding bells and/or children', while older women were simply too old. This prompted some intellectual questioning surrounding the nature of discrimination being experienced – is it predominantly gender discrimination? Is it mainly discrimination on grounds of age? Or is it some combination of the two? A small body of research has wrestled with these questions and has tried to shed some light on why older women are often in the least advantageous positions in the labour market.

### 5.2.1 Disadvantage arises primarily from gender discrimination

One perspective is that gender discrimination is the main factor and that this is compounded by age. The dominance of patriarchy in the workplace prioritises male careers and penalises discontinuity (Duncan and Loretto 2004; Granleese and Sayer 2006). Therefore, the devaluation of older women arises partly from a lifetime of subordination (Buoncore Porter 2003–4) and partly from always being the less favoured group. In support of this view, Gorman and Kmec's (2007) interrogation of work-effort data from the US and the UK showed that women consistently reported that their jobs required higher levels of effort. They put forward a persuasive case to suggest that this is because requirements for women are greater than those for men, even in the same job. They then make the connection with age by questioning the extent to which these greater requirements for women subsequently dissuade women from continuing or seeking advancement in their careers over the course of their working lives. Furthermore, Clarke and Griffin (2008) point out that the collective impact of work discrimination is worse for women because they live longer, have fewer financial resources and are less likely to have accrued a pension.

### 5.2.2 Disadvantage is caused mainly by age discrimination

A second view is that age discrimination is the chief disadvantaging factor. The UK Employment Equality (Age) Regulations 2006 outlaw age discrimination in employment and cover discrimination on grounds of *any* age (see Chapter 3). Nevertheless, in research and employment practice much of the focus has been on discrimination on grounds of *older* age, which is often thought to arise from a deeply rooted underlying fear of illness and death.

> As such, ageism is rooted in an insidious social obsession with youthfulness and results in the assigning of social value, resources, and opportunities based on actual and perceived chronological age.
> (Clarke and Griffin 2008, p. 655)

This results in older women being discriminated against by younger women (Buonocore Porter 2003–4), because the older women (employees) personify younger women's own fears of ageing (Handy and Davy 2007). However, this is not sufficient to explain why older women appear more disadvantaged than older men in the labour market. This brings us back to examining the interactions between gender and age.

### 5.2.3 Age discrimination and gender discrimination are additive

It may be that older women suffer discrimination both on account of their gender and on account of being older, and that these two forms of discrimination added together serve to especially disadvantage them. Building upon Itzin and Phillipson's (1995) work, Duncan and Loretto (2004) investigate several aspects of gendered ageism in a UK financial services company. Their findings suggest a bipolar distribution of age discrimination for both sexes. However, older women are more likely than older men to suffer age discrimination (Duncan and Loretto 2004). Other research supporting this position has drawn attention to the current cohort of older women, suggesting they may be particularly vulnerable to the effects of gendered ageism because of the prevailing norm of gender relationships based on male-breadwinner and female-carer roles (Handy and Davy 2007) and because of their life experience of discrimination. For example Walker et al.'s (2007) study of women aged 50 and over highlight how this cohort experienced employer discrimination as mothers in the 1960s and 1970s or faced explicit age barriers in jobs at a time when these were neither prohibited by legislation nor much challenged by society.

### 5.2.4 Age discrimination and gender discrimination are mutually reinforcing: the sum is greater than the parts

Finally, there is also strong support for the claim that gender and age discrimination are mutually reinforcing and that this mutual reinforcement puts women in a disadvantaged position. This perspective draws upon the notion of sexualising women's value to work (and beyond) in youth, in a way that is simply not the case for men. For example, Duncan and Loretto (2004) found that many of the accounts of age discrimination given by the women contained a sexualised element.

> One senior team member sent an e-mail when I forgot to sign a form .... 'Tell the dried up old maid to get her teeth in'. On another occasion a Team Leader called us a bunch of 'old *******' .... A coach asked us which was greater, our team's combined ages or [Finserv's] bank balance ... to name but a few incidents.
>
> (Female, 35)

The authors find that women in their thirties appear to suffer because they are perceived as being both too old *and* too young. Such discrimination is frequently based on their appearance. Other work has shown how appearance brings a gender dimension to job–age typing. Handy and Davy (2007) quote research from UK and from Australia which suggests that employers prefer younger women – aged around 25 – as clerical and reception staff. Their own study, in New Zealand, is based on interviews with female job seekers aged between 45 and early sixties, and with some private employment agencies. A former secretary in her mid-fifties commented that 'the best thing older women could do to improve their job prospects was to lose weight, invest in high-heeled shoes and become as glamorous as possible' (Handy and Davy 2007, p. 91)

From the employer's point of view, one (male) agency owner denies that women employees become less effective as they get older, but states that physical appearance could count against them – being older they are not perceived as being attractive. Walker et al. (2007, p.43) find that concern over appearance and being perceived as less attractive is greater among older women in professional, male-managed and hierarchical organisations. Paradoxically, these are the very areas where women are often seen as successful only if they can suppress the feminine side of their characters (Wilson 2004, p. 92).

### 5.2.5 The invisibility of older women

Work from Canada explores the significance of appearance in more detail. Clarke and Griffin's (2008) study of 50 women aged 50–70 reveals a common theme of feeling invisible, which the authors note is 'ironically ... grounded in their acute visibility as old women' (2008, p. 669). The women felt this invisibility meant they were overlooked in the workplace, and for those seeking jobs that it was further compounded by the social exclusion associated with not being in work.

> regardless of their employment status, the women were very aware of the impact of their changing physical appearances on their ability to obtain and retain jobs as well as maintain credibility to others and themselves in their chosen careers.
>
> (Clarke and Griffin 2008, p. 663)

Many of the women addressed this problem of invisibility by minimising the visible effects of ageing through beauty work – ranging from hair dye and make up to non-invasive and invasive cosmetic techniques. Some felt that youthful appearances were required in order to work with the public, especially in health-oriented jobs. Even one health-care worker commented on this, saying that appearance was important to her patients. Although the authors do not draw attention to this, it would seem that looking younger is associated not just with being more attractive but also more healthy. Respondents also referred to the tension caused by being aware of ageism but at the same time submitting to it by accepting the importance of physical appearance and engaging in beauty work. Some spoke of how retirement had offered them the 'luxury' of having these appearance pressures lifted.

A study of female academics (Granleese and Sayer 2006) also finds that older women are concerned about being invisible. In addition, the authors' research highlights the fact that younger female academics view (their) attractiveness and the associated visibility as counterproductive. Being attractive makes them vulnerable and liable to control, so they play down this attractiveness in order to blend in with the (male) environment. Walker et al. (2007, p. 44) highlight how these processes of 'self-denial' and self-separation' differentiate (gendered) ageism from the other 'isms'.

This research undoubtedly supports the continued dominance of patriarchal mores. It also highlights how women's unchallenged acceptance of these mores results in internalised discrimination and perpetuates segregation and disadvantage. For example, in Duncan and Loretto's survey, respondents were asked at what age they perceived performance of men and women to decline (they were asked to differentiate between men and women in manual and non-manual jobs). While all respondents felt that performance among women (especially women undertaking manual work) declined at an earlier age than that of men, the harshest judges were women who themselves had experienced age discrimination.

As a final comment on invisibility, and a supremely ironic twist of the concept, analysis by Ainsworth and Hardy (2007) of a public enquiry into problems faced by older unemployed workers in Australia demonstrates how older female job seekers were rendered invisible, on this occasion because they were constructed as privileged, and consequently less in need of government assistance. Women were viewed as relatively successful in gaining employment because of their experience of and greater propensity for flexible working. It was also felt that gaps in women's employment history could be accounted for more easily than could gaps in men's careers. In contrast, men's work continuity and greater economic success were viewed as constraints – and thus made it difficult for them to change and to take lower-paid jobs. There was also greater public sympathy for older male workers because of the perceived greater impact on men of loss of self-esteem – this was seen to be detrimental to the individual male and also to the family he heads, which in turn feeds into a wider burden on society.

> Ideas about the lesser social and economic power of women in the labour market were inverted to construct a position of their relative privilege.
>
> (Ainsworth and Hardy 2007, p. 273)

## 5.3 Extending working lives: focus on older women workers

In the face of ageing populations across Europe, governments are keen to encourage older workers to extend their working lives and to delay retirement. In the UK there has been a steady increase in the numbers of workers aged 50 years or more who are in employment. This trend is accounted for by the rising labour market activity rates of women. We have already discussed how these activity rates for older workers are gendered and noted that there are significant differences in the kinds of work that men and women typically undertake across the life course. Given these relatively profound differences in women's and men's experiences of paid work, it is curious that much of the emerging literature on older workers and extending working life is gender-blind. Policy pronouncements on the need to work longer and to delay (and to save more for) retirement typically depict their target as the de-gendered and individualised 'adult worker' (see Lewis 2002 on the adult worker model). Women and men are typically retiring from different kinds of work.

The factors that dispose older workers to leave the labour market in advance of state pension age are in reality gendered: while health is a major predictor of early labour market withdrawal for both women and men, for older women looking after family or home is the second-most common reason given for labour market inactivity (Phillipson and Smith 2005, pp. 25, 27). As through much of the life course, caring responsibilities have a key role in older women workers' ability and willingness to take up or remain in paid employment. As Marshall, Clarke and Ballantyne (2001, p. 384) have put it,

> The meaning of both work and retirement thus differs significantly by gender.

In addition, the impact and significance of individual factors such as health, caring responsibilities or finance are normally played out in the context of specific domestic relationships, what Pienta, Burr and Mutchler have called 'work–family pathways' (1994, S231). It is becoming more clear from a range of research (both old and new) that the timing of a married or cohabiting person's retirement tends to be contingent upon the trajectory his or her partner is taking (Banks and Tetlow 2008; Johnson 2009; Vickerstaff et al. 2008; Szinovacz 1989; Pienta, Burr and Mutchler 1994). This suggests that it is important to view the incentives and disincentives to stay in paid work for different genders. This is significant not only for governments seeking to encourage us to work for longer but also for employers who have older women and men in their workforces. In this section of the chapter we look at gendered motivations to work through recent empirical work undertaken by the authors.

### 5.3.1 Decisions about work and retirement: a qualitative perspective

We know from research that health, financial situation, job security, job satisfaction and caring responsibilities all have an effect on the manner and timing of individual retirement decisions (see, for example, Emmerson and Tetlow 2006; Phillipson and Smith 2005; Humphrey et al. 2003; Evandrou and Glaser 2003). What is less well understood is how these variables interact to produce different outcomes and to what extent they are gendered variables. In a qualitative study in which 96 men and women in three different locations were interviewed about their motivations and attitudes towards extending their working lives, we endeavoured to explore how different factors condition withdrawal from the labour market at the end of working life. We found major differences between women's and men's work histories, accumulated pension entitlements and responses to continuing work (Vickerstaff et al. 2008).

The majority of interviewees were in what can be characterised as male-breadwinner households. Many of the women had worked part time throughout their lives in order to accommodate caring responsibilities, initially for children and subsequently for other relatives or grandchildren. The part-time work they did was typically chosen for convenience (for example, proximity to home or the availability of flexible hours) rather than for its interest or challenge. Giving up such work in the face of health or caring demands was therefore comparatively easy if finances allowed. In contrast, the men often had long work histories, having started work at ages 15 and 16 and worked continuously since. Hence, by their mid-fifties many had worked for 40 years.

As the majority of our respondents were from low- or middle-income households, this pattern of women working part time meant that their income, though not insignificant, was typically not a predominant factor in the household income overall. This more fragmented and part-time pattern of employment also meant that most of the women did not have occupational pensions from their own employment, or that, where they did, they were relatively modest. As a result, their actual and expected contributions to the household's post-retirement income were also not predominant.

When respondents were asked about their willingness to extend their working lives, we found considerable gender differences. Women were much more likely to mention social reasons for continuing to work, whereas the men were more inclined to feel that they had already 'done their bit'. Generally, women tended to cite non-financial reasons for continuing with work such as the sociability of work or the need to 'keep busy':

> Just a case of ... I don't know ... I felt that I would maybe quite like to have a wee job again. Partly because hubby's not one for doing

> very much and I like to be busy and while I keep myself busy ... how can I put it? I just feel I need something just to stretch me a bit more than going out for lunch and meeting friends and ... it's all very enjoyable but ...
>
> (ES40Female)

> And then I began to get a little bored, you know. It [retirement] was fine at first, but then I sort of missed the company, you know. So, since I've gone back to work I've thought, 'well maybe I'll just work on a wee bit longer', you know.
>
> (ES44Female)

The theme of working to 'help people out' was noticeable among women but not mentioned at all by men. For many of the married women the decision about when to retire was taken in response to their husbands' retirement (whether planned or not). Some women were also continuing to work beyond state pension age in order to retire at the same time as their husbands.

### 5.3.2 Working past retirement age

For those, both women and men, who expressed an interest in, or willingness to consider, working for longer and extending their working life there was a strong preference for flexible work. However, sometimes the degree of flexibility desired was somewhat unrealistic and acknowledged as such:

> the thing is about any job that I would want, is I need the sort of job where I can say ... I'm maybe just on the internet and looking at flights and things and 'God, look at ... I could fly to so and so next week for that' and I'll go and in the meantime you're on the shift that they need you at B&Q or whatever ... I would need to be able to say 'oh I'm not coming in next week' and very few employers would give you that flexibility.
>
> (EC35Male)

In addition to access to flexible work options, the issue of job satisfaction was mentioned by many of the interviewees, and for many women retirement beckoned as a release from a boring part-time job. This suggests that, in addition to providing flexible work options, employers may also need to consider job quality as a factor that affects the intentions and behaviours of older workers.

> But if it's a job that you really, really enjoy ... then I think yes you would carry on as long as you've got that job satisfaction there you have a reason .... I wouldn't have left that last job ... if it had been a good job I would have carried on.
>
> (TC28Female)

This research suggests that views about working for longer are often gendered in the sense that the incentives and disincentives differ as between women and men. In particular, it is very important to view the incentives and disincentives to stay in paid work for older women in the context of their domestic circumstances. The factors which may encourage many women to work for longer (social contacts, keeping busy) are likely to be different from those that will motivate many men (financial situation), although both share an interest in job satisfaction.

## 5.4 Summary and conclusions

It is clear throughout the discussion in this chapter that we cannot divorce age from gender. The older workforce is gendered as well as aged, and this has an effect on the kinds and amounts of work done, the level of remuneration and, crucially, the motivation and incentives to continue working. The gendered nature of the labour market has been well researched and understood for some time in the academic literature; but, as Krekula (2007, p. 157) comments, little attention has been paid to age in the construction of women in gender theory. The impact of domestic roles, in particular caring, has long been understood to condition or constrain women's participation in paid employment; but even here the focus of attention has tended to be women as mothers of small children. This has often had the effect in discussions of family-friendly or work–life balance issues of rendering younger women, childless women and older women invisible (Krekula 2007, p. 58). The impact of caring on labour market activity for many women may thread through the life course, including not only looking after children well into their teenage years and beyond, but also caring for elderly relatives, ailing spouses and grandchildren as they get older.

Gendered ageism is undoubtedly one of the 'less visible gendered mechanisms' (Gorman and Kmec 2007) affecting women's experiences of work. We have focused primarily on women and that is a limitation (Russell 2007; Krekula 2007): clearly, older male workers will also be facing discrimination, as older men may acutely feel the pressure to make way for younger men, especially in the context of recession and job losses.

Discussions about extending working life and delaying retirement have tended recently to assume that retirement decisions are the outcome of individual 'adult worker' calculations; but it seems much more plausible that retirement decisions are often made jointly by couples and reflect work–family pathways (Pienta et al. 1994) that have been laid down through the life course. Public policy needs a much keener awareness of this reality if the extending working life agenda is to have an impact.

Employers face an ageing population, which is especially acute in some sectors, for example the public sector in areas such as local government, health and education. We have shown that these workforces are gendered as well as older. We would argue that employers need to pay attention to their current and future workforce, to recognise the 'untapped potential' represented by older women. Our discussion of gendered ageism has provided some insights into the ways in which older women are marginalised, often by being rendered invisible – to employers and to society as a whole. Challenging this requires serious and deep questioning of the extent to which human resource management policies and practices can ever be 'objective', and may, in the case of accepted notions of good practice – for example, the importance of team fit in effective team working – be merely rationalising and reinforcing gender and age divisions in the workforce.

# 6

# The Prism of Age: Managing Age Diversity in the Twenty-First-Century Workplace

*Marcie Pitt-Catsouphes, Christina Matz-Costa and Melissa Brown*

Increases in older adults' labour force participation rates have resulted in a workforce that is 'more grey' than it was at the turn of the millennium (see Chapter 2 for workforce ageing statistics). Between 1997 and 2007, the labour force participation rates of adults who were aged 55–64 years increased from 49.6 per cent to 57.1 per cent in Canada, from 41.1 per cent to 51.3 per cent in Germany, and from 54.1 per cent to 61.8 per cent in the United States (OECD 2009a). This extended labour force attachment among older adults reflects a set of new economic realities, emergent priorities of today's 50+ age group and altered expectations for the productive roles that different societies around the world are setting for older adults, including continued participation in paid employment. (Morrow-Howell et al. 2009)

Managers at many workplaces are aware of these demographic changes; indeed, top executives report that shifts in the age demographics of the workforce are among the most important economic, social and demographic trends that are reshaping today's business environment (McKinsey and Company 2007). Although managers may appreciate that the ageing of the workforce can have strategic implications, managers and supervisors may find it challenging to anticipate *which* age-management policies and practices are likely to be the most *effective* in *which* circumstances.

In this chapter, we first discuss examples of age-management policies and practices adopted by some organisations that view age management from a strategic perspective. We then present a conceptual framework, the 'Prism of Age', which employers (as well as researchers) can use to factor in the diversities of age when considering the outcomes associated with different age management strategies. Finally, using data from the Age and Generations Study, a study that gathered information in

2007–8 from 2210 employees working in the United States (described in more detail later), we demonstrate how various age-related factors can interact with age-management approaches to effect important outcomes, such as job satisfaction.

## 6.1 Age management strategies

Managers who are interested in leveraging the potential benefits of today's multigenerational workforce – which includes a higher percentage of older workers than in decades past – want to select policies and practices that augment performance and positive work experiences. In this section, we provide an overview of some approaches that have been used as age-management strategies.

Managers can choose from a wide range of human resource policies and practices to accomplish their age management goals. As noted by Walker (2005, p. 685):

> The term 'age management' may refer specifically to the various dimensions by which human resources are managed within organisations with an explicit focus on ageing and, also, more generally, to the overall management of workforce ageing via public policy or collective bargaining.

Since the turn of the millennium, a number of different age management models have emerged at the workplace, each of which may respond to different age-related issues. The models vary from worksite to worksite, but might include programmes that promote knowledge transfer, the acquisition of competencies and skills, career development for employees of all ages, the utilisation of workplace flexibility, valuing diversity/generational differences, succession planning, extending relationships with former employees (for example, by establishing alumni activities), job redesign (including the creation of temporary and project-based work), wellness/ergonomic fit, and age-sensitive benefits (see Chapter 11 for more details of age management practices). Figure 6.1 presents examples of two age-management practices that will be discussed later in this chapter.

Managers often raise questions about the efficacy of different age-management strategies. The Prism of Age framework, discussed in the following section, can provide managers with insights about the complexities of age that, in turn, can help them to gain a better understanding of the outcomes they can expect from different age-management strategies.

*Flexible work options:* There are a number of strategic reasons why employers offer flexible work options to their employees. Given the transitions and changes that employees experience with their work and personal/family responsibilities over the course of their lives, flexible work options can offer employees opportunities to customise certain aspects of work situations so that they fit in the context of their work–life experiences. MITRE, USA (an organisation that works in the domains of aviation, defence, intelligence and enterprise modernisation) offers a range of flexible work arrangements, including flexitime, reduced hours part time, compressed work week, job sharing, telecommuting, phased retirement and 'Reserves at the Ready' (opportunities for retirees to work on specific term-limited projects as temporary or contract work). According to MITRE's human resources department, 'Just about everyone flexes some day of the week.'

*Training/development and knowledge transfer:* One concern voiced by employers about the ageing of the workforce is the potential for workers' skills and competencies to become outdated. Employers may develop either formal or informal approaches to training and development. At Central Baptist Hospital, Lexington, Kentucky (an ANCC Magnet-designated hospital), over 48 per cent of the employees are over the age of 40 and the average age of retirement is 64. Central Baptist launched the Evolving Leaders Programme in 2001 as part of its emerging strategy to retain leaders, create opportunities for tactical and implicit cross-generational knowledge transfer and to provide additional opportunities for learning and development within the organisation. The Evolving Leaders Programme is a formal education and mentoring programme consisting of five different levels, each building upon the knowledge acquired in the previous levels. The curriculum is based upon four critical elements: organisational culture and customer relations; workforce development; performance and critical care improvement; and finance and performance accountability. The programme has a self-governing Steering Team, which evaluates the programme using a number of different metrics for success. The majority of leadership positions at the hospital are now filled from within by identifying individuals who have participated in the programme.

*Figure 6.1* Two examples of age-management strategies

## 6.2 The Prism of Age: Factoring age factors into the management of today's multigenerational workforce

It seems as if 'age' is a straightforward demographic characteristic; however, it is actually more complex than it might seem. Consider this example. A colleague recently introduced himself at a meeting. He first commented on the fact that he was very enthusiastic about his 'new career'. Then, he recounted his experience with his registration at the hotel. Apparently, he took out a senior citizen's card (to receive a hotel discount), and then proceeded to ask for two cribs for his children. So how old would you say he is?

Typically, we assume that age is simply the answer to the question, 'How old are you?' For many decades of the twentieth century, chronological age was often accepted as a reasonable indicator of career development and life-course events, as well as human development. Unfortunately, this led to an oversimplified understanding, and some people began to assume that age could be used interchangeably with other age-related labels. Assumptions about the tight connections between age-related experiences are depicted in Figure 6.2.

Today, the realities of people's lives (at work and at home) are less predictable than in decades past with regard to chronological age; as a consequence, managers might need to think about these age-related factors more independently. Why might this matter to managers? As noted by Wagner (2007), it is important that managers do not confuse different sets of age-related factors because the programmes and policies designed to respond to variations in human development that reflect chronological age might be quite different from programmes and policies developed at the workplace to respond to other age-related factors (such as generational influences).

Building on the important work of noted gerontologists (see, for example, Kooij et al. 2007; Sterns and Miklos 1995; Sterns and Doverspike 1989), the Sloan Center on Ageing and Work at Boston College in Massachusetts refers to the multiple dimensions of age and age-related factors as the 'Prism of Age'. The lenses in this prism focus our attention on different perspectives of age, each of which may have different relevance for experiences at the workplace.

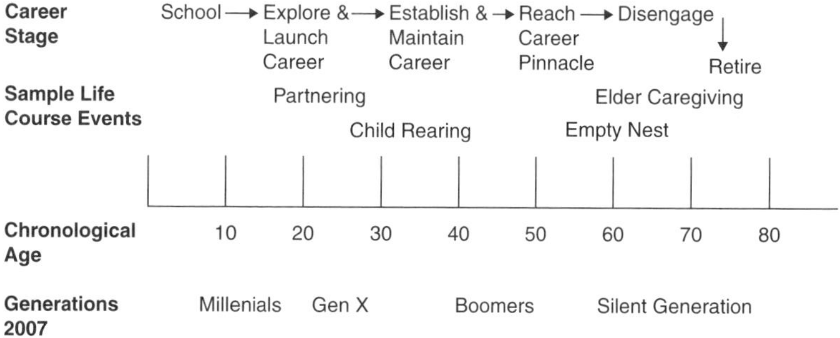


*Figure 6.2* Assumptions about the connections of age-related experiences

### 6.2.1 Physical–cognitive age

The ageing process has often been depicted as reflecting biological changes in capacities and functions at specific points in time (Bryson and Siddiqui 1969). Contrary to the myth that human development stops at age 21, changes in virtually all aspects of human development continue throughout our lives. An employee's physical–cognitive age reflects a complex interaction between: (*a*) the person's capacities (physical, intellectual/cognitive); (*b*) the tasks that need to be completed (for example, routine tasks, timed tasks, physical tasks, and tasks requiring problem solving based on experience); and (*c*) the supports and demands in work environments (such as ergonomic work stations). As a consequence, depending on either the demands made in certain environments or the resources available to help the person meet those demands, a worker's level of functioning might be lower or higher. The term used at the workplace to depict this situation-specific level of functioning is 'workability' (Ilmarinen 2005). Even if most people experience some declines in physical capacities with age, this might not become a performance concern in jobs that do not require physical labour (Johnson 2004). Consequently, the age at which a construction worker becomes an older worker would be different from the age at which a scientist might be deemed an older worker. Similarly, although on average older adults might experience some decline in how rapidly they can memorise de-contextualised information (whereas their abilities to synthesise new information may remain the same or actually increase), few jobs actually require this competency, so there would not be a perceived performance decline among these older workers (see Cleveland and Lim 2007).

Managers might use the perspective of physical–cognitive age when they consider options for changes (including ergonomic adjustments, technological resources, or job redesign) that could expand opportunities and compensate for challenges associated with employees' physical–cognitive age.

### 6.2.2 Socio-emotional age

Psychologists focus on developmental tasks that gain salience at different points in our lives. For example, during later adulthood many people focus on issues of generativity (Erikson 1950). Levinson, in his book, *Seasons of a Man's Life* (1978), discussed the linkages between adult development and work-related transitions and experiences. Managers could use insights gained from an understanding of socio-emotional age to gain a better understanding of employees' interest in pursuing specific roles and responsibilities at the workplace, such as mentoring new employees.

### 6.2.3 Subjective age

It has often been observed that 'You are only as old as you feel'. Subjective age reflects an employee's overall assessment of his or her life stage or the feeling of being younger or older (see Baum and Boxley 1983; Cleveland and Shore 1992; Kastenbaum et al. 1972; Kooij et al. 2007). This assessment might take into account a variety of factors, including how old one feels, looks and acts; the person's identification with a particular age cohort; and how old the person 'wants' to be.

The construct of subjective age can help managers to remember that employees' sense of their own age might be different from their chronological age. For example, 53.1 per cent of the respondents to the Age and Generations Study (Pitt-Catsouphes, Matz-Costa and Besen 2009) who were aged 50 years and more designated themselves as being in mid-life. Understanding subjective assessments of age can help to prevent disconnects where an employee feels that he or she is 'young' and has much more to contribute at the workplace, whereas a supervisor might focus on chronological age and wrongly assumes that the same employee is getting ready for retirement.

### 6.2.4 Social age

In contrast to subjective age, social age measures how other people gauge an individual's age (see Cleveland and Shore 1992; Kastenbaum et al. 1972; Mead 1934). Social age introduces the social context into the calculus of age.

Social age is relevant at the workplace in situations where employees try to decipher how their supervisors or colleagues perceive them (for instance, in situations where there could be questions of age bias). During times of transition (decisions about hiring, promotion, and so on), employees may wonder whether their employers see them as 'too young' or 'too old' for the tasks at hand. Managers should consider whether the language used in their workplaces expresses expectations or assumptions about age that employees may perceive as biased. These biases could discourage workers from applying for a particular job, despite being qualified.

### 6.2.5 Generational age

Anecdotal observations suggest that managers prefer to use generational age when they discuss older workers or design different age-management strategies. In part, this reflects their assessment that generational labels are less stigmatising than others, such as 'mature workers' or 'older workers'. However, gaining an understanding of generational influences proves to be one of the most complex ways to look at age.

The study of generations recognises that macro-societal factors (such as economic circumstances, historical events and dominant cultural values) can have a sustained impact on the ways that large groups of people who are of approximately the same age see the world and understand their experiences (Green et al. (in press); Parry and Urwin (2010 forthcoming); Strauss and Howe 1991; Elder 1974). Although there is variability in their designation, specific generations are defined by birth years, so the link to chronological age is apparent. It is important to recognise that the major events which can affect generational groups will not only vary from country to country but are also likely to have different effects on sub-populations within the generational groups. For example, the macro-influences might affect older adults in high-income brackets differently from those in low-income brackets (even though the older adults are all in the same generation). The concept of generations is discussed in detail in Chapter 7.

### 6.2.6 Relative age

The notion of relative age places age in a social context because it reflects a person's perception of his or her age relative to a referent group, such as a work group (see Cleveland and Shore 1992; Kooij et al. 2007; Lawrence 1988; Pfeffer 1983; Baum and Boxley 1983; Kastenbaum et al. 1972). As a consequence, a person's perspective of his or her age could vary depending on the referent group.

Managers might want to keep in mind that an employee working with much younger people might *feel* old whereas that same person working with older peers might *feel* young. Focusing on employees' perspectives of their relative age can help managers to better understand employees' experiences of inclusion (a sense of belongingness at the workplace), which is related to a number of important outcomes, including job satisfaction (Mor Barak and Levin 2002).

### 6.2.7 Normative age

Societies as well as individuals have different expectations about age-appropriate activities that might characterise a 'young' or an 'old' person (see Sweet 2009). Individuals might gauge their progress against normative calibrations, getting a sense about whether they are 'on time' or 'out of sync'.

At the workplace, tacit normative expectations might become visible in situations where employees anticipate that certain opportunities or rewards might occur at specific times. For example, norms might be established at some workplaces for ages when it is appropriate (or inappropriate) for an employee to assume supervisory responsibilities (Lawrence 1988). Managers should consider whether age norms have been institutionalised in their workplaces and the costs incurred when qualified candidates are overlooked because they do not meet these normative expectations.

### 6.2.8 Life events age

The emergence of the work–life field during the 1980s and 1990s drew attention to the importance of life-course events (such as establishing a partnered relationship, having children and assuming responsibilities for the care of ageing parents) in the lives of employees (Kossek and Lambert 2005; Sweet and Moen 2006). Key life events and transitions can shape the roles and responsibilities people might assume both at work and outside of work (Elder and Giele 2009; Lange et al. 2006; Sweet and Moen 2006; Sterns and Doverspike 1989; Sterns and Miklos 1995; Cleveland and Shore 1992; Lawrence 1988; Pfeffer 1983). Life-course events are different from human development for three primary reasons (O'Rand and Campbell 1999). First, not everyone experiences all life-course events (for instance, not everyone experiences a divorce, although divorce has become a normative experience in some societies). Second, people may experience life-course events in different sequences. For example, some adults live with their parents until they marry whereas others establish an independent household before they marry. Finally, although it is possible to calculate an average age when a specific population group has a particular life course experience (for example, the average age of parents when their oldest child enters school), the range of ages for specific life-course events is very wide. Data gathered for the Age and Generations Study (Pitt-Catsouphes, Kossek and Sweet 2006) found that 7.8 per cent of the respondents aged 55 and older have children under the age of 18 years.

For several decades many managers have recognised the importance of work–life issues and understood that employees' responsibilities for family and other life roles could affect their behaviours at work. There is ample evidence that employees' lives outside of work often cross the threshold of the workplace; that is, experiences at home often affect the ways that employees manage their work responsibilities. Similarly, work experiences often affect how employees manage their responsibilities at home (Pitt-Catsouphes, Kossek and Sweet 2006). Although research has found that experiences in one domain can have a facilitative effect on performance in the other domain (Barnett and Hyde 2001), interference between work and home role demands can also occur (Bond et al. 2003). This interference can have a deleterious impact on employee well-being and job performance (Frone, Yardley and Markel 1997), leading some employers to offer resources to assist employees in managing work and home responsibilities.

Some organisations have linked some of their benefits and employee programmes to life-course events (for example, benefits related to childcare) to ensure that employees can get the most out of workplace-based resources. However, since the relationships between age and specific life-course events are a little more tenuous than the relationships between age and some of the other age-related factors, managers should not jump to the conclusion that a programme, such as an employee affinity group created for parents of special needs children, would have exclusive appeal to employees in a particular age range.

### 6.2.9 Occupational/career age

Career development theories are based on assumptions that jobs provide employees with opportunities to develop (and then master) sets of skills, responsibilities and roles that enable them to progress from more basic to more advanced levels (Kooij et al. 2007; Super 1990). Although managers are likely to find that the average age of employees who report they are in early-career stage is lower than those who are in late-career stage, this is not always the case. Some career theorists, such as Hall and Associates (1996), have noted that our notions of career development need to be updated so that they account for trends, such as the diminution of internal labour markets at most organisations (resulting in limited opportunities for steady, upward advancement unless the employee moves to another organisation), the shift of responsibility for career development from the employer to the employee and the possibility that an employee might pursue a career that engages him or her in several different occupations over the course of his or her work life. For this reason, managers should consider an employee's occupational/career age (rather than chronological age) when developing opportunities for career development. Occupational/career age differs from organisational age (described below) because career development may take place at multiple organisations (and could, therefore, be distinct from tenure).

### 6.2.10 Organisational age

Organisational age takes into account the length of time (tenure) that an employee has had relationships with his or her organisation, supervisor and possibly department or team (see Kooij et al. 2007; Bedeian, Ferris and Kacmarl 1992; Sterns and Doverspike 1989). Tenure, typically defined either as the number of years that an employee has worked for a specific employer or the number of years an employee has held a specific position, is a commonly used indicator of organisational age. Employees with a long organisational tenure can be a tremendous source of institutional knowledge that managers would be remiss to overlook. Managers should ensure that employees making the shift to a new 'career' within the organisation are still regarded as an important source of institutional knowledge.

In summary, although chronological age and generations might provide managers with some clues about the ways that age can affect experiences and interactions at work, other age-related factors should also be considered. Perhaps the biggest challenge which managers face is remembering that individual employees are likely to deviate from the 'average' descriptors of any particular lens in the Prism of Age. An employee at mid-career might not share some of the priorities and needs that are typical of mid-career employees (reflecting a range of diversity characteristics including gender, race/ethnicity and chronological age); similarly, not all Baby Boomers will share the same preferences for certain types of work styles. The following anecdote illustrates why age is a complex construct and we need to be careful to refrain from applying group stereotypes to any individual employee.

A few years ago, the lead author of this chapter was asked to participate in a panel discussion where people presented information about different generations. The first speaker had completed some research on Generation Y (currently the youngest cohort at the workplace). She began to describe this group as being technologically hip, seeking meaningful work, working well when goals are clear but when they are given the autonomy to figure out how to complete the work, and wanting developmental opportunities so that they can expand their competency set and feel proud of their accomplishments. I was the last speaker, and was supposed to focus on the work experiences of the Baby Boomers. I went to the podium and removed the earplugs from my iPod, methodically unclipped my BlackBerry and cell phone and proceeded to announce that I was a Baby Boomer and, like many in my generation, I sought meaningful work, worked well when my goals were clear but I was given autonomy (okay, a lot of autonomy) to figure out how to complete the work, and wanted developmental opportunities so that I could expand my competency set and feel proud of my accomplishments.

In the next section of this chapter, we use the Prism of Age framework to consider how individuals' work experiences might vary depending on some of these various age-related factors.

## 6.3 Putting the Prism of Age framework to work

One of the challenges associated with the Prism of Age framework is that the idea that employees will have multiple 'ages' at one time can seem confusing. Managers eager to put the Prism of Age framework to work might be asking which lens they should consider when making an assessment about the most appropriate age-management strategy to implement. Ultimately, the Prism of Age framework encourages managers to adopt a more holistic perspective of age, providing a tool that reminds them to consider age from more than a single dimension. This understanding is critical for the implementation of effective age-management practices.

For this section, we have used data from the Age and Generations Study to illustrate how managers can use the Prism of Age framework as they design and implement different age-management strategies. The Age and Generations Study was conducted by the Sloan Center on Ageing and Work between November 2007 and September 2008. The Center collaborated with nine US workplaces (12 worksites) on this study. In total, 2210 employees participated in this study (for more information about the sample see Pitt-Catsouphes et al. 2009). The survey included questions that measured seven of the ten age-related factors included in the Prism of Age framework.

We found wide age ranges associated with several of the age-related categories. For example, the ages of those who reported that they were in early career ranged from age 17 to 61 years; mid-career, from 22 to 62 years; and late career, from 28 to 81 years. Similarly, using a 'life events' lens, the ages of those who provide care for the elderly on a weekly basis ranged from 20 to 65, while the ages of those who report having retired from a previous job ranged from 27 to 74 years. These results reinforce the notion that managers might need to consider that some employees could be 'younger' according to some age-related factors and 'older' according to others. For example, managers may need to be prepared to take some time to get early career (but older) employees who have retired from a different occupation assimilated into their new career (often called "onboarding" in the US).

Can the Prism of Age framework help managers to understand whether different age-management strategies are more or less effective with regard to important outcomes, such as job satisfaction?

To measure job satisfaction, the Age and Generations Study asked respondents to indicate how satisfied they were with their jobs. Response options ranged from 1 ('very dissatisfied') to 6 ('very satisfied'). For the sample (overall), the mean score was 4.9, indicating that, overall, people were satisfied with their jobs. We found differences in the levels of job satisfaction among employees when we looked through certain age-related lenses, but no differences when we looked through other age-related lenses. Results suggest variation by: physical–cognitive age (those who were 'not at all' limited at work by their physical health were more satisfied with their jobs than those who reported that their physical health limited them 'a little bit' or 'some'); subjective age (those who perceived themselves as older adults were more satisfied with their jobs than those who perceived themselves as young adults); generational age (Traditionalists/Silent Generationers (born before 1955) were more satisfied than Millennials/Generation Y'ers (born after 1980) and Generation X'ers (born 1965–80); life events age (those who were married/ separated/ widowed/ divorced were more satisfied than those who had never been married or who were living with someone); occupational/career age (those who perceived themselves to be in late career were more satisfied than those who perceived themselves to be in early career, and those who had retired from a previous job were more satisfied than those who had not); and organisational age (those with 10.01 or more years of tenure were more satisfied than those with 0–10 years of tenure).

How can a manager translate this knowledge into effective age-management strategies? The Prism of Age framework can help managers focus a variety of age lenses when selecting appropriate age-management strategies. For example, managers offering mentoring opportunities as a strategy to increase the job satisfaction of early-career workers might easily overlook early-career workers considered to be older adults. The Prism of Age framework is an important tool, reminding managers that age is a multidimensional construct.

Managers, of course, will be interested in the relationship between selected approaches to age management and job satisfaction. We focused on two age-management strategies (workplace flexibility and opportunities for training and development) and explored whether the positive relationships between these age-management strategies and job satisfaction varied according to the different lenses of age. We did find differences in the relationship between flexibility fit (the extent to which respondents perceived that they had access to the flexible work options needed to fulfil their work and personal needs) and job satisfaction, and we also found differences in the relationship between satisfaction with opportunities for learning/development and job satisfaction for two of the age lenses, namely, physical–cognitive age and occupational/career stage.

In terms of physical–cognitive age, among those who did not have any access at all to the flexibility they needed, those whose work activities were 'very limited' by their physical health were significantly less satisfied with their jobs than those whose work activities were only 'somewhat, a little, or not at all limited' by their physical health. However, when these respondents perceived that they had the flexibility they needed – even to a limited extent – this difference disappeared (see Figure 6.3). In other words, having flexibility fit may help to narrow the gap in job satisfaction between those who do and those who do not have physical disabilities that make getting their work done more difficult.

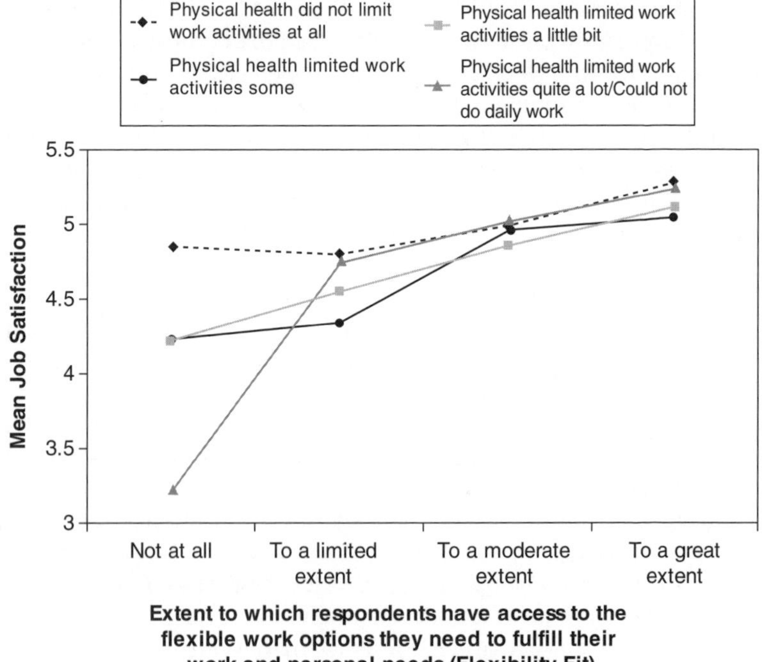


*Figure 6.3* Mean job satisfaction by physical–cognitive age and flexibility fit

For occupational/career age, among those who reported low or moderate satisfaction with opportunities for learning and development, late-career employees had higher job satisfaction than early-career employees; however, these career-stage differences were not present among those who were highly satisfied with their opportunities for learning and development (see Figure 6.4). Having access to opportunities for learning and development may help to narrow the gap in job satisfaction between early-career employees and late-career employees.

Why are these results important to managers? The findings reinforce the importance of understanding age as a multifaceted construct, which would allow, for example, for the possibility that an older worker might have dependent care responsibilities or be in early or mid- (rather than late) career. While recognising that opportunities for learning and development and having flexibility fit are important for the job satisfaction of all workers, our findings reveal interesting intricacies about the ways that this relationship may or may not differ for employees depending on their physical–cognitive age and career stage. For example, opportunities for learning and development may be particularly relevant to the job satisfaction of early-career workers; however, this finding would not have emerged if we looked only at the chronological age of employees. Therefore, in this case managers would be remiss to overlook this particular age-related lens in making decisions about

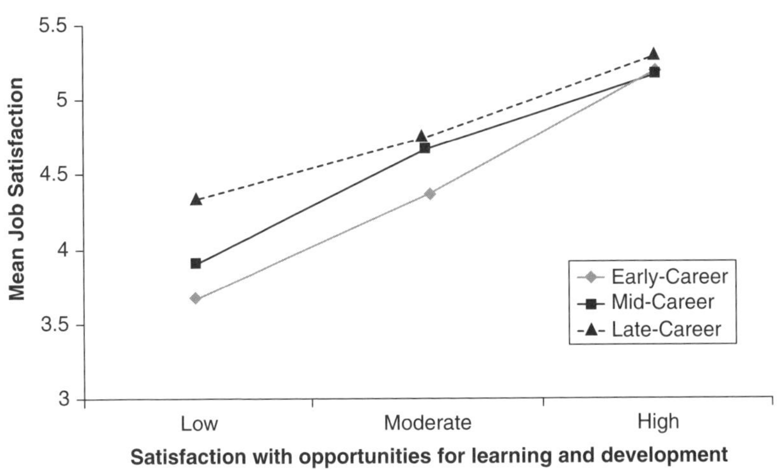


*Figure 6.4* Mean job satisfaction by occupational/career age and satisfaction with learning and development opportunities

training and development. Ultimately, if managers are interested in promoting the job satisfaction of all employees, they might consider how they can adjust the various supports that they provide to employees of different age diversities (that is, not making the assumption that a given type of support will have the same impact on job satisfaction for all employees).

## 6.4 Summary and conclusions

In this chapter, we have provided managers with a conceptual framework – the Prism of Age – which can help them to appreciate the complexity of age and generations. This framework can serve as a check on the tendency to stereotype the members of the different generations, and to overlook some of the important diversities within each generational group that might reflect either life-course events or age at the workplace (such as career stage).

The findings from the Age and Generations study underscore the importance of extending managers' understanding that the realities of today's multigenerational workforce offer a number of challenges as well as opportunities. Employees are likely to bring both assets and needs to the workplace, some of which are related to age and age-related factors. Managers that want to maximise their effectiveness with age management will develop strategies for responding to the needs and priorities of the twenty-first-century workforce by taking steps such as expanding support for employees' use of flexible work options or increasing the availability of meaningful learning and development opportunities.

# 7
# The Impact of Generational Diversity on People Management

*Emma Parry and Peter Urwin*

The issue of generational diversity has received growing attention in recent years, as management and business consultants, together with the popular media, make increasing reference to the different generations in the population (Parry and Urwin 2009). Within the area of management practice much attention has been paid to generational differences in workplace attitudes and behaviours (Filipczak 1994; Kupperschmidt 2000). In this chapter we draw on this growing practitioner literature and consider how this relates to the academic underpinnings of the study of generations. The aim is to draw together an understanding of how generational diversity may affect the workplace, the relationship that this concept has to 'age' and ultimately the implications for practitioners.

As other chapters in this collection underline, there is a commonly held belief that firms will have to learn how to manage an ageing workforce. Implicit in this is the suggestion that an ageing workforce raises new challenges for managers, and that older and younger workers are therefore different on a number of dimensions. Chapter 6 touches upon the potential drivers of this difference that arise from the complex nature of ageing, with an emphasis on distinguishing between the different facets of age, such as chronological, functional, relative and psychosocial age, as well as between career stages and life-course events. These potential drivers of difference in values, expectations and behaviours of older and younger workers can be grouped into two broad categories. The functional, relative and psychosocial aspects can be thought of as arising from a process of ageing or 'maturation' that affects us all to a greater or lesser extent. In contrast, career stages and life-course events are not necessarily related to the process of ageing; rather, they are driven by the passing of chronological time.

In addition, scholars and practitioners have begun to consider the possibility that differences between age groups can be driven by varying 'generational' experiences. Since the turn of the millennium this focus on generations has predominated in the popular media and within the practitioner-focused marketing and human resource management (HRM) literature. The essential underlying assumption is that the shared social, political, cultural and economic experiences of distinct age cohorts cause them to differ in their values, attitudes, consumer preferences and behaviour at work (Parry and Urwin 2009; Alsop 2008). There would seem to be a strong argument for us at least to consider generational diversity in the workplace. If it is true that different generational groups have different values and preferences at work, then this needs to be considered alongside age-related factors; one can then consider arguments that people need to be managed differently.

There are a number of assumptions implicit in this line of reasoning. First, many readers will consider that their own experience supports the assumption that different age groups/cohorts have different workplace values. However, as we shall see, the wider evidence base on which we can draw to support such an assumption contains very few reliable studies; and there is also some conflation of terms in the literature, with 'cohort', 'age', 'generation' and other terms being used interchangeably. In following the reasoning that generation affects the workplace, one must also make the leap from an assumption that different generations have different workplace values, but also that this is manifested in different workplace behaviours. One of the potential flaws in the existing academic and practitioner approaches to the issue of generations is in the (often automatic) adoption of the same four generational categories. Are such categories still appropriate when one considers the distinction between groups of workers in a variety of workplace settings?

In this chapter we attempt to provide some direction on the possible answers to these questions through a close examination of the concept of generations, and ultimately to identify the implications for HRM. First, we explore the concept of generations in some detail, beginning with an account of what exactly we mean by a 'generation' and then contrasting this with the generational cohorts that are commonly discussed across the Western world. Second, we discuss the theoretical rationale for the study of generations and the associated empirical studies that consider the evidence for the existence of generations. We are then able to consider the possible impacts that generational differences could have within the workplace and the implications of these for people management. We draw throughout on both academic and practitioner literatures to provide an overview of the current position with regard to generational diversity.

## 7.1 What is generational diversity?

A generation can be described as 'an identifiable group that shares birth years, age, location and significant life events at critical developmental stages' (Kupperschmidt 2000, p. 66). In the next section of this chapter we dig a little further and unpick this interpretation. However, much of the practitioner and academic literature espouses this definition of a generation, that is, as a group of individuals born at a certain time who have had similar life experiences. The potential importance of generations as a focus of study is driven by the assumption that their differing social and economic experiences then lead to differing behaviours and preferences (Parry and Urwin 2009).

This generational effect is not the same as the change in values and behaviours that arises from the process of ageing. Whether one is born in 1958 or 1978, one may expect some common impacts from the ageing process – for instance, a growing focus on retirement and pensions among both cohorts. However, one may also expect generational differences between individuals from these two cohorts to persist (irrespective of age). Those reaching age 16 in 1974 (born in 1958) experienced a social, economic and political upheaval during their formative years while those reaching age 16 in 1994 (born in 1978) experienced political stability and economic plenty. Such differences in the shared experiences of cohorts can be expected to affect values, attitudes and ultimately behaviours throughout the life course.

The majority of studies of generational difference has been conducted in Western societies, and much of the thinking on this subject originates from the US, where it is generally accepted that there are four main generations in the workforce. These are Veterans, Baby Boomers, Generation X and Generation Y. Authors discussing generations do not necessarily agree about the exact years that mark the cut-off points between these generational groups, but they do cover approximately the same time periods. These four groups are presented in Table 7.1 (taken from Strauss and Howe 1991, p. 32).

The workforces in the US and the UK are currently dominated by Baby Boomers (44 and 45 per cent respectively) and Generation X (34 and 31 per cent) (Burke 2004; Labour Force Survey 2009). As a result of this predominance, in both countries the literature on generational diversity has focused on these two groups. However, the practitioner

*Table 7.1* Generational groups currently in the workforce

| Generation | Years of birth | Also known as |
|---|---|---|
| Veterans | 1925–42 | Silent Generation, Matures, Traditionalists |
| Baby Boomers | 1943–60 | |
| Generation X | 1961–81 | Thirteenth Generation, Baby Busters, Lost Generation |
| **Generation Y** | 1982– | Millennials, Nexters, Echo Boomers |

*Source*: Strauss and Howe (1991, p. 32).

*Table 7.2* Characteristics of four generational groups

| | |
|---|---|
| Veterans | Plan to stay with the organisation long term<br>Respectful of organisational hierarchy<br>Like structure<br>Accepting of authority figures at work<br>Give maximum effort |
| Baby Boomers | Give maximum effort<br>Accepting of authority figures at work<br>Results-driven<br>Plan to stay with the organisation long term<br>Retain what they learn |
| Generation X | Technologically savvy<br>Like informality<br>Learn quickly<br>Seek work–life balance<br>Embrace diversity |
| Generation Y | Technologically savvy<br>Like informality<br>Embrace diversity<br>Learn quickly<br>Need supervision |

*Source*: Burke (2004).

and academic literature has considered the characteristics of each of these four generations in relation to their attitudes and preferences at work. A good summary by Burke (2004), based on research from the Society for Human Resource Management, is reproduced in Table 7.2.

It can be seen from Table 7.2 that there are common elements across some of the four groups, as experiences of social, economic and political histories can be similar for very different cohorts. For instance, we may be on the verge of a new generation (post-Y) as the cohort of individuals born in the early 1990s contemplates an economic and political environment more akin to that faced by Generation X. However, this serves only to further highlight the assumption underlying the analysis of generations, namely, that experiences are shared by members of a cohort as they grow up and this then results in shared values, attitudes and behaviours. For instance, members of Generation X saw their parents being made redundant and entered the labour market at a time of economic uncertainty without expecting job security. This has led them to believe that each job is temporary (Filipczak 1994). In addition many members of Generation X were 'latchkey kids' and therefore grew up to be independent and self-reliant. Veterans, on the other hand, grew up during the Great Depression and therefore believe in hard work and loyalty to employers in return for job security. Table 7.3 summarises the events in the US that may have affected the values of each of the four generations.

Up to now our discussion of generations has been rather focused on the US. This is reflected in Table 7.3, where we can identify a number of events that will clearly not be relevant to the experiences of cohorts in different parts of the world. This US-centric viewpoint is common in the literature on generational difference, particularly the practitioner literature.

*Table 7.3* Events affecting the values of four generations

| Generation | Event |
|---|---|
| Veterans | Great Depression<br>New Deal<br>Second World War<br>Korean War |
| Baby Boomers | Civil Rights<br>Sexual revolution<br>Cold War<br>Space travel<br>Assassinations (for example, of US President John F. Kennedy) |
| Generation X | Fall of the Berlin Wall<br>Watergate<br>Women's liberation<br>Desert Storm<br>Energy crisis |
| Generation Y | School shootings<br>Oklahoma City<br>Technology<br>Child-focused world<br>Clinton–Lewinsky scandal |

*Source*: Parry and Urwin (2009).

In order to consider the possible implications of generational differences for human resource management practices, we must adopt a wider viewpoint. The notion of generational diversity may have been widely accepted by practitioners and consultants. In fact, it is difficult today to open a professional magazine or attend a management conference without coming across the concept. However, as academics we can hope to contribute by taking a critical view of such concepts and seeking evidence of their validity. These findings can then feed into the discussions of those who wish to consider the implications of generations in practice.

## 7.2 Theoretical basis of generational diversity

We begin by considering the extent to which accepted approaches to generations are based upon a sound theoretical framework and empirical evidence base. The theoretical basis for generations can be traced back to the 1950s and the work of Karl Mannheim (1893–1947). In his paper 'The Problem of Generations' (1952) Mannheim proposed that generations were important to understanding the structure of social and intellectual movements. Mannheim likened a generation to an individual's class position in society, in that a generation is not a concrete group but rather a 'social location'. Individuals within a generation share the same year of birth and so have a common historical social location, which means that they have a limited range of potential experience. This predisposes them to a certain characteristic mode of thought and experience. However, it is important to note that Mannheim's work does not suggest that simply sharing a birth year is sufficient for a group of individuals to be considered as a generation. They must also share common experiences so that they share 'an identity of responses, a certain affinity in the way in which all move with and are formed by their common experiences' (1952, p. 306). Straightaway we can see how important it is to question an approach to generations that is based primarily on experiences of US citizens.

Sessa et al. (2007) have summarised Mannheim's definition of a generation by suggesting that there are six characteristics that a generation must possess. They must have experienced, first, a traumatic or formative event such as a war; second, a dramatic shift in demography that influences the distribution of resources in society; third, an interval that connects a generation to success or failure (such as the Great Depression); fourth, a 'sacred space' that sustains a collective memory (for example, Woodstock); fifth, mentors or heroes (for example, Martin Luther King); and, finally, the work of people who know and support each other.

Bourdieu (1977) suggested that differences between generations were the result of conflict over economic and cultural resources. As different generations see different resources as important, this leads to inter-generational conflict such as the anti-youth movement (Bourdieu 1993). This idea has been adopted by Eyerman and Turner (1998), who proposed that a generational cohort has strategic access to collective cultural and material resources and maintains its cultural identity by stopping others having access to these resources. A generation promotes its survival by retaining a collective memory of its past, through historical and political events and characters. This focus on the fight for resources distinguishes the work of Turner and his colleagues (Turner 2002; Eyerman and Turner 1998; Turner 1998) from that of Mannheim, although it should be noted that the basic characteristics of a generation, as detailed by Sessa et al. (2007), remain the same.

More recently, sociologists have focused on cultural events such as music or popular culture as defining characteristics of a generation, as opposed to historical events (Turner 2002; Eyerman and Turner 1998; Turner 1998). Eyerman and Turner (1998) emphasised the idea that members of a generation share a collective cultural field of emotions, attitudes, preferences and dispositions and a set of embodied practices such as sport and leisure activities. Generations are therefore linked through shared cultural symbols such as music or fashion (McMullin, Comeau and Jovic 2007). This is an idea that has been adopted by the marketing industry through the use of music or other nostalgic symbols to advertise products and services (Arsenault 2004).

The notion that a particular generation shares collective memories, whether they are of historical events or of popular culture, has received some support in the literature (Schuman and Scott 1989; Holdbrook and Schindler 1989; 1994; Schuman and Rogers 2004). There is, therefore, some evidence that people who experience during their formative years particularly significant national or international events will form a shared memory of them ('generational imprinting'). However, it is these two notions of (*a*) *shared* experiences, which (*b*) then translate into *shared* future attitudes, preferences and behaviours that distinguish the sociological perspective on generational differences from that of the demographic cohort analysis. In the latter it is only the case that different cohorts *may* have shared experiences that cause them to have different outcomes (in contrast to generations that *must* have shared experiences to be considered as such) and it is not necessary for any shared experiences to be manifested as differences in behaviours and attitudes. These are important distinctions for our understanding of generational diversity and how it has been operationalised by researchers and practitioners.

### 7.2.1 Cohort analysis

A cohort is defined, more broadly than a generation, as 'a set of individuals entering a system [i.e. being born] at the same time', who are 'presumed to have similarities due to shared experiences that differentiate them' (Mason and Wolfinger 2001). Edmunds and Turner (2002) make a clear distinction between chronological or birth *cohorts* and social or political *generations* that form around particular formative experiences and adopt distinctive cultural symbols expressive of those experiences. This view is reflected by Ryder (1965), who considered the term 'cohort' as a 'more neutral construct' (Gilleard 2004, p. 108). When dealing with cohort analysis there seems only to be a *presumption* that cohorts exhibit differences in outcomes due to shared experiences (Mason and Wolfinger 2001). In contrast, it would seem that a generation *must* exhibit such differences in order to be considered as such (and that this is expected to result in a common set of behaviours and attitudes).

The empirical approach we would therefore expect when considering cohorts is, first, to define the cut-off birth date for those being considered and then test where the 'outcomes' (including perhaps values and attitudes) of this group exhibit particular differences from other cohorts. In contrast, with the theory of generations one *begins* with a social, political or economic event; change in resource, demography or other social characteristics and from this one would search for appropriate cut-off points to define a generation. A cohort would be counted as a *generational* group only if it exhibited separate and distinct values and attitudes because its members shared social, economic and political events that other cohorts did not.

## 7.3 Empirical evidence of generational diversity

The use of generational differences to segment the population is not limited to HRM. The modern notion of generations in business has mainly stemmed from the field of marketing, where it has been used to segment the consumer population into groups which may have different preferences (Bradford 1993; Noble and Schewe 2003). However, while this approach has been increasingly adopted by those interested in people management issues, the jump from one discipline to the other has been accompanied by a degree of scepticism.

A number of commentators have criticised the concept of generational diversity for lack of evidence. For example, Lyons, Duxbury and Higgins (2007, p. 339) suggested that 'there has been relatively little academic work either to confirm or refute popular generational stereotypes'. Giancola (2006) went one step further than this to describe the notion of generational differences as 'more myth than reality' (p. 32). Giancola's (2006) literature review found a lack of 'major published articles' in the US in the 25 years up to 2005 and therefore concluded that there was an absence of support from independent sources. Macky, Gardner and Forsyth (2008) also commented that, while there was some evidence for differences between generations, effect sizes tended to be small and some findings were inconsistent with the popular stereotypes of generations. Our search of the academic literature on generational differences in work values identifies some empirical studies in this area, but as we will see from the discussion below, these do not provide the strong evidence for generational diversity that we are looking for.

We found a number of studies that support the existence of generational differences in work values. For example, Wong et al. (2008) found differences between generations in their scores on the Motivation Questionnaire for affiliation, power and progression. However, the authors concluded that these differences may stem more from career stage than from generational differences. A similar study conducted by Chen and Choi (2008) found that Baby Boomers rate personal growth more highly than younger generations, while Generation Y values work environment more highly than Generation X or Baby Boomers. Cennamo and Gardner (2008) also found significant generational differences in some work values (status and freedom) but not in others (extrinsic, social and altruism-related values). Lyon, Duxbury and Higgins (2007) found differences between the four generations in scores on the Schwartz Values Survey (Schwartz 1994), although a number of these did not support the popular stereotypes of generations. Gursoy, Maier and Chi (2008) use in-depth focus groups to identify differences in generations' attitudes towards authority and the perceived importance of work.

We also identified a number of studies that fail to find support for generational differences. For instance, Kunreuther (2003) failed to find differences between the qualities of older and younger employees using interviews. Appelbaum, Serena and Shapiro (2005), Parker and Chusmir (1990) and Mahoney (1976) fail to find differences in motivational factors, work values, and work goals respectively, using cross-sectional surveys. Jurkiewicz and Brown (1998), who conducted a survey of public sector employees, also found that the work-related values of Veterans, Baby Boomers and Generation X were similar. Repeating this study, Jurkiewicz (2000) again found that Baby Boomers and Generation X were more alike than different.

These examples show that, of the few studies that do exist, there are as many that fail to find differences, or find differences that are contrary to popular stereotypes, as those that do find the predicted differences. However, across studies that find evidence both for and against generational differences, there are questions over the methodological approach used. First, as Rhodes (1983) suggests, it is standard practice when analysing cohorts to distinguish between 'cohort effects', 'age effects' and 'period effects'. We have already made the distinction between generational/cohort effects and age effects that stem from psychosocial, physiological or anatomical changes that occur as a result of 'maturation'. If any differences are observed in a cross-sectional empirical study between an older and a younger age group, it is impossible to distinguish generational from age effects. Cohort/generational effects would be expected to remain relatively stable as people age, whereas any differences arising from age effects would result in younger people becoming more like the older people as they age – something that cannot be distinguished in a study that considers only one point in time.

Period effects represent a further confounding factor, as they arise from characteristics of the environment at the particular point in time at which a study is taking place (for instance, studies carried out in a period of rapid social change such as the 1960s would likely overstate any differences between generations). In order to accurately distinguish between these three effects, longitudinal and time-lag (comparisons of people who are the same age in different time periods) data are needed, as opposed to the cross-sectional data used in the studies discussed above. This means that, regardless of their results, the above studies are incapable of truly identifying generational or cohort effects, and therefore do not constitute evidence for or against generational differences.

Smola and Sutton (2002) provided a rare example of a longitudinal study of generational differences in work values. Smola and Sutton found significant differences between Baby Boomers and Generation X in desirability of work outcomes and moral importance of work that were in keeping with popular stereotypes. However, as this study used different samples at each time period, it is difficult to establish whether these findings actually arose from sampling differences. Lippmann (2008) used standard age-period-cohort logistic regression techniques to separate out the effects of age, period and cohort in his examination of cohort effects on unemployment and re-employment, and found that the cohort effect was a better predictor of displacement than age. Twenge and Campbell (2008) found significant differences between generations by taking archival personality data from different generational groups at different time periods and comparing them. These few studies may provide hope that evidence of generational differences can be found. However, they cannot be taken as evidence of the validity of the categorisations set out in Table 7.1, for which considerable further work is required.

This brings us back to consideration of the difference between cohort effects and generational effects. The sociology literature suggests that generations cannot be defined purely by birth year and that their formation is based on a more complex combination of birth cohort, a shared experience of historical and political events, and collective culture (Mannheim 1952). This seems to be in direct contradiction to the approach taken to the issue of generations in most studies where predefined cohorts (Veterans, Baby Boomers, Generation X and Generation Y) are taken as representing distinct generations. The a prior assumption would seem to be that there are four generations grouped according to birth year; and implicit in this approach is the assumption that the job of proving proximity to historical events and social, cultural and economic phenomena has already been carried out. When we consider the empirical evidence, there is little clear justification for the use of birth-year cut-off points similar to those set out in Table 7.1. As a result, in studies that utilise these four existing cohort categorisations, a lack of evidence of differing values, behaviours or attitudes can mean either that (*a*) these cohorts are not good proxies for the four generations described or that (*b*) these are the correct categorisations but there are genuinely no differences between the generations. This raises an issue for all of the empirical evidence on generational difference (for more detail, see Parry and Urwin forthcoming)

### 7.3.1 The importance of individual differences and national context

As one might expect when working from such a weak methodological base, a number of authors have suggested that generations may be more heterogeneous than homogeneous (Denecker et al. 2008). Research has found differences between men and women within generations (Lippmann 2008; Parker and Chusmir 1990; Eskilson and Wiley 1999) and differences based on region (Griffin 2004) and educational level (Schuman and Rogers 2004). These findings remind us that any notion of homogeneity within generations is too simplistic, and, what is especially relevant for HRM, we need to consider differences between generations alongside other cross-cutting differences that may be driven by a variety of socio-demographic factors.

One of the more obvious potential drivers of heterogeneity between individuals within a generation is that which exists across national boundaries (an issue we have already touched upon when noting the US-centric nature of the literature). Thus, there is some evidence to suggest that generational characteristics in eastern countries are different from those in the West. For example, a number of studies (Egri and Ralston 2004; Ralston et al. 1999) established a different generational structure in China based on events such as the Great Cultural Revolution and rise of Communism. Similarly, Murphy, Gordon and Anderson (2004) found differences between generations in the USA and Japan; and Whiteoak, Crawford and Mapstone (2006) provided evidence of differences between generations of manufacturing employees in UAE. However, Hui-Chun and Miller (2003) found that generational differences among manufacturing employees in Taiwan were actually similar to those suggested in Western societies. This is an area that needs considerable research in order to establish the extent to which differences between generations are consistent across cultures and where national experiences make talk of shared generational values defunct. In today's globalised society we can expect that the workforce, even within a particular location, will consist of employees of different nationalities and cultures. In these situations we may find that the use of generations as an axis of diversity is not appropriate.

We have considered the empirical research that has been carried out about generational differences in work values and discussed some of the problems inherent in the evidence base for these differences. It should not be forgotten that these need to be addressed before generations can be accepted as a valid basis for segmenting the workforce. However, the idea of generational differences does have a strong theoretical foundation on which we can build; the main problem seems to be that this theoretical foundation has not been used in the building of an empirical literature.

One is also struck by the extensive consultant and practitioner interest in this issue of generations and the wealth of advice that is available on how one manages the generations, based on 'evidence' of their differing work values. As readers will understand from our review of the empirical evidence, the next section of this chapter, which details the existing advice on how the differences between generations can be best managed, must come with a health warning. Most importantly, we begin the following section with some discussion of how practitioners should interpret the 'findings' that we present from the existing literature, given the criticisms raised here.

## 7.4 Advice on the impact of generational diversity on people management

Despite the lack of consistent and reliable evidence of generational differences, much has been written, particularly in the practitioner arena, about the impact of generational diversity and the approaches that have been adopted by consultants and managers alike. How are practitioners able to gain some direction from the existing evidence base we present here when it suffers from quite substantial flaws?

First, it is important to note that, while the existing research does not provide evidence *for* generational differences, the methodological limitations of most studies also mean that they do not represent evidence *against* this concept. The following 'evidence' is, we hope, useful for practitioners who are advised to take a critical perspective.

Following a format adopted in earlier work for the Chartered Institute of Personnel and Development (CIPD) (Parry and Urwin 2009), we consider the impact of generational diversity on the five areas of (*a*) recruitment and selection, (*b*) training and development, (*c*) career development, (*d*) rewards and working patterns and (*e*) generational conflict.

### 7.4.1 Recruitment and selection

The potential differences between generations have been suggested as reasons why they may have different experiences of looking for work. For example, Baby Boomers will have searched for jobs using newspapers and industry press and employment agencies, whereas Generations X and Y are more likely to look for work online, through jobs boards, search engines and social networking sites. The implication would be that employers need to take this into account and use a wide range of sources when advertising vacancies so that they can reach job seekers of all ages.

There is also a suggestion that Generations X and Y will be particularly interested in the 'employer brand' of an organisation, as they are more used to brand marketing. In addition, the different generations will be interested in different things from an organisation, so the employer brand will need to take this into account. For example, Generation X might be looking to learn marketable skills, build relationships with people who can help them, tackle challenges and produce results as evidence of their ability, manage their own time, work in an entrepreneurial environment, be creative and innovative, work as part of a team and receive feedback and credit for valuable contributions (Tulgan 1997). In contrast, Generation Y might be looking for an employer who invests heavily in training and development, cares about employees as individuals, provides clear career progression opportunities, provides variety in daily work and has a forward-looking approach to the business (Terjesen, Vinnicombe and Freeman 2007).

### 7.4.2 Training and development

The practitioner literature suggests that training is very important to Generation X in particular. This means that, in order to retain members of this generation, it is important for employers to create an environment that supports continuous learning (Corley 1999). Generation X also values mentoring relationships in the workplace, where managers lead by example.

The generations may differ in the nature of the training that best suits their learning. The most notable possible difference is the fact that Generations X and Y are likely to be more used to learning using technology, so like to see innovation in training. However, it is further suggested that Generations X and Y both have the ability to concentrate on multiple tasks and assimilate several pieces of information at once, and the younger generations also like learning to be fun and memorable. The implication would be that organisations should create training programmes that involve all six senses and should allow time for practice. Generation X is seen to particularly value independent, self-paced learning and flexibility of training; and members of this generation like to understand *why* they should learn something before they will agree to do so. Baby Boomers, on the other hand, are seen as preferring traditional classroom-based training with personal interaction, while Veterans prefer traditional lectures, seminars or topic experts. The important point here is that employers should deliver training in a variety of ways, rather than presuming that one size fits all.

### 7.4.3 Career development

Probably the most striking difference that has been proposed between generations is in their attitudes towards careers. Baby Boomers were brought up to believe that a job was for life, and therefore the assumption is that they do not tend to change organisations often and will rely on their employer for career development. In contrast, members of Generation X are more likely to assume responsibility for their own career development and to make frequent sideways or even downward as well as upward career moves across organisations as opportunities arise. They also generally see jobs as a 'stepping stone' to something else (Filipczak, 1994). Members of Generation Y are generally seen as being similar to Generation X, with tenure in any one job being short, although recent research from the Chartered Institute of Management (2008) showed that there was still a significant proportion of Generation Y who stayed with their organisation on a longer-term basis.

Any change in employees' attitudes towards careers has important implications for employers. Baby Boomers might value traditional methods of career management and formal career advancement schemes linked to pay, but for Generations X and Y organisations will need to move away from a linear, hierarchical view of career management to a broader view that incorporates both subjective and objective career goals and promotes learning opportunities, networking and work–life balance.

### 7.4.4 Rewards and working patterns

It has also been suggested in the practitioner literature that the different generations have different preferences for rewards. While all four generations see money as important, Baby Boomers see money as a form of recognition while Generation X sees money as valuable for its own sake. Baby Boomers place particular emphasis on economic security, while Generation Y wants competitive salaries, good benefits and learning opportunities. Generation X, on the other hand, is also driven by non-financial rewards such as increased responsibility, opportunities for creative expression and exposure to decision-makers.

Employers should consider these preferences when putting together reward packages for a multigenerational workforce. One way of addressing this issue is for employers to provide a flexible or cafeteria approach to benefits that allows employees to select their own benefits package within a predefined financial limit. Generation X, in particular, is seen to value rewards based on performance and wants to know what is being rewarded. If this is the case then it is essential to link pay to clear performance-management systems (Filipczak 1994).

It is also important to note that Generations X and Y are believed to place more importance on work–life balance than do Baby Boomers. Whereas Baby Boomers are seen as being willing to work long hours in return for recognition, the younger generations prefer to work more flexibly, with recent research from the CIPD (2008) showing that 49 per cent of Generation Y managers worked away from the office at least some of the time. Employers should therefore ensure that they have flexible working arrangements in place.

### 7.4.5 Generational conflict

It is worth also mentioning another area that has received much attention in both the popular media and the industry press – that of generational conflict. A number of commentators have suggested that the 'generation gap' between the four generations currently in the workforce may lead to conflict. Survey research from the Society for Human Resource Management (Burke 2004) found that 40 per cent of HR managers were aware of intergenerational conflict at work, demonstrating what a significant issue this is thought to be. In particular, the considerable differences between Baby Boomers and Generation X have been suggested as having a negative effect on working relationships. Baby Boomers are seen by Generation X as being self-righteous workaholics, while Generation X is seen by Baby Boomers as 'slackers' who lack social skills. The situation is made worse by the fact that Generation X is waiting for Baby Boomers to retire so that it can move into their positions.

A number of suggestions have been made for overcoming intergenerational conflict in the workplace. Schizas (1999) emphasised the importance of creating an atmosphere of fellowship where employees could learn from each other, training line managers in supporting and facilitating rather than controlling, providing training and development opportunities and keeping open communication channels. Burke's (2004) research also emphasised the importance of communication, training and team-building activities.

## 7.5 Summary and conclusions

Many practitioners believe that the differences between generations are self-evident. Practitioners may therefore see 'generation' as a defining characteristic, cutting across gender, ethnicity and industry sector. However, we must conclude that the academic research currently available in this area does not provide robust support for this idea, at least in respect of work values (Parry and Urwin, forthcoming). In fact, most of the literature in this area is not academic or empirical but is located in practitioner publications and in the material produced by management consultancies. The academic research that does exist provides at best mixed evidence of generational differences in work values.

However, as we have detailed in the previous section, one is struck by the extensive consultant and practitioner interest in this issue; and as part of our review we detail some of this 'evidence' and advice. We hope that this chapter is useful for practitioners who, given the state of research, can now consider the existing management advice from a more critical perspective.

As an example of this more critical perspective, for those considering generational difference in the workplace the concept of generations seems to have a theoretical (from the academic literature) and intuitive (from the work by practitioners) appeal. However, our study would suggest that one of the largest flaws in the approach to generations is the assumption, before any research has taken place, that there are four specific cohorts of individuals and these are *the* generations (with some variation in the specific years used as cut-off points). From what we have detailed, managers may find consideration of generational difference as a diversity axis useful, but they should do so outside of the confines of the categories used in Table 7.1 (which are highly US-centric).

Within each workplace, managers need to consider the generational context as unique to that setting; and in this instance management literatures should be treated as only a point of reference rather than a guiding philosophy. Ideally, we would sit down with each individual and put together a bespoke employment package that fully accommodated their diversity of needs. In reality we are forced to consider dimensions of diversity as a half-way house towards such a bespoke approach. In doing so, we must be careful that we do not spuriously add more dimensions than are strictly necessary; and in the case set out here, in the majority of cases it seems to be unnecessary to distinguish four generations.

In order to move this area of study forward, a comprehensive body of research must be undertaken using a clear definition to establish the nature of generations within and across national cultures, the characteristics and values of these generations and any differences between them. Such research requires the use of longitudinal and time-lag design to enable us to distinguish between the effects of age, generational cohort and transient environmental influences. Smola and Sutton (2004) have provided us with the first step on a journey that was originally suggested by Rhodes back in 1983, but there is a still long way to go.

# Part III
# The Employee's Perspective

Now that we have considered the nature of both age and age diversity as well as the reasons why employers and individuals might want to develop age-management practices, we can move on to examine the implications of an age-diverse workforce, the impact of age discrimination and potential age-management practices in more detail. When looking at the implications of an age-diverse workforce it is necessary to consider these from more than one perspective. Therefore, we adopt two perspectives within this book, that of the individual or employee and that of the organisation or employer. In Part III we present three chapters that approach the issue of managing an age-diverse workforce from the employee's perspective.

In Chapter 8 Fiona Carmichael and colleagues examine ageism and age discrimination from the point of view of older workers. This chapter reports on the existing literature and some empirical research on older workers' perceptions of ageism in the workplace and investigates the impact of this on the participation of older workers in the labour market.

In Chapter 9 Dianne Bown-Wilson looks at the factors that might affect older workers' motivation for career progression. Much research has focused on the impact of employer policies and practices in retaining older workers within organisations, but few scholars have examined the influence of the motivation and attitudes of the older workers themselves. This chapter also considers differences in older workers' motivation by gender.

In Chapter 10 we move away from our focus on older workers and look at the other end of the workforce. Wolfgang Mayrhofer and colleagues investigate the employment needs and preferences of younger workers (specifically Masters graduates), through an examination of qualitative research data, and discuss the implications of their findings for HRM and leadership.

# 8
# Ageism and Age Discrimination: The Experiences and Perceptions of Older Employees

*Fiona Carmichael, Claire Hulme, Lorna Porcellato, Barbara Ingham and Arvin Prashar*

This chapter explores reasons for the lower employment participation rates of older people by considering the views and perspectives of older people themselves. The chapter begins by setting out some contextual issues. In section 8.2 some recent qualitative research that provides an 'insider perspective' on the views of older men and women is reviewed. Within this body of work, a range of factors that constrain the employment of older people has been identified. Among these factors, ageist attitudes are found to be of particular importance since these are manifested in discriminatory practices. In section 8.3 new research by the authors is presented which explores in detail how ageism can restrict the opportunities of older people in employment. Section 8.4 concludes.

## 8.1 Employment participation rates of older people

According to data from the European Union Labour Force Survey the employment participation rate in 2006 for British men aged 20–49 was 86.1 per cent, but for men aged 50–64 was 72.6 per cent (see Table 8.1). For women the participation rate was 73.9 per cent for those aged between 20 and 49 but only 57.7 per cent for women aged 50–64. Significant age gaps in employment rates also exist in other European countries, as indicated in Table 8.1, where the data indicate that these gaps are particularly evident in Austria. A similar pattern exists across all OECD countries, where less than 60 per cent of those aged 50–64 were employed in 2004, compared with 76 per cent of those aged 24–49 (OECD 2006).

A wide range of seemingly diverse explanations for the lower employment participation rates of older people has been put forward in the literature. These include ageist attitudes, higher incidences of ill-health

*Table 8.1* Employment rates in the UK, France, Greece and Austria, 2004–6

| | **UK** | | **France** | | **Greece** | | **Austria** | |
|---|---|---|---|---|---|---|---|---|
| **Age group** | **< 50** | **50–64** | **< 50** | **50–64** | **< 50** | **50–64** | **< 50** | **50–64** |
| Year | Male participation rates (%) | | | | | | | |
| 2004 | 86.4 | 71.5 | 81.5 | 58.3 | 84.9 | 67.2 | 86.3 | 53.3 |
| 2005 | 86.2 | 72.1 | 81.4 | 57.5 | 83.9 | 69.1 | 88.2 | 57.3 |
| 2006 | 86.1 | 72.6 | 79.6 | 55.9 | 84.8 | 69.2 | 88.4 | 60.0 |
| | Female participation rates (%) | | | | | | | |
| | < 50 | 50–64 | < 50 | 50–64 | < 50 | 50–64 | < 50 | 50–64 |
| 2004 | 73.1 | 56.0 | 67.9 | 47.1 | 55.5 | 48.3 | 74.9 | 34.9 |
| 2005 | 73.7 | 56.6 | 68.1 | 48.8 | 55.4 | 48.8 | 75.4 | 39.1 |
| 2006 | 73.9 | 57.7 | 66.8 | 48.1 | 57.2 | 50.2 | 76.0 | 42.4 |

*Source*: European Commission, Eurostat. European Union Labour Force Survey, quarterly data (Eurostat has no responsibility for the interpretation of this data).

and lower levels of educational attainment among older people as well as organisational practices such as seniority wages, redundancy agreements and retirement rules and personal choice (Herz and Rones 1989; Schwartz and Kleiner 1999; OECD 2004; House of Commons 2004; McNair et al, 2004; OECD 2004: Irving, Steels and Hall 2005; Siebert and Heywood 2009). Ageist attitudes are important since they can lead to discriminatory practices in the workplace that negatively affect older people in employment as well as those seeking work (Taylor and Walker 1994; Redman and Snape 2002; Taylor and Walker 2003; Duncan and Loretto 2004; Loretto and White 2006a). Widespread ageist attitudes that have been internalised (Lorretto and White (2006a) further disadvantage older workers if they lead to negative perceptions of self in the workplace.

Appropriate policy interventions that address some of these factors could raise the employment rates of older workers in the current labour market. This is more likely to be achieved with a clearer understanding of how older workers themselves perceive these constraints. Maltby (2007, p. 164) emphasises this point when he argues that 'outcomes of political decision making will reflect the concerns of older people if and when activities and views from "ordinary" people's lives are incorporated in the process of a political democracy'. However, knowledge concerning the experiences and perceptions of older people in the workforce is less extensive than that relating to the attitudes of employers to the employment of older workers (Loretto, Vickerstaff and White 2006;

2007; McNair 2006; Lundberg and Marshallsay 2007; Maltby 2007). Consequently, in much of the literature on ageism and age discrimination the behaviour of older workers has been treated in a passive manner, simply as a response to opportunities and constraints emerging in the labour market. Roberts (2006) argues that this represents a missed opportunity since

> the relationship between changes in the labour markets, the labour process, structures of age and patterns of work are never simply issues of the use of impersonal human resources. They imply issues that go way beyond the individual workplace to arguments about what kind of society we want to live in and the role that institutions including work organisations, have to play in such a society.
>
> (Roberts 2006, p. 82)

Giles and Reid (2005) also stress that research on ageism should focus much more on the individual worker. They point to a gap and a bias in empirical work in that individuals are not asked about their own feelings. Of the few studies that do consider the perspectives of the older employee directly, most are quantitative in design (Chiu et al. 2001; McGregor and Gray 2002). This reflects a reluctance noted by Giles and Reed (2005) to use respondents' own words to explain their experiences of ageism and age discrimination. Researchers tend to use instead 'contextually-defined and coded qualities' that fail to convey the distress experienced by older people who are subjected to ageist behaviour.

Some recent attempts to redress this imbalance using qualitative research methods are briefly reviewed in the next section. We then report findings from the authors' own research.

## 8.2 Qualitative evidence of constraints on older workers' employment

Irving, Steels and Hall (2005) have explored factors influencing participation in and withdrawal from the labour market as well as barriers to continued labour market participation by older workers (those aged 50–69). Seventy-one interviews were conducted followed by six focus groups attended by 52 of the interviewees. Their sample of respondents included people both in and out of work, and reflected a wide range of diverse socio-demographic characteristics. The sample was domiciled in four locations in the UK: Newcastle, Christchurch, East Dorset and Walsall. The authors identified push (involuntary) and pull (voluntary) factors that explain labour market exit of older people. Push factors include health conditions, redundancy, reduction in job satisfaction, changes in work, caring responsibilities, recession, restructuring and fixed retirement ages. Pull factors include financial security, proximity to the eligibility age for the state pension, looking after home, time with family and quality time or hobbies. Both push and pull factors such as ill-health, redundancy, caring responsibilities and bereavement were found to influence attitudes towards planning and saving for retirement.

Barriers to labour market re-entry for those out of employment were categorised as either external or personal, although barriers rarely operated in isolation. External barriers include economic restructuring, labour demand and age discrimination. Personal barriers include a range of factors such as health, family and caring responsibilities, skills and experience, limited awareness of opportunities, the benefits trap and personal attitudes to income and employment expectations, and lack of confidence or fear. Some of these barriers were classified as real by Irving, Steels and Hall (2005), but others were thought to be imagined (that is, not based on actual experience but on how employers might or ought to behave). One worrying finding from this research is that there are over-50s who want to work but are outside the labour market and see no place for them in the labour market.

Loretto and White (2006b) have explored the preferences and expectations of employed older workers regarding work and labour market exit on retirement. They employed focus groups with 33 participants from four areas within Scotland chosen to represent a diversity of geographic characteristics, types of employment, local labour markets and levels of economic buoyancy. Participants were employed in finance, education, local government, hospital and catering, and had been with their employers for up to 37 years. Employing organisations varied in size from 2 to 18,000 employees. The majority of participants in this research (Loretto and White 2006b) expected to work past state pension age or were already doing so. The main drivers for this were financial, but there was also a sense of *filling a vacuum* and making a positive contribution. Those who wanted to retire as soon as possible cited workplace stress and a negative effect on their health. Other drivers for retirement included a culture of retirement that inflicted peer pressure.

Barriers to continuing in employment included lack of choice (contractual retirement age and rigidity in pension schemes) and lack of career advancement and promotion opportunities. In large organisations early retirement was the norm while smaller organisations were thought more flexible. Older workers were seen as an easy target for redundancy or early retirement. There were also perceived barriers to moving jobs as organisations were believed to favour younger workers with discrimination in the recruitment process and a lower quality of jobs available to older people. Older workers themselves exhibited some age bias and discrimination, and they believed that, particularly in lower-skill jobs, performance declined with age. Loretto and White (2006b, p. 503) conclude that there is an array of personal, financial and institutional factors 'which interact to influence older employees' expectations of work and retirement'.

Age Concern England (Collins 2006) published work detailing the personal experiences of 49 men and women aged over 50 who were looking for employment in London and the north-east and the south-west of England. Focus groups were used to explore the experiences and views of the sample members. In line with Irving, Steels and Hall (2005) the research found that the important reasons for being out of work were redundancy, health problems and caring responsibilities. The study showed how being unemployed affects self-esteem, morale and confidence levels, and often leads to severe anxiety because of financial insecurity. In contrast, paid work was believed to be the key to leading a fulfilling life and was also linked to personal identity, self-esteem, self-motivation and general interest in life. However, the participants had experienced multiple rejections and a lack of response when applying for jobs, and the ageist attitudes of potential employers were thought to be a contributory factor. Age discrimination was thought to be a rational explanation for the difficulties they had faced and consequently some had felt forced to lie about their age in job applications. However, other external constraints on job opportunities, such as rapid technological change and the decline of manufacturing industry, were acknowledged. Gaps in knowledge were identified by some respondents, although others thought that older people could be overqualified for some jobs and therefore too expensive. Personal factors such as ill-health, lack of confidence and unwillingness to take risks were also discussed.

Lundberg and Marshallsay (2007) conducted focus groups with over 30 active and retired officials from Australian unions representing three industrial sectors: finance, care work for the aged in the health sector, and construction. One of the aims of the focus groups was to shape and test the relevance of the issues that the authors proposed to incorporate in a subsequent survey of older workers on retention and training. The focus groups highlighted increasing workloads, the physical demands of work as workers became older, pension rights, tax issues and lack of employer support as factors affecting incentives to remain in work. The union representatives also raised concerns about employer support for training for older workers, and suggested 'train the trainer' training of older workers that could enable them to transfer their experience to younger workers. In the subsequent survey of older workers, Lundberg and Marshallsay found that around 80 per cent of the sample saw value in 'train the trainer' courses that would enable older workers to act as trainers or mentors to younger workers, and 70 per cent 'saw a need for training of supervisors and younger workers against age-biased stereotypes' (Lundberg and Marshallsay 2007, p. 29).

The gendered dimension of ageism in employment has been explored by Walker et al. (2007), who focus on older women's experiences in paid employment. Twelve women aged between 50 and 65 were interviewed, eight of whom were in paid employment. Participants expressed their views concerning age-related matters in their current or past employment and, where relevant, in relation to transitions into retirement or unpaid work. Seven participants had experienced discrimination earlier in their career based on age, gender or both. For four this related to motherhood and care of their family. Time taken out of the workplace after having children had a detrimental impact on availability and choice once they returned to work, and had a long-term psychological impact. It was suggested that gender discrimination was compounded or exacerbated by ageism over time. Within the workplace age stereotyping was reported in relation to appearance and performance. Concern for the former was particularly prevalent for women in 'professional, male managed and hierarchal organisations' (Walker et al. 2007, p. 43) where ageism tended to be centred on technology.

Walker et al. conclude that 'while most of the women had faced (to differing degrees) gender and age discrimination, the experiences and interpretations revealed were not static, nor isolated from the wider historical, cultural and social contexts in which these women had grown up and grown older' (2007, p. 37). By implication, policy should take into account the gender dimension of ageism.

In summary, the evidence of these studies is that there is a wide range of factors that negatively affect the employment of older people, including external social and economic factors. Institutional arrangements, health and other personal circumstances are also involved. However, a common theme is that ageism and ageist attitudes can adversely affect the opportunities of older workers in the labour market. These effects are discussed further in the next section.

## 8.3 Older workers' perspectives on ageism and age discrimination

The research discussed in this section was conducted by the authors of this chapter and based in the north-west of England. It provides a regional perspective on the relationship between age and work from the viewpoint of older people themselves. The relative position of older workers in the British labour market has a regional dimension, and in the north of England in particular there are many older people (particularly men) now approaching state pension age who were made redundant in the 1980s and 90s in traditional industries such as engineering and steel. While economic activity rates at all ages are lower in the north-west than nationally, these gaps widen in the 50–64 age groups (Cox 2004; Meadows 2004). However, the north-west of England is not unique in being plagued by a history of high rates of unemployment and re-employment (McCormick 1997), and thus insight from this research will be applicable to other older people.

The research builds on the existing qualitative research base by interviewing a sample of older people from the full spectrum of the employment cycle: those who are in and out of work, those economically active and inactive, both voluntarily and involuntarily. Fifty-six individuals were interviewed between April and October 2006. Over half (31) were male. Their ages ranged from 50 to 68, with a mean age 58.9 years. Of the 22 people who were in paid employment at the time of interview, 14 were employed full time. Five participants were self-employed, 12 were unemployed and 17 were retired (only one retiree was looking for employment). Six sample members who were not in paid work were involved in voluntary work.

Semi-structured interviews were used in conjunction with occupational–life events calendars (Axinn, Pearce and Ghimire 1999; Engel, Keifer and Zahm 2001; Martyn and Belli 2002) to collect information about previous employment experiences and perceptions of the past and present labour market. The calendar was developed to provide visual cues and historical markers, thereby facilitating the recollection of both occupational history and life events in a sequential manner (Holland et al. 1999). Detailed work histories on a job-by-job basis were recorded by the researchers in reverse order from the present day to first-ever job. Upon completion of the calendars, participants were asked a series of open-ended questions about influences on their employment over time and their views on ageism and current anti-age discrimination policy. In the interviews the relevance to the sample members of factors found to be influential in previous research was examined without setting pre-ordained boundaries on the topics explored. This was achieved in two main ways. First, while completing the calendars the participants were encouraged to talk about reasons for any job or career changes, periods of unemployment or other reasons for not working, and retirement. Second, and on completion of the calendars, the open-ended questions were used to establish whether respondents had been unfairly disadvantaged in any way in their employment and, if so, when and how.

This approach indicated that as the respondents aged the most commonly cited influences on their employment (those leading to career or job changes, redundancy, becoming unemployed or retiring) were factors relating to health, lack of human capital, and ageism, linked in some cases to age discrimination. Ageist attitudes were thought to be widespread and had even been internalised by some older workers, leading to negative perceptions of the self. Ageist attitudes of employers were also thought to be involved in the under valuation of the skills and experience of older people and an over emphasis on the costs of employing them. These findings in relation to ageism and age discrimination are discussed in more detail here.

### 8.3.1 Ageism and age discrimination

Age discrimination is a poorly understood complex social construct (Taylor 2002) that can operate indirectly and subliminally. Those affected are often unaware that they are being disadvantaged. Participants generally defined age discrimination as 'not being allowed to do something that you're capable or willing to do just because of your chronological age'. In the employment context, most of the sample felt that ageism manifested itself as 'a lack of opportunities for ... older and younger people', acknowledging that workers from either end of the labour market could be affected. For those individuals who were struggling to regain employment, perceived ageism often engendered a sense of futility ('If you're over 50, you haven't a bloody chance') or a lack of utility ('You're just useless, I mean that's how I feel now').

Age discrimination was felt by most to be perpetuated by deeply entrenched societal attitudes. These were thought to give rise to misplaced, stereotypical assumptions about older workers' abilities which constrained their labour force participation. One participant spoke of older people being perceived as suitable for only certain types of work 'because they're [seen as] old and sort of degenerate and not very fit and not very bright and losing their marbles', which in turn limited the work opportunities available to them.

Eleven participants felt that they had personally been affected by age discrimination in employment. For these people, the sense of frustration this had created was acute. While several participants raised the issue of the double burden of discrimination often faced by women in work, one participant who believed that 'we live in an ageist society' talked about how older males could be disadvantaged in the labour market as well. This participant spoke of training a younger female colleague who subsequently was appointed to a position they had both applied for. His perception was that the post had been awarded on the basis of gender and age: 'I was too old ... I was a man.'

Other participants were aware of cases where negative perceptions of age had influenced employer decision-making and led to discriminatory practices. Many of these respondents believed that such attitudes led to older workers being 'written off' as valuable contributors to the labour market: 'You know if you're over 50, it's hard work getting a job even though you might be skilled.' One participant, who had worked in a managerial role and was familiar with some of the functions of human resource (HR) departments, highlighted the overt nature of age discrimination within this particular context in as much as when a position was advertised in his department 'HR would get the CVs, and if they were over 45 I wouldn't even see the CV. It wouldn't even come to me.'

While participants demonstrated knowledge and awareness of age discrimination in the workplace, there may still be a need for a better understanding of what constitutes ageism and age discrimination. An awareness of the policies and interventions that are in place to tackle these issues is also needed in order to heighten sensitivity to age prejudice in general. Given the potentially detrimental effects of discrimination on health and well-being, the provision of psychological and emotional support for unemployed older workers (Collins 2006) should also be considered.

The ages of managers and co-workers relative to the ages of those being interviewed for a position was considered to be an important factor. It was felt that managers do not want to work with employees who are older than themselves, and older employees were sometimes perceived to be a threat or considered 'difficult' to work with. Moreover, the age of co-workers was also considered an important determinant of whether someone aged over 50 would be employed, whether the older person would 'fit in' with other employees. The issue of respect (or lack of it) on the part of younger managers was also raised. A few interviewees were of the opinion that younger employees were preferred because they had the potential to be more easily manipulated.

The perception of ageism in the workplace was debated on the basis that there was scope for personal interpretation – that some potentially ageist policies were implemented for legitimate reasons, with physically demanding jobs for example. It was felt that what may be perceived by one individual to be a discriminatory practice may be considered appropriate by another. Indeed, a small minority were of the opinion that many older people were not necessarily victims of age discrimination but rather needed to 'lower their standards', to accommodate the natural progress of ageing 'because as you get older you do slow down'. Notably, and in contrast to the discussion above, some participants identified themselves as fitter, healthier and more capable and sustainable than previous generations. However, they expressed concern that this was not universally recognised. Instead, older people were still plagued by enduring negative perceptions that characterise traditional concepts of 'old age', reflecting incongruence between the individual experiences of some contemporary older people and the wider socio-political and economic context.

Ageism and ageist attitudes towards older people were considered to have a substantive negative impact on the employment of older workers. Such attitudes arise from a more general 'culture of ageism' (Stoney and Roberts 2003) and are associated with negative stereotypes of older workers (Taylor and Walker 1994; 1998; Lyon and Pollard 1997; Loretto and White 2006a). They can lead to employer preferences for young workers who are deemed to fit in better and likely to be around longer (Loretto and White 2006b), perpetuating the notion of aesthetic labour, that is, selecting applicants on the basis that they need to 'look good or sound right' (Warhurst and Nickson 2007).

### 8.3.2 Emphasis on the costs of employing older workers

Almost a quarter of the sample put forward perceptions of cost as a motive for not employing older workers. While such costs may be real, a tendency for employers to focus on the costs – the negatives – rather than the benefits of employing older workers may reflect ageist attitudes. Among the sample, the belief that older workers were more costly to employ derived from employers' expectations in relation to the anticipated time employees would be with the company. It was believed that employers take a long-term view and therefore prefer to recruit workers who they believe will stay with the company or institution for a prolonged period. This preference was justified in terms of training costs, higher incidences of ill-health and turnover costs that lead some employers to favour the employment of younger workers. However, a focus on the looming retirement of older people undermines the importance of 'dependability' factors such as reliability, job commitment and loyalty, which are commonly associated with older workers (McGregor and Gray 2002). One participant pointed out, 'I can offer them a minimum of nine years, a minimum. Now which one of the younger ones can offer anybody nine years? I've got staying power and I can prove it.'

The participants were of the opinion that employers' preference for employing younger workers was reinforced by seniority wage systems which meant that older, more experienced workers were more expensive; that older workers might require a more adaptable and potentially more costly approach from employers, such as flexible hours of work, or in relation to the type of work (for example, physical work) or the amount of work that employers could expect older workers to perform if they wanted to tap into the experience that older workers could offer. Notably, two felt that they had been effectively pushed out of a job because employers did not want to pay the wages appropriate to their age and experience. Among many older people there was a belief that employers consider aged workers' skills to be obsolete and non-transferable and that new skill acquisition was expensive (Schwartz and Kleiner 1999). Focusing on the perceived costs associated with an older workforce rather than the value of its contribution is arguably a consequence of ageism and negative stereotyping (Peterson and Spiker 2005). It is also potentially costly as the underutilisation of the available supply of experienced labour is estimated to cost the UK economy £16 billion annually (Cabinet Office 2000).

### 8.3.3 Employers' undervaluation of the experience of older workers

The value of older employees' work-related experience was considered to be largely ignored by many employers. In contrast, the interviewees themselves maintained that it was an indispensable attribute for three main reasons: skills and knowledge acquired over time could improve effectiveness and thereby raise the productivity of employees; experienced workers could teach younger or new employees how to do the required work in line with the practices of the employer; and the experience of older workers embodied valuable knowledge in relation to a skill or process or about how an organisation or a piece of equipment or machinery functioned, and in essence could compensate for older employees' relative lack of formal qualifications.

Other research findings have highlighted how older workers are disadvantaged by a vague appreciation of the value of experience that leads to a devaluation of their contribution. However, there is evidence to suggest that the intellectual capital they gain from experience can be beneficial to employers (Trade Union Congress 2005), and the loss of their 'cultural wisdom and organisational knowledge' (Hewitt 2008) when they leave the workplace can be disadvantageous to employers. Many respondents were under the impression that this undervaluation of older workers by employers in the current labour market had also manifested itself in poor-calibre job opportunities, typified by low pay and low-skill work of the type advertised in garden centres and 'do-it-yourself' stores. Although some older workers move into inferior, low-wage jobs to accommodate a changing preference regarding type of work, others are reluctant to undertake 'McJobs' (Lindsay and McQuaid 2004); and for those that do, the move is often not one of choice but rather of circumstance, exacerbated by ageism and institutional discrimination (McNair 2006). The lack of appropriate employment has encouraged calls for more flexible work opportunities for older workers, including self-employment, part-time work and home working.

Although there was some recognition that employers were starting to view older workers more positively, notably in the voluntary and retail sectors of the labour market, the general consensus was that the 'intellectual capital' (Geisler 1999, pp. 18–26) older people bring to the workplace is not necessarily valued by employers. Participants were of the impression that, in the context of the current labour market, employers generally held qualifications and (by implication) education in higher esteem than experience. The fact that older people have not had the same educational opportunities as younger people was felt to be overlooked by some employers. In the 1950s and 60s only a very small minority of young people studied for degrees, and many people, particularly females, left school with very few or no academic qualifications.

Given that older workers tend to be disadvantaged by lack of qualifications (McGregor and Gray 2002), employment policies need to recognise the value of experience as well as of education, and employers should encourage older workers to undertake training for further qualifications to ensure that they are not penalised for the educational norms of their generation (see Chapter 12 for a discussion of training and learning by older workers).

### 8.3.4 Negative self-prejudice

While discriminatory practices of employers act as an external barrier affecting the employment of older people, some older people may be constrained because they have 'internalised negative prejudice' (Loretto and White 2006a, p. 327). As a result they 'discriminate "against themselves" by not coming forward for training or promotion' (Loretto and White 2006a, p. 327). Ageist attitudes that promote negative attitudes towards oneself in this way can therefore lead to what one participant described as 'self-fulfilling prophecies'. This type of negativity kept at least five participants from embarking on further training or applying for jobs. Participants quoted lack of confidence, perceived inability to cope with the demands of the job, the unfamiliarity of new situations, increasing changes in the workplace, and decline in mental or physical health as factors that acted as potential barriers to employment. While age was not explicitly held accountable for all of these factors, there was an inherent implication that such variables were affected by the ageing process.

Resistance to change or non-acceptance of workplace alterations was perceived as another obstacle facing older workers, one that could lead to stress related ill-health. Typically those interviewed recognised that change was difficult to embrace as one grew older. For some, resistance to change sprang from fear or a deep-seated conviction that the old ways are best. Others cited unacceptable falling standards in the current labour market which, sadly, compelled them to opt out: 'I said no, that's not for me and walked away.' For some participants this meant retirement (possibly early retirement) from a lifelong career; for others their unwillingness or inability to change was perceived to reduce the probability of employment or re-employment.

This research has indicated that older people themselves adopt negative 'adaptability' stereotypes (fear of new technology, resistance to workplace change and lack of interest in training) that emulate those held by employers (Taylor and Walker 1994; 1998; Lyon and Pollard 1997; McGregor and Gray 2002; Loretto and White 2006a). Given that such negative perceptions of the self can inhibit uptake of training (Lundberg and Marshallsay 2007), which affects employability, incentivised training that is responsive to older workers' needs should be considered.

## 8.4 Summary and conclusions

By situating research within the qualitative paradigm, the studies reported here were able to obtain the 'insider perspective' on older workers' views on the relationship between age and employment, which gives further credence to the validity of the results. This research highlights the areas where strategies to address participation in the labour market should be directed in order to ensure successful engagement and retention of the older workforce.

To summarise, the evidence discussed in this chapter suggests that older people are disadvantaged in the labour market by a range of factors that include prevailing ageist attitudes. These can lead to negative self-perceptions, the devaluation of older workers' labour market skills and experience, and a focus on the negative aspects relating to the employment of older workers rather than the contributory value of their labour market experience.

Prevailing ageist stereotypes embedded in work culture need to be challenged, as such attitudes can hinder the progression and mobility of older workers currently in employment by eroding their confidence and impeding their uptake of training opportunities. Age discrimination also disadvantages the unemployed who are seeking work by creating barriers to re-entry into the labour market, and can drive older workers out of the labour market into early retirement. More in-depth knowledge about such factors can provide a better platform upon which to build policy that helps to increase the participation of older workers in the labour market.

# 9

# The Role of Age in Career Progression: Motivation and Barriers to Fulfilment in Older Employees

*Dianne Bown-Wilson*

For the majority of older employees the workplace today is very different from what it was when they started their career. Restructuring and globalisation have created flatter and less hierarchical organisations with fewer promotional opportunities and reduced security of tenure (Wilson and Davies 1999). This, in turn, has redistributed responsibility for career progression from employers to employees themselves (Baruch 2006). These changes affect all employees, but for those who are categorised as 'older' they may be compounded by wide-ranging additional changes occurring because of, or in association with, the ageing process (Kanfer and Ackerman 2004).

Few studies have investigated the links between age and drivers of work motivation and the specific factors that represent 'progress' in the subjective view of older workers themselves – whether that progress represents the continuation of their current career or a change of occupation or focus. In order to address this gap it is necessary to find out more about what motivates older workers in careers in which 'progress' and 'promotion' are no longer likely to be synonymous, and about what drives them if they are now contemplating working for longer than they may once have envisaged, even past the age at which they could draw their pension. It is also necessary to examine how motivation may differ in later life from earlier in the career, and what part, if any, is played by factors such as gender, organisational context and life-stage changes in respect of opportunities for career progression. Equally important, a review is also required of the barriers to the motivational fulfilment of older employees, whose desires may include 'remaining in work, but on their own terms' (Standard Life 2009).

This chapter investigates the role of age in career progression, its links to motivation and some of the subjective barriers that older employees may encounter by in the later stages of their career. These may emanate from within the workplace, from older employees' broader lifestyles, or from individuals themselves through their own attitudes, orientations, perceptions and behaviours. In order to clarify how such diverse and wide-ranging influences may affect older workers' career progression, they are organised here into three groups of variables: motivational drivers, individual identity and lifestyle, and career opportunities and barriers. Following an explanation of the significance of career context, each group is considered in turn, leading into a discussion of the ways in which these variables may interact and the overall implications for employers, society and older workers themselves. This review concludes with brief recommendations for further research in order to address the considerable knowledge gaps in this particularly significant field, together with a description of actions that might usefully be taken by practitioners based on what is already known.

## 9.1 Career context

At a fundamental level, career context affects two significant areas relating to motivation for career progression: the meaning of 'career' and the meaning of 'progression'. As mentioned above, the profound changes that have taken place in corporate structures and technology in recent decades have combined with other social and economic developments in areas such as demographics, working women and the nature of family life to exert a considerable impact upon what is meant by 'career' in the twenty-first century. Consequently, numerous definitions of 'career' now exist reflecting aspects such as content, mobility and perspective. For older workers, the notion of a career has a fundamental temporal aspect:'It is not simply about what one does for a living, but about what one has done, does now and might do in the future' (Adamson, Doherty and Viney 1998). Older workers' careers are thus more likely to be more diverse in terms of their representation of a range of experiences, planned or not, creating differing motivations and expectations for the future based on personal assessments of what has gone before.

Perhaps because of this diversity of concepts, the meaning of 'career progression' has not to date been made explicit. Researchers have focused on similar but not identical paradigms – for example, progression as continuing *career development* (Arthur and Kram 1989) or progression as continuing *career success* (Sturges 1999). These paradigms accentuate the notions of 'more' or 'new' but do not in themselves account for all the underlying psychological variables that may drive careers. In the absence of any other definition, 'career progression' is used here to mean, within an individual's career, 'a gradual movement or development towards a destination or a more advanced state' (Compact Oxford English Dictionary 2009). To understand more about the impact of age upon such developments at an individual level, it is important to understand the interaction of objective and subjective factors represented in today's career arena.

## 9.2 Objective and subjective career progression

In the traditional hierarchical career structures in which the majority of today's older employees would have started their careers, individuals worked for only a small number of employers over the course of their working lives, and career progression and tenure were seen as employer-created and controlled. Career-stage (Super 1957) and life-span theories (Levinson et al. 1978) maintained that careers developed through a number of orderly stages relating to developmental stage and/or age, with the career end point represented by age-related decline and withdrawal. These theories are based on a pattern of full-time male employment (Reitman and Schneer 2003) and subsequently have been heavily criticised for factors including their failure to recognise the influence of different types of roles and workplaces, varying individual circumstances, and psychological variables such as individual motivation and personality (Latham and Pinder 2005).

Within traditional career contexts, career progression generally ceased in later life, resulting in *career plateauing,* a situation where older employees were no longer promoted, developed or incrementally rewarded (Ference, Stoner and Warrren 1977). Generally, career plateauing was regarded negatively (Near 1984) as representing lack of employer support. Such an approach, however, paid little heed to the importance of people's own views about their career experiences, choices and achievements judged by such measures as job and career satisfaction, embodied in the notion of the *subjective* career (Ng et al. 2005). The distinction between *organisational plateauing,* involving restricted progress because of a lack of employer-generated opportunities for, or management attitudes towards, those with the capability to progress and perform well, and *personal plateauing,* involving those who, because of lack of ability or motivation, no longer wanted progression (Appelbaum and Finestone 1994) acknowledged that later life plateauing was not necessarily employer-driven. This concept, combined with the notion of job-content plateauing, which occurs when there is no longer scope for growth within an individual's job and it ceases to be personally challenging (Allen et al. 1999), underlines that older workers' career progression, regardless of career context, may be much more subjective than earlier career progression. It appears, then, that two key issues lie at the heart of how age may affect career progression in later life: first, even within traditional contexts employees themselves are able to make decisions regarding their own career progression and are not totally at the mercy of their employers; and second, the subjective career may become increasingly important in influencing future choices and decisions based on what has gone before. This means in practice that career progression may equally reflect both employer-controlled circumstance and employee choice and be evaluated according to both objective and subjective measures (Bown-Wilson and Parry 2009).

As traditional hierarchical career environments disappear, career progress is becoming increasingly defined in terms of job mobility and marketability linked to each individual's repertoire of skills and achievement. As a result individuals increasingly measure success in subjective psychological terms, such as pride and achievement rather than status related to upward progression within a single organisation (Clarke 2008). Clarke's (2008) study also highlights the significant point that many older workers' careers have been less a result of planning and focused choices than a response to chance, random opportunities and luck. This appears to have little impact on future career opportunities; a psychological orientation towards flexibility and career goals turned out to be more important than past career structures, particularly for older workers:

> "When assessing perceived employability the critical issues did not seem to be whether careers had been unplanned, semi-planned or planned but the extent to which individuals had exhibited both job mobility and a career orientation. Those with experience across a range of roles and organisations as well as a focus on developing themselves for the future were more confident in their employability and more optimistic about the future."
>
> (Clarke 2008, p. 23)

This said, although the meanings associated with career progression may have changed and the emphasis shifted from objective to subjective variables, both may still be highly influential motivators, although operating in different ways. For example, salary, promotion and job satisfaction represent conceptually distinct variables and are unlikely to be linked in motivational terms, although studies have shown that all may continue to be important (Ng et al. 2005). Many significant aspects of individuals' self-image may continue to be derived from their objective career status while their personal development and the goals and expectations they relate to in subjective terms may closely relate to achievements within that framework (Doherty and Tyson 2002).

## 9.3 Career ownership

As traditional career explanations for career progression waned, new theories emerged to explain the nature of contemporary careers. Most significant are the 'protean' career (Hall 1976) and the 'boundaryless' career (DeFillippi and Arthur 1996), theories which embody the notion of self-managed careers and horizontal movement – often across a number of roles and employers. Building on these notions are the 'kaleidoscope' career (Mainiero and Sullivan 2006) and the 'authentic' career (Svejenova 2005), which further emphasise both the uneven nature of today's career paths and the shift in emphasis to the subjective career experience of the individual. A common thread running through these theories is the issue of responsibility for career development and its shift from the physical actions of the employer to the psychological drivers of the individual (Mirvis and Hall 1994), thereby equating career progression with individual psychological success. How, under what circumstances and to what degree this is taking place still requires further investigation. In the absence of a series of moves up the hierarchical ladder, a 'good' working life and a valuable and desirable work history now may be one that demonstrates a rich experience of work and great flexibility through vertical and horizontal moves – and even career breaks – across and within organisational boundaries (Adamson, Doherty and Viney 1998). Thus it may well be that in today's workplace an individual configuration of these variables is truly what represents 'career progression' for both employers and employees themselves. If so, how does this affect career progression in older employees? And how, if at all, does it affect their motivation? Clarke's (2008) study reveals that ,regardless of past career patterns (traditional, boundaryless or protean), the critical issue for older individuals' future career success is the extent to which they are flexible and open to change and have accepted responsibility for their own career development, motivating them to set goals and seek opportunities for change and advancement.

It would appear that new career contexts have led older individuals not only to assume ownership for their careers but also to reassess what 'career' and 'career progression' mean in terms of their own boundaries between work and the remainder of their lives. For example Wilson and Davies's definition of 'career' as representing the long-term accumulation of education, skills and experience that an individual sells to an employer (or employers) to try to provide the lifestyle that they want for themselves and their dependants (1999, p. 102) moves away from the achievement of employment-related success as a career driver and focuses instead on the attempt to achieve individual work–life balance. From those interviewed in their study (which focused on the changing career strategies of managers) three key aspects of careers emerged as being individually important: first, work-related events; second, an individual's relationship to work; and third, an individual's overall lifestyle, with individual drivers focused on achieving and retaining equilibrium across all three aspects. As changes in one area can affect other areas, people acted either to restore balance that had been disrupted or to avoid what they foresaw as future disruption and imbalance.

As new boundaryless and protean career contexts mean individuals are increasingly tasked with managing and developing their own careers, they may also find themselves faced with greater responsibility for managing the relationship between work and non-work aspects of their lives (Sturges 2004). Additionally, whereas in the past education, work and leisure were generally conceptualised as separate aspects of life linked respectively to youth, middle age and old age, in today's society a more cyclical framework exists in which education, work and leisure interact in a range of transition points. Under this model career entry and exit may occur at many points throughout the lifespan for individuals of both genders; and career planning and development is a lifelong activity (Ozanne 2001). Wilson and Davies's study showed that changes to the nature of organisations had led older managers to adopt responsibility for developing and managing their own careers but without the same single-minded commitment to work that they may have exhibited in the past. They now balanced work with domestic and lifestyle issues with some evidence that as a group they had redefined the nature of the psychological contract with their employers, moving towards one which assured the continuation of lifestyle rather than the survival of an employer-defined career. Relationships were important and they concluded that the dominant psychological contract of some managers was with those outside work, such as their partner.

## 9.4 Motivational drivers

The questions of the extent to which older workers are motivated by other factors than either their younger colleagues or their younger selves in respect of their careers, and how motivational drivers may vary under different circumstances and by gender have so far received very little research attention. These drivers, which are heavily influenced by both context and individual variables (Claes and Heymans 2008), are complex and are subject to change over time (Kanfer and Ackerman 2004). In itself the concept of motivation is complex and wide-ranging, and includes both internal factors that drive action and external factors that can prompt action (Locke and Latham 2004). Within this there are *extrinsic* motivators – outcomes that exist apart from the work itself, such as pay and benefits, profile and status, and working conditions (Amabile 1993) – and *intrinsic* motivators – those which derive from the inherent value and interest of the work itself such as achievement, meaning and autonomy. Motivation can affect not only the *acquisition* of skills and abilities but also how and to what extent people *utilise* them, which in turn affects the direction (choice), intensity (effort) and duration (persistence) of action on an individual basis (Steers, Mowday and Shapiro 2004).

The majority of studies concerning motivation in a workplace context have involved younger workers (Kanfer and Ackerman 2004) and have focused on *work motivation* – 'a set of energetic forces that originate both within as well as beyond an individual's being to initiate work-related behaviour and to determine its form, direction, intensity and duration' (Latham and Pinder 2005, p. 486). *Career motivation* is a multidimensional construct which goes beyond this to apply motivation theory to understanding career plans, behaviours and decisions (London 1993, p. 55). According to London, career motivation encompasses *career identity* – the extent to which people define themselves by their work; *career insight* – how realistic people are about themselves and their careers and how accurately they relate these perceptions to career goals; and *career resilience* – the extent to which people resist career barriers, obstacles or disruptions to their work. Changes to these elements in later life can result in both reduced or enhanced career growth, with career resilience and insight both being positively related to age (London 1993).

Career motivation theory represents a general conceptual approach to understanding frequent experiences and perceptions. Understanding how the theory relates to older workers' motivation for career progression at an individual level in today's workplace involves reviewing each of its components alongside what is known about the numerous and interrelated changes which take place in the later years of individuals' working lives. For example, in later life survival needs are likely to be less urgent than previously. Older workers may be affected by greater knowledge about the likelihood of effort paying off (Sterns and Miklos 1995) and by their attitudes to what they have already achieved (Sturges 1999). How these and other factors might exert an influence on an individual basis is examined below.

## 9.5 Career identity

Career identity is the extent to which people define themselves by their work. Various studies have produced differing typologies relating to career identities (for example, Derr and Laurent 1989; deLong 1982). Perhaps the most enduring is the notion of *career anchors*, an individual's self-concept of his or her career which includes 'self-perceived talents and abilities, basic values and ... [an] evolved sense of motives and needs as they pertain to the career' (Schein 1996). Schein's career anchors framework relates motivation to fundamental work orientations which develop over time and may play a significant role individuals' predispositions to pursue certain goals. As strong self-concepts which hold internal careers together even in the face of significant external changes, career anchors that are linked to considerable stability and consistency within individuals' careers over time are useful for helping to predict individuals' future career choices (Feldman 2007). However, this usefulness comes with a warning: career anchors may change in older workers because of the increasing significance of other drivers (for example, work–life balance) which in some cases may lead to motivational conflicts such as that caused by a shift from the drive for functional competence to the drive for security and autonomy (Ettington 1998).

## 9.6 Career insight

Career insight relates to the degree of realism people possess about themselves and their careers and how accurately they relate these perceptions to their career goals. Feldman and Bolino (1996) suggested that a number of moderating variables may affect the relationship between career anchors and career outcomes, including such factors as the availability of alternative jobs (a key factor for older employees), personal life constraints, career anchor–occupation fit, and career anchor–organisational culture fit – all of which depend, to a degree, on individual career insight. Career insight can best be understood in terms of Vroom's expectancy theory (1964), a wide-ranging approach to explaining how individuals make conscious choices between alternative actions. In this theory, motivation is affected by the interrelationship between an individual's beliefs about an outcome, its desirability and the relative effort to be expended in achieving it. This in turn affects their perceptions about the attractiveness of the tasks and actions involved in attainment (for example, in achieving further promotion) and the energy which they would have to invest. In respect of older workers, expectancy theory may help explain the basis on which they make decisions relating to, for example, a drive to seek further promotion or increased responsibility, or to take part in training and development activities. Expectancy theory may also provide a useful framework for considering older workers' individual goals and their motivational drivers in terms of the *de-motivators* they may experience.

## 9.7 Career resilience

> "Goals may not change with age but expectations of achieving these outcomes (promotions, salary increases and other rewards) can diminish."
>
> (Sterns and Miklos 1995, p. 256)

The extent to which people can withstand and overcome barriers, obstacles or disruptions to their work appears fundamental to motivation for career progression in older workers. The study by Wilson and Davies (1999) into the changing career strategies of managers showed that the impact upon them of unpredictable external events such as redundancy was closely linked to their resilience, beliefs and the range of actions they were prepared to take in response. Prior to this Goffee and Scase (1992), researching the restructuring of managers' job aspirations in response to organisational change, found that many older individuals gradually and consciously reduced their psychological dependence upon employment, seeking instead ways of achieving overall balance and fulfilment. As for how career resilience may be specifically affected by age, a number of factors may play a part. For example, relative position may be important; those who reach higher levels before further promotion ceases may be more likely to believe they have been successful in their career and be better able to accept the situation (Allen et al. 1999).

## 9.8 Career embeddedness

Outside of London's career motivation framework, a further concept, *career embeddedness*, is particularly useful for understanding older workers' motivational drivers in respect of their careers. Career embeddedness (Feldman 2007; Mitchell et al. 2001) acknowledges that an individual's ability and motivation to progress may be subject to numerous external constraints. Feldman used the concept to investigate older-worker career stability in terms of the individual-level, job-level and occupational-level factors that influence them, particularly in terms of what older individuals saw as the predicted sacrifices that would result from making changes and the real or perceived barriers to doing so. Having found that lifelong career decisions were based largely on work skills and personal values developed early in the career, Feldman suggests a need for future research to examine the relationship between career anchors and career embeddedness, an approach which would investigate how much individuals are willing and able to change careers (embeddedness) in light of how far away from their current career they are prepared to move (career anchors).

From this discussion it can be seen that, although underlying motivations in respect of older workers' career progression are considerable and wide-ranging, the impact of individual variables and lifestyle as mitigating influences is equally significant. What these are and why they are important is examined next.

## 9.9 Individual identity and lifestyle

> "There is little evidence ... that employers are cognizant of the need to develop different policies for different groups of older employees ... it is essential for employers to get away from thinking of older employees as an homogeneous group."
>
> (Patrickson and Ranzijn 2006, p. 734)

Many studies and practitioner policies relating to later-life careers are based on the concept of 'older workers' as though this represented a homogeneous group with shared characteristics, aims and aspirations. But older age is not an attribute like gender or ethnicity that is either present or not (Sterns and Miklos 1995). There is no clearly recognised and accepted definition of 'older' employees; and the age at which workers' objective career progression tends to slow or cease may vary by industry or job role (Heslin 2005). As it is clearly established that older workers lack meaningful shared characteristics based on chronological age alone (Kooij et al. 2008), it appears more helpful to use the concept of 'late career' as a lens through which to study the choices and reactions of workers aged 50–70 and the economic social and organisational factors that influence them (Greller and Simpson 1999). Compared with focusing purely on chronological age, the notion of a temporal career state is helpful for understanding the potential range of individual factors, such as life stages, which may be involved and the influence this may have on career opportunities (see Chapter 6 for a discussion on career stage).

Careers are not experienced similarly by all (Sullivan and Arthur 2006). For example, some older workers may have working lives which represent a series of individual unrelated jobs or a series of moves in the same job role across employers (Reitman and Schneer 2003), whereas others such as managers tend to have relatively structured careers based on vertical or horizontal role development founded on a cumulative process of skills development and experience over time (Baruch and Rosenstein 1992). Because of the nature of what constitutes a 'career' for this latter group, it may be a more productive hunting ground for researchers seeking to understand how career-related changes take place over time.

Although ageing is an individual process and older people do not consistently, if at all, relate to a group that is defined primarily by age (Sherman 1994), the extent to which older individuals consciously or unconsciously adopt an ageing identity may shape their choices, attitudes and behaviour in late career (Bultena and Powers 1978). How individuals perceive themselves, how they perceive themselves in relation to others and how they perceive themselves relative to their past and future selves, particularly in terms of career progress, may all be significant factors in the pursuit of opportunities leading to older individuals' further career progression (London and Greller 1991). From an individual, psychological perspective age norms, age-related expectations or even age stereotypes may provide a standard that people use to gauge whether their behaviour or attitudes are age-appropriate and also whether their achievements are above or below those of their peers (Giles and Reid 2005). The extent to which individuals consider themselves, or are considered by others, as 'old' may also depend on their age relative to their colleagues' and to organisational norms of what constitutes 'old' or 'senior' (Lawrence 1988). This aspect, in particular, may influence career opportunities and an individual's predisposition to pursue them. Position relative to others of the same age may be significant; age norms that reflect age-related expectations and the likelihood of goal attainment may not only directly affect motivation and limit what individuals see as realistic options, but also lead to the development of coping processes in order to deal with goals which may become seemingly unattainable (Freund 1997).

Numerous changes may take place within individuals as they age, affecting career decisions and leading, in some cases, to dramatic changes of direction. In one of the few papers to have examined the qualitatively different career experiences of managers, Sturges (1999) showed that for many the importance of material criteria for career success declines with age, to be replaced by an emphasis on factors such as influence and autonomy. She maintained that aspects of employment such as innate meaning, quality of relationships, inclusion, stimulation and continuing opportunity to contribute may become paramount in later years. In a comment which may help explain why even those who could advance further may prefer not to, she surmised, 'Those managers who are "successful" in hierarchical terms, may value external criteria for success less once they have achieved them' (1999, p. 250).

Studies show that, today, people judge their careers and their position according to a wide range of individually significant, subjective variables such as influence, job satisfaction and peer recognition (Heslin 2005). Outside this, however, both their careers and their position may be affected at a fundamental level by factors such as gender, ethnicity and physical ability – of which gender is perhaps the most prevalent. In respect of career progression, numerous studies have shown that women's career needs and drivers are quite dissimilar to those of men (Armstrong-Stassen and Cameron 2005; Powell and Mainiero 1992; Roberts and Friend 1998). For example, women's careers have been found to be *relational*, with both careers and families being equally significant (Mainiero and Sullivan 2005) and self and social development being important to notions of success (O'Neil and Bilimoria 2005). Also, women may be more likely to describe what success means to them in terms of *internal criteria*, whereas *position*, *pay* and *status* are seen as indispensable to men's career success (Sturges 1999). However, little is so far known about the needs and drivers of older working women and how these may change according to such objective factors as job role, time at work and caring responsibilities in combination with internal variables such as identity, personality and resilience.

With age, factors such as health, outside interests and family and other responsibilities may have a greater and more diverse effect on individual motivation than earlier in the career (Near 1984), leading to changes in career identity. Today older employees are increasingly unlikely to define themselves solely in terms of their work but to do so more in terms of their overall lifestyle. In general they are likely to reduce their psychological dependence on work alone, adopting a greater focus on achieving a balance between work and the other important spheres of their lives (Wilson and Davies 1999). Personal circumstances, including those that are financially based and driven by proximity to retirement, can also strongly affect individual career decisions in later life. The extent to which they affect career progression may depend on whether individuals have adequate or good pension provision (or other financial means) that will allow them to choose when to retire (Arnold 1997) and their perceptions regarding what they – and other people – regard as 'retirement age' and the degree to which they start to see themselves in these terms (Karp 1987). These variables can lead to entirely different outcomes: in practice some older workers will remain in the same position rather than endanger their pension rights (Sterns and Miklos 1995), whereas others may be forced or tempted into job or career changes both to increase their income and to sustain what they envisage will be a considerably extended working life (Kooij et al. 2008). Those who define themselves as 'pre-retired' may simply cease to seek further progress altogether (Ettington 1998).

Studies have examined the extent to which older individuals may develop a greater orientation towards improved work–life balance, the role played in this by spouses – particularly in relation to establishing a retirement date – and the role of external responsibilities and obligations such as providing financial support and care for older dependants or grandchildren (Greller and Simpson 1999; Near 1984). However, there is no evidence of how and under what circumstances these consistently affect older workers' career progression – these are individual decisions although they may be heavily influenced by cultural and societal factors.

## 9.10 Career opportunities and barriers

> "Employment is becoming confused and tendentious creating problems for individuals who are attempting to develop strategies for their long term survival through work."
>
> (Wilson and Davies 1999, p. 101)

In contemporary career contexts, where the responsibility for career progression has shifted, if only in part, to the individual and the 'old rules' governing promotion and security of tenure have eroded, it appears that career progression for individual older workers is dependent on their ability and willingness to identify, recognise and respond to career opportunities whenever and wherever they may occur. At the same time such workers may also need to acknowledge and, if necessary, seek to overcome a range of external and internal barriers which may prevent them from succeeding. For example, their employer's nature of business and size may correlate with enhanced or restricted opportunities for career progression. Other variables, for example training and development, may act as an opportunity in one career context, while the lack of these may provide an equally significant barrier to career progression for older workers in another. It is important that this is kept in mind when reviewing the issues relating to opportunities and barriers, which follow.

## 9.11 Career opportunities

Although career opportunities are commonly thought of as emanating from policies and practices devised by employers, they can be equally affected by a wide range of individual variables including employees' own perceptions and interpretations (Irving, Steels and Hall 2005). As with careers themselves, opportunities for career progression can have both objective and subjective elements; and how people individually recognise, respond to, and even create career opportunities may be heavily influenced by subjective individual variables such as personality, values and identity, which are either relatively stable (Judge et al. 1999) or, like motivation and attitudes, linked to context and subject to change over time (Sterns and Miklos 1995; Sturges 1999).

One consistent age-related characteristic affecting perceived opportunities may be the fact that many older workers who now operate in contemporary career environments will have commenced their careers under traditional hierarchical promotional systems (Goffee and Scase 1992). Today's careers, career paths, skills requirements and organisational settings may bear little relation to those which were in place when they started out (Feldman 2007); and this may set them apart from younger colleagues in both experience and expectations, thereby restricting the career progression avenues available to them. For certain careers, for example those relating to the requirement for a high level of technological skills, these may be further affected by restrictions relating to the range of opportunities which older workers themselves are prepared to consider.

For older individuals, it appears that two key variables – age and type of career – are particularly important in respect of career opportunities, whether objective or subjective. As discussed earlier, blanket workplace policies and procedures aimed at older workers cannot adequately address the needs of all older employees who have no more in common with each other than they ever did. While some older workers will eagerly seek new challenges and increased status and recognition, other individuals will prefer to maintain the status quo, deriving their motivation from the security of familiarity and the satisfaction of a job well done. Similarly, other older workers may seek to increase their commitment to work as their caring responsibilities reduce, while others may wish to achieve better work–life balance and more time for external interests through working flexibly or adopting reduced hours.

With regard to job type, undoubtedly some occupations and roles are more likely to fall into either linear or protean career types (Heslin 2005), and certain jobs also may be perceived as age-typed (stereotypically young or old) or gender-typed (stereotypically masculine or feminine) (Goldberg et al. 2004). To a degree this may affect career progression, although whether this results from an employer's unwillingness to overturn these stereotypes or an individual's own reluctance to attempt to breach these perceptual barriers has not been investigated. A further element to take into account is older employees' exact age and career stage; although they may all be considered 'older', there can be marked differences between those in their early fifties who are still aspirational and those who may be some 15 or so years older who may wish to focus on gradual workplace withdrawal and winding down (see Chapter 6).

## 9.12 Barriers to career fulfilment

Barriers to career fulfillment and their effect on the motivation of older workers may be founded on external factors such as nature of the business, business size, labour demand and age stereotyping. At an individual level barriers to career fulfillment include a wide array of factors which may differ greatly in importance according to individual circumstance, identity, insight and resilience. These may include health, absence of support from employers, peers and colleagues within the workplace and family and friends outside it (London 1990), lack of confidence and lack of role models for career progression within today's work contexts. There also may be a mismatch between what older workers believe employers want and what employers are actually seeking, contributing to, for example, older workers' lack of success in securing new jobs (Patrickson and Ranzijn 2006) and presumably also to other job transitions. However, of all the important variables three key ones appear to be worthy of particular investigation – health, attitude and confidence.

Health can form a key aspect of individual's identity in later life and may also affect employer decisions concerning individual promotion and development (Taylor 2002). In fact, stereotypes about older individuals' inevitable descent into ill-health in later life still abound (Sherman 1994) even though most older workers are able to perform at a similar level to younger colleagues (Czaja 1995). However, ailments which prevent older individuals from effective job performance will tend to curb both employer- and employee-driven career progress and may result in individuals with chronic health conditions choosing to operate on a plateaued level up to early retirement (Tremblay, Roger and Toulouse 1995). A full examination of health issues for older workers can be found in Chapter 13.

One health-related problem which may be growing in rate of occurrence and in importance for some older workers is stress and burnout (Carlson and Rotondo 2001). Stress and burnout generally have been regarded as negative motivators for older individuals (Appelbaum and Finestone 1994) but this is not universal. Some older workers as their energy levels start to slow may selectively downscale their ambition in order to better withstand stress and to avoid burnout. In doing so they may be deciding that their greater usefulness – to themselves, their colleagues and their employer – may lie in remaining *in situ* and pacing themselves (Baltes and Baltes 1990). For others maximum stress will have been experienced earlier in their career; by late career they will either have developed resilience and coping mechanisms or withdrawn from a highly stressful arena (Baruch 2006). Nevertheless, for some avoidance of stress may remain more of a motivator than the negative effect of stress itself (Carlson and Rotondo 2001).

With respect to attitude, ageist stereotypes often portray older employees as inflexible and having negative attitudes towards change which restrict their ability to progress (Loretto and White 2006). However, it is unlikely that age per se is the reason for this; resistance to change is more likely to be linked to tenure (Bedeian, Ferris and Kacmar 1992), a greater concern for security as retirement approaches (Karp 1987) or a drive to try to hold on to what has already been achieved through maintenance of the status quo (Warr and Fay 2001). Attitude towards change can be all-important; for example, Patrickson and Ranzijn (2006) examining job change in older individuals concluded that those who were successful in gaining employment were likely to have done so through responding to opportunities generated through personal networks or by developing new skills in areas where the competition for jobs was less intense – in short, by recognising and acting upon the need for change.

Although for many older workers career progression depends on skills updating and even reskilling, attitudes towards training can vary (see Chapter 12). Barriers to older workers' pursuit of training and development have been shown to include personal attitude, lack of access and the cost of training if not employer-sponsored (Irving, Steels and Hall 2005). But attitudes themselves are often context-dependent and can be changed. For instance, Irving et al.'s study showed that attitudes towards training were positive if the individual was or had been in a career with frequent training to update skills; if not, many older workers felt that training was 'not for me' or that it was too late to train or that they were too old. Other studies have demonstrated that, given the right opportunities and support, many 'attitudinally plateaued' workers will show enthusiasm for ongoing development and change. Even those who have refused to participate in workplace-provided training may still be prepared to pursue other types of work-related development which they perceive as personally relevant (Robson and Hansson 2007).

Linked to attitude as a potential barrier to career progression in late career is the issue of confidence, otherwise known as self-efficacy for development and defined as an individual's confidence in learning totally new things or developing new skills (Maurer 2001). Maurer argued that self-efficacy may play a role in learning and development behaviour independent of perceived benefits of participation, which goes some way to explaining the drive for individual development in hierarchically plateaued employees. Overall, Maurer found that age per se negatively affects individual and situational variables that predispose a person for development, although many other variables seemingly counteract this:

> "A person who is oriented toward employee development will be someone who has participated in development activities before, perceiving themselves as possessing qualities needed for learning, having social support for development at work and outside of work, being job involved, having insight into his or her career, and believing in the need for development, in his or her ability to develop skills and to receive intrinsic benefits from participating."
>
> (Maurer 2001, p. 718)

This seems to underline that, as with many other motivational drivers, a propensity for development in later life will depend much on an individual's earlier personal and career experiences or existing attributes; it does not operate within a vacuum in a situation where older workers are clean slates. Maurer concluded that voluntary participation in development activities by ageing employees is a behaviour that increasingly needs to be understood, although it may be questioned how much this is actually understood in younger individuals in the workplace if the link to direct reward is removed.

## 9.13 Discussion

It appears that few employers so far are translating the 'demographic time bomb' into policies and practices to meet the requirements of their older workers and their own underlying, if largely unrecognised, business needs (CIPD 2007). Wide-ranging global evidence suggests that the greatest immediate impact of longevity is on the lives of employees who are already aged 50 and over, many of whom – for a wide range of reasons – have to or want to keep working. For many older employees in the UK and throughout the majority of developed economies, longer working lives are being driven by pure economic necessity, resulting in older individuals now having to work longer and even beyond what is regarded as 'normal' retirement age (ONS 2009). For others however, regardless of their economic position, something much more fundamental is driving their decisions:

> "[45–65 year olds] want a future that involves travelling more, spending more time with family and friends, developing new skills and remaining in work, but on their own terms."
>
> (Standard Life 2009, p. 2)

To date, research into older individuals' careers has been sparse and generally undertaken from the employer perspective. Studies have typically examined factors relating to older employees' abilities in later life (for example, Maurer, Weiss and Barbette 2003), their reactions to career plateauing (Near 1984) or issues concerning retirement (Wang et al. 2009). Currently our knowledge about the benefits for employees themselves of remaining in work – such as maintenance or enhancement of physical and mental well-being, increased learning opportunities and more positive retirement prospects – is increasing on what seems a daily basis (for example, Beehr and Bennett 2009). But the business case for retaining older workers is only slowly being recognised by employers; and their decisions about older workers in many cases fail to fully appreciate the complexity of the issues involved. Some employers introduce policies and initiatives based on the assumption that all older workers, simply on the basis of their age, share the same motivation in respect of their careers and will respond and react uniformly. Yet, as has been shown here, motivation is individually variable and relates to a wide range of extrinsic and intrinsic factors which may change over time and according to life stage and shifting perceptions of identity and ability. Other employers fail to take age into account at all, introducing organisation-wide policies and practices based on variables such as pay and promotion that may no longer be highly relevant for the careers of older individuals. The result may be not only lack of positive engagement and commitment in older individuals but negative reactions: for instance, some older employees will become demotivated and disengage, although remaining in the workplace, while others will withdraw entirely (Duncan 2003; Greller and Stroh 2004).

Because of changes in career contexts, 'career progression' as a concept has now changed from traditional notions of career plateauing and decline for older individuals to a drive to maintain individual employability and marketability in the face of reduced job security and strong competition from younger employees. The extent to which older employees themselves recognise this shift and are willing and able to respond is a key element in terms of their ability and optimism regarding future career opportunities and progression. This chapter has demonstrated that among the majority of older workers changes may take place in respect of the individual boundaries between 'work' and 'life', leading them to re-evaluate their motivation in terms of what is important to them in their lives, of which their career is just one aspect. This may differ according to gender, exact age, job role, personality and numerous other factors. What appears to be important is that older workers recognise and utilise their past experiences and existing skill sets, and use this as a basis for identifying future development opportunities in the areas and ways they want. By doing so they are helping define what later-life career progression may look like in a world where older workers still have much to contribute but want to do so on their own terms.

## 9.14 Summary and conclusions

This chapter has reviewed what is known about motivation for career progression in older workers and has emphasised that improved knowledge about the motivational drivers for career progression in older workers would be helpful for both employers and employees themselves. For employers, retaining, developing and maintaining the engagement of older workers and benefiting from the advantages associated with a flexible, mixed-age workforce requires an understanding of what motivates different groups of older employees in order to assist them to progress their careers in ways which are both attractive and meaningful to them and achievable for the business. On the other hand, for the majority of older employees the absence of employer programmes, role models and case studies of successful later-life working means they have to work out for themselves what 'career progression' might mean for the remaining years of their working life.

A number of barriers to fulfilment have been identified in terms of both contextual and individual factors. Although motivation for career progression ultimately links to individual drivers, the significance of context – the type, size, sector and structure of an organisation, human resource policies and practices, and peer group and social influences – cannot be overlooked. What emerges is a picture of the ageing individual in interaction with his or her environment both inside and outside the workplace being driven by complex and individually diverse sets of variables in relation to his or her ongoing career progression. However, beyond this the picture is unclear. Further research is needed into motivation for career progression in today's workplace context.

Research is needed to explore factors relating to the career motivation of managers and how this may differ over time and by individual differences such as gender. Studies will be needed into both how motivation may differ according to workplace context and role, and how – if at all – generalisable results may be derived from across the older worker population as a whole, both in the UK and internationally.

Many practitioner policies are still founded on the premise that individuals share the same concerns about the objective success they attain in their careers. Even if they are recognised, as individuals' underlying wants and needs are disparate the challenge of satisfactorily meeting them can be problematic (Patrickson and Ranzijn 2006). Within this chapter it has been possible to provide only a brief summary of what is known thus far about older workers' motivation for career progression, but there are nevertheless a number of key points which practitioners may wish to build on to develop and support their older workers. These include

- treating older workers as individuals and devising a range of policies to meet their different needs and aspirations;
- recognising that changes – positive and negative – take place within individuals as they age, which may mean they respond differently from younger employees and perceive things on a more individual basis;
- providing training and development opportunities for the entire span of individuals' careers, ensuring that such programmes are perceived as relevant by older employees and delivered in a manner which is appropriate, with confidence issues taken into account;
- enabling older workers to balance work–life commitments and withdraw from working life gradually should they wish through providing flexible working and flexible retirement policies; and
- establishing role models which older workers can use to guide their career aspirations and providing support to assist them in fulfilling them.

Beyond this, it is important for employers to understand the bigger picture and to be clear about their own business case for better managing and supporting older employees. Now and in the future, there is plenty to be gained at commercial, societal and individual levels for those who are prepared to effectively manage the issues surrounding their older employees' career progression.

# 10
# Younger Academics' Expectations about Work and Future Employers

*Wolfgang Mayrhofer, Odd Nordhaug and Carlos Obeso*

This chapter looks at expectations of younger people – specifically, graduates of the CEMS Master's in International Management (MIM) program where students take their 'home master' and then add another year at one of the partner universities of the network – about work in general, the role of work in their lives and about future employers. Against the backdrop of different streams of literature looking at 'typical' expectations of different generations of graduates, the chapter not only outlines concrete empirical findings in this respect but also identifies broad emerging themes. In this way, it provides a potential contrast to the ageing workforce and its characteristics, the major focus of this collection, thus generating insights into similarities and differences between age groups.

Generations encompass individuals who are born within a certain period of time and basically share similar life experiences in relation to both historical events and social life at large. Moreover, it is commonly held that these experiences affect these generations throughout the individuals' lives: 'A cohort develops a personality that influences a person's feelings towards authority and organisations, what they desire from work, and how they plan to satisfy those desires' (Smola and Sutton 2002, p. 365). There are a number of typical categorisations for different generations entering the labour market since the early twentieth century (see Chapter 7 for a detailed discussion of generations).

The generations commonly discussed can be summarised as World War II-ers (born between 1910 and 1933), Swingers, Traditionals, Matures or The Silent Generation (born between 1933 and 1945) (Schaeffer 2000; Kupperschmidt 2000; Jurkiewicz and Brown 1998; Dries, Pepermans and De Kerpel 2008), Baby Boomers (born between 1940 and 1960 or between 1946 and 1964) (Smola and Sutton 2002) and Generation X (persons who were born between the early or mid-1960s and 1980, although some set the upper limit to 1975 or 1982) (Adams 2000; O'Bannon 2001). Generation Y consists of individuals born between the early 1980s and the mid-1990s. It is also referred to as the Millennials or the Next Generation (Jennings 2000). This generation is believed to have even higher expectations than Generation X. At the same time there are indications that its members worship material values less strongly than Generation X (Birkelund, Gooderham and Nordhaug 2000). Generation Z, born since the mid-1990s, is the first generation growing up with continuous access to various kinds of media and communication technologies such as the internet, mobile computing and mobile phones (Palfrey and Gasser 2008; Tapscott 2008). These individuals are starting to enter the labour market now, and few systematic studies are available shedding light on work-relevant issues.

Given these views, it is therefore hardly surprising to see researchers as well as practitioners becoming interested in the younger generations. Graduates from business schools have received considerable attention since they are looking forward to playing crucial roles in organisations and society, thus exerting substantial influence. In recent years, the number of studies of business school students has soared. The focus has frequently been on the properties of generations and cohorts of students (Gooderham and Nordhaug 2002; Gooderham, Nordhaug and Birkelund 2004; Mayrhofer, Meyer and Steyer 2005; Nordhaug, Gooderham, Zhang and Birkelund 2010). It has been commonplace to study factors such as values, job preferences, career preferences and industry or sector preferences.

The purpose of this chapter is to shed light on work-related preferences among CEMS students who take MIM degree. Founded in 1988 in Europe, CEMS (the Global Alliance in Management Education) is a strategic alliance of leading business schools and multinational companies. Currently 28 world-class academic institutions collaborate with more than 62 corporate partners to offer international postgraduate students a unique blend of high-quality education and professional experience. Based on the analysis of a survey comprising 339 individuals from 37 countries, 34 interviews and the analysis of 52 contributions to an essay competition on 'The Future World of Work', from young professionals from a variety of European countries in 2007, we identify major themes that have relevance beyond the specific group analysed and outline consequences for research and organisational practice.

## 10.1 Conceptual background

Conceptually, our study rests on theoretical and empirical insights from a number of areas. A first discourse relates to studies looking at changing values over time and between different age groups. Baethge (1992) has contended that Western societies are taking an increasingly individualistic path as a result of modernity processes supported by the safety net provided by the welfare state. More emphasis is being put on developing one's own personality and opportunities for self-expression. Like Baetghe, Maccoby (1988) also believes the emergence of new work-related values is caused by modernity processes and structural changes implying leaner, less hierarchical and less bureaucratic business organisations. As a result, the number of traditional opportunities for advancement and managerial power has shrunk, and in this context it may be considered rational to offer less status-oriented and more self-development directed forms of incentives and rewards. Less hierarchy and bureaucracy also implies greater uncertainty and the need for increased flexibility in many areas. Inglehart and colleagues (Inglehart 1997; Inglehart Basáñez and Menéndez Moreno 1998; Welzel and Inglehart 2005) claim that there has been a swing from materialistic to post-materialistic motives in relation to work. This is interpreted as partly resulting from general prosperity in Western countries, making many people look for qualitative rewards instead of more material goods and higher status. Vansteenkiste et al. (2006, p. 2892) argue that 'according to an environmental-match perspective regarding the content of values, extrinsic or materialistic values should positively predict well-being in populations, in which extrinsic values match the environmentally promoted values (for example among business students)'. The authors also find that business students ascribe greater importance than education students to materialistic values. Gooderham and Nordhaug (2002) report strong similarities between the values of students coming from the various business schools, indicating a significant pan-European convergence of values. This is partly supported by a study conducted on foreign exchange students and native Danish students at the Copenhagen Business School (Kragh and Bislev 2005).

A second relevant discourse deals with careers (for an overview see Gunz and Peiperl 2007). The concept of career can be approached in various ways. Inkson (2004; 2006) provides a typology of different concepts and images of careers (see Chapter 9). In our context, the following metaphors are particularly fruitful. 'Career cycle' refers to the various phases individuals go through in their working lives. Researchers who work with this perspective are preoccupied with the chronological development of employees working lives. The 'action metaphor' signifies that the focus is predominantly on the choices and decisions that individuals make in regard to their own careers. The notion of 'fit' points to the needs for, and challenges related to, mutual adjustment between employers and employees. The 'role perspective' focuses on matters such as professional identity and commitment, work–life balance and dual-career couples. 'Careers as stories' refers to the literature on storytelling within organisational contexts. The focus may be on public stories about great men and excellent careers that bear resemblance to heroic sagas and myths. Finally, the 'resource perspective' conceptualises individuals as repositories of various work-related resources, such as motivation and competencies. The notion of 'psychological contracts' is central in this context, since it represents a more or less tacit agreement or understanding of individual resource mobilisation weighed against returns in the form of compensation and rewards from the employer. Against this backdrop, so-called new careers were central in career research since the year 2000. The concept of 'boundaryless careers' was introduced in the mid-1990s (see Arthur 1994 and the contributions in Arthur and Rousseau 1996), and since then there has been a growing body of research based on the concept (see, for example, Sullivan and Arthur 2006; Arthur, Khapova and Wilderom 2005). It is conceptualised as self-development through inter-company mobility rather than through intra-company learning. 'Protean careers' (Hall 1996; Hall and Mirvis 1996) are characterised by developing independently of traditional career development arrangements (Segers et al. 2008). This approach centres on individual career management as opposed to career planning and development arranged by the organisation. Protean careers have been characterised as involving greater mobility, a more whole-life perspective, and a developmental progression (Hall 1996). In later conceptualisations of protean careers, Briscoe and Hall (2006) have defined it as involving both a values-driven attitude and a self-directed attitude towards career planning (a discussion of careers in older workers can be found in Chapter 9).

A third discourse focuses on the changing relationship between individuals and organisations in Western countries. The notions of job security and long-term employment have been weakened at the same time as job mobility has increased. In other words, the psychological contracts between individual and organisation (Rousseau 1995; 2001; Rousseau and Schalk 2000) have changed substantially. Relational contracts, typically characterised by mutual loyalty, have to a large extent been substituted for transactional contracts. The increased job mobility between employers indicates decreased loyalty on the part of the employees, whereas processes such as outsourcing signify a lower commitment on the part of the employers. In a similar way, the concept of incomplete labour contracts was developed to account for the fact that, in reality, employers are unable to specify in great detail what the employees are expected to do in their jobs. Hence, the actual written contracts have to be supplemented by more or less tacit, implicit bonds tying the interest of the two parties together. From the employees' standpoint, it is a question of their expectations and preferences relating to what can be gained from working in the organisation. Therefore, knowledge about changes in psychological contracts provides a major guide to understanding and managing employment relationships in a better way (Conway and Bringer 2005).

Finally, a fourth discourse comprises gender and diversity studies primarily concerned with similarities and differences arising from various facets of diversity, in particular sex or gender. Gender is critical in career research not only because it leads to different career experiences (Mallon and Cohen 2001; Powell, Butterfield and Parent 2002) but also because it is a central determinant of career success (Melamed 1995). There is ample evidence that gender either directly (see, for example, Stroh, Brett and Reilly 1992) or indirectly (see, for example, Ng et al. 2005) influences career success. Gender also affects career motivation and choices (Correll 2001), progress towards top positions (Tharenou 1999) or income (Bornmann and Enders 2004). Gender not only is important for careers in general; it is also related to university education, for example in terms of congruency between students' characteristics and values on the one hand and, on the other hand, the fundamental values of the profession pursued (Segal 1992), work attitudes among German and Polish students (Maurer, Oszustowicz and Stocki 1994) or cultural differences between business school students from 11 European countries where substantial gender differences were uncovered (Gooderham and Nordhaug 2002).

## 10.2 Sample and methods

The data was collected in two ways: through a comprehensive survey for which a questionnaire was developed, and through in-depth interviews with students. The survey sample included 339 students from the CEMS-MIM classes of 2007–8 and 2008–9, representing 39.2 per cent of a total of 1330 individuals constituting the CEMS-MIM classes of 2007–8 and 2008–9). Students from 37 countries were included, and the most strongly represented groups were from Germany, Italy, Poland, the Czech Republic, Austria, Switzerland, France, Denmark, Norway, the Netherlands, Hungary and Finland. The sample comprised 53 per cent female and 47 per cent male students, and the average age of the respondents was 24 years.

The interview sample consisted of 34 CEMS-MIM students from ESADE in Spain and WU in Vienna who were interviewed using an interview guideline emphasising the narrative component (Hermanns 1991; Froschauer and Lueger 2003). The average length of the interviews was 45 minutes. All interviews were recorded and fully transcribed. In addition, 52 contributions to an essay competition on 'The Future World of Work' were available. Contributors consisted of young professionals from a variety of European countries.

The texts resulting from transcription were coded, using NVivo 7.0 data analysis software. In general, qualitative content analysis (Mayring 2003) was applied to respondents' statements and available essay contributions. Additionally, special issues emerged – for example, the importance of the psychological contract – which were analysed in more depth in order to obtain a richer picture. The results were compared with those of contemporary generations research derived from the literature.

## 10.3 Core findings

This section presents key findings (for additional results see Mayrhofer, Nordhaug and Obeso 2009) of the study, which had the following research questions:

- What are the preferences among CEMS master's students who take the MIM degree concerning the role of work in their lives and their future employers?
- What relevance do emerging themes which have relevance beyond the specific group analysed have for research and organisational practice?

### 10.3.1 Role and meaning of work

Notwithstanding current theories maintaining that a culture of consumerism is central to younger generations, our group places work and effort at the very centre of their lives. For them work means effort, working hard and working a lot:

> Work is a big part of my life and for me it is very important because when I don't have to do something or I don't have work I really don't know what to do with my time, it's fine to have two or three or maybe even more months of holidays, but after that I really need

> to do something because I feel bad, useless, whatever, so that's really important and crucial that it's challenging and you have new experiences not every day the same ... yeah.
>
> I could work 10, 12, 14 hours at the moment, I don't feel any difficulties with that now though I would like to have some time for the personal life ....

Work is central to their lives and they are prepared to devote time and energy to it. But it has also a moral meaning:

> Working means having significance for society, contributing to society in some way. I think working is being part of society, and it helps the growth as well as the improvement of the society.

In addition, the results of work must be perceived as morally clean and meeting high ethical standards:

> And then also knowing the culture of the company, being part of social responsibility, and the fact that do what they say they will do. Because it is very fashionable to say that you have corporate social responsibility but it can be that it is just words, and I think for example or for what I have seen here, when I was working in internships, there were at least, I know, out of all the teams there that there were two blind people, maybe that sounds like nothing, but from what I have seen, it's very costly to have a blind worker because you have special machines and the fact that there are two people who are really smart, I am sure they are a big part of this company. And at least there was an effort made to keep them.

For the respondents in our sample, a good place to work is not just a nice place but a challenging, positive and results-oriented environment with good working relationships with people who share a similar approach to work and results:

> I can't stand people who don't work but I don't think this would happen too often. I can't stand people who are always late and who haven't done their homework!
>
> Work means effort, of course, and means ... working hard! But it also means relationships. For me it's very important to have a good environment. It means reaching some personal goals ... I think it's a lot

> of hours you have to spend in your work so it's an important thing in your life and there's a lot of people that you meet in the work, so it's an important part of your life, it's not only effort as I have said – that it is, of course! – but it is not only effort.

Somewhat surprisingly, the respondents did not put too much emphasis on having a great deal of personal freedom in their jobs. What they demanded, however, was something that could be defined as 'structured freedom' whereby somebody sets the limits and the objectives. This issue is probably related to their growing personal experience, nurtured by their parents, with very few instances in which they feel obliged to make important decisions completely on their own.

> I would like to have some very good colleagues, that is very important for me, especially the people who are above me, like my managers.

> Then, to have a good critical team as in to say to be able to go somewhere and have some guides. To be able to go and see someone, and say what they think about without throwing the paper back in your face.

### 10.3.2 Expectations from jobs and employers

#### *10.3.2.1 Choosing one's first job*

When respondents were asked about the importance of a range of factors influencing their choice of first post-graduation job, the following picture emerged (see Table 10.1)

The five highest-scoring factors are interesting work, opportunities to develop competencies, opportunities for personal development, good social relations at the workplace and opportunities to work abroad. These are followed by variety in work tasks, the employer's reputation, high annual earnings, good personnel policy, the employer's reputation, good personnel policy and opportunities for fast promotion. Although the group will normally obtain a substantial initial salary, money is clearly not everything. It seems that respondents are, to a certain extent, willing to let pay take second place in order to secure qualitative rewards such as interesting work tasks, opportunities for development and good social relations at work.

Female students put more weight than male students do on interesting work, opportunities for personal development, good social relations among colleagues, variety in work tasks, systematic career planning, good job security, a large amount of project work and opportunities to work at home. On the other hand, male students emphasised opportunities

*Table 10.1* Perceived importance of a range of factors influencing choice of first job, on scale of 1 to 10

| Factors | | Average | Men | Women |
|---|---|---|---|---|
| 1. | Interesting work | 9.37 | 9.26 | 9.49** |
| 2. | Opportunities for competence development | 9.18 | 9.10 | 9.25 |
| 3. | Opportunities for personal development | 9.15 | 8.99 | 9.29** |
| 4. | Good social relations among colleagues | 8.93 | 8.71 | 9.12*** |
| 5. | Opportunities for spells of working abroad | 8.71 | 8.63 | 8.78 |
| 6. | A lot of variety in work tasks | 8.62 | 8.39 | 8.81*** |
| 7. | The employer has a good reputation | 8.32 | 8.23 | 8.40 |
| 8. | High annual earnings/salary | 8.22 | 8.34 | 8.10 |
| 9. | Good personnel policy | 7.87 | 7.48 | 8.21*** |
| 10. | Opportunities for fast promotion | 7.83 | 8.10 | 7.59*** |
| 11. | A lot of freedom in the job | 7.68 | 7.76 | 7.61 |
| 12. | Pay based on individual performance | 7.53 | 7.90 | 7.21*** |
| 13. | Systematic career planning | 7.41 | 7.19 | 7.61** |
| 14. | The position has a high status | 6.94 | 7.20 | 6.70** |
| 15. | Good job security | 6.88 | 6.26 | 7.44*** |
| 16. | Flexible working hours | 6.82 | 6.65 | 6.97 |
| 17. | Large amount of project work | 6.29 | 5.96 | 6.59*** |
| 18. | Opportunities to work at home | 4.80 | 4.52 | 5.06* |

*Notes*: 1 = low; 10 = high; average score on a 1–10 scale. ***p-value < 0.01; **p-value < 0.05; *p-value < 0.10.

for fast promotion, pay based on individual performance, and high status more strongly than female students did. The greatest difference was related to good job security (men 6.26, women 7.44). Overall, female students in the sample were more preoccupied with qualitative aspects of their prospective jobs, while male students put more weight on factors related to fast careers, high job status and individually based compensation.

### *10.3.2.2 Views on good leadership*

Asked to rank a set of statements about good leadership in order of importance, respondents ranked 'manages primarily through trust and empowerment' first (8.97), followed by 'possesses a lot of natural authority' (7.87). There is a leap down to the two next statements that could be supported: 'obtains power to be better able to manage' (6.66) and 'manages primarily through power and authority' (4.30). Further analyses revealed two main underlying dimensions: emphasis on relational leadership and emphasis on hierarchical leadership. The former was clearly regarded as the preferable mode of management and leadership. Hence, organic forms of management were preferred to traditional mechanical management relying on hierarchies, duties and rules.

In order to gain an insight into how CEMS master's students view leadership, we asked them to rate the importance of a set of selected managerial competencies (Table 10.2). The question was how important these competencies were for a person to be a good manager.

Social and communicative competencies, firm-specific knowledge and skills in handling stress and uncertainty were regarded as vital competencies for high-quality managerial action. In the lower end of the distribution, competencies such as high ethical standards, creativity, political skills and professional skills were regarded as less important. Still the scores indicate that the respondents attached substantial value to these competencies, too. With a few exceptions, women gave higher scores than men did.

*Table 10.2* Perceived importance of competencies needed to be a good manager

| Competence | Average | Men | Women |
|---|---|---|---|
| Communication skills | 9.41 | 9.27 | 9.53*** |
| Ability to listen to others | 9.09 | 9.04 | 9.13 |
| Knowledge about the firm's strategy | 8.93 | 8.76 | 9.08** |
| Stress tolerance | 8.77 | 8.54 | 8.97*** |
| Ability to delegate tasks | 8.70 | 8.66 | 8.74 |
| Knowledge about the firm's culture | 8.65 | 8.38 | 8.88*** |
| Ability to handle uncertainty | 8.51 | 8.25 | 8.74*** |
| Knowledge about the industry | 8.22 | 7.99 | 8.44** |
| Analytical skills | 8.21 | 8.15 | 8.26 |
| Ability to command/ control subordinates | 8.19 | 8.06 | 8.30 |
| Personal flexibility | 8.06 | 7.85 | 8.26** |
| International competence/experience | 8.05 | 7.90 | 8.20 |
| High ethical standards | 7.90 | 7.61 | 8.19*** |
| Creativity/innovativeness | 7.62 | 7.44 | 7.67* |
| Political skills (power related) | 7.59 | 7.51 | 7.67 |
| Professional/technical skills | 7.28 | 6.92 | 7.63*** |

*Note*: ***p-value < 0.01; **p-value < 0.05; *p-value < 0.10.

### *10.3.2.3 Intrinsic and extrinsic rewards*

Respondents emphasised non-material rewards such as a good, trusting environment, personal development in the job, having interesting work with adequate responsibility, quality of work and receiving recognition for one's results:

> [What things motivate you at work and why?] A good environment, of course, I think it's very important. People that at the beginning help you because at the beginning you feel very lost and you need … like … the others to help you, that if you have any questions you have the confidence to go and ask them …
>
> Results. Get something from what you do. I think that basically all you need is to see that something's happening. Like you have an impact … and for what you do it's really important that it's noticed in the organisation. If you do a good job that somebody says you did a good job.
>
> [What importance do you attach to professional recognition?] It's very important because I am studying in a business school; I have an international background so I think everyone does it for recognition and for the life. But I think recognition is not only important in your working life but also in every part of the life. Yeah but it is important.
>
> I would say I need recognition, I need an appropriate salary, I need flexibility and I need … a good atmosphere.

Still, money is important since it reflects the deserved recognition and objectively expresses the deserved admiration:

> [Salary.] A good salary. If I am being well paid then, especially if there is a bonus and it is the bonus part that changes. Also propositions of moving; so if you have done a good job then maybe you can be moved to another post.
>
> I think salary is maybe the most important because it's the way you support your lifestyle. I think recognition is very important for me personally. And also, of course, promotional perspectives. Promotion is a good outcome.

The importance of being recognised and admired points towards an individual-centered 'me–me' personality. Focus is set on the immediate work environment and not so much on the company or the broader industry.

> [What importance do you attach to professional recognition?] Yeah, just like I said it is very important, that my colleagues recognise that I have some skills from my education, they recognise my work and yeah just recognise my presence and the person that I am, that matters a lot in a professional environment.
>
> A lot. Well, I mean it depends on what you call professional recognition. But being, I mean if it is work recognition then it means a lot. I feel that it's important that if you do something, then it is said that this was good and this was done by me.

#### *10.3.2.4 Psychological contract*

The psychological contract with future employers, at least in the first years, was conceived of as primarily transactional. Individuals were not too passionate about a concrete company and, as a consequence and compared with previous generations of students entering the labour market, it was more difficult to tie them to one concrete employer:

> Yes, definitely. I mean I have changed jobs various times, I have already worked at three companies now and on my fourth now, and it is different positions but usually I change job because I see another interesting job offer so I am like 'OK, I am tired of this job...'. It is also to do with the knowledge of different businesses, different functions and learning as much as possible, a big part is learning, I mean you learn the most a half year.
>
> Maybe it is my generation culture again, but I think to learn things you have to change companies.

What emerges is a picture of a more or less calculating engagement based on a quid pro quo relationship, that is, what you can do for your company and what can the company do for you. At the same time, these students are ready to devote all their energies to the company if they feel the company gives them a lot:

> To give my best every single day. To do marketing for [a] company and for my job and in my private life and my social life, when I get to know more people, I don't have to say 'I have this shitty job and it is a pretty bad job', but I think you really have to promote it and … I think

> continuous improvement, he can expect suggestions for improvement and, yeah that's it.
>
> My obligation towards the company is to contribute in terms of my job. My obligation is also to create a workplace for people around me, to be friendly towards the people who surround me. And to perform the task from the company at 100 per cent, to try to contribute all that I can in the most intensive way I can do .... My internal obligation is to feel that I contributed the most that I could. And that I feel satisfied.

Interestingly, the picture seems to change in their future. Anticipating their situation at age 30, interviewees emphasised the prospective need to settle down, accompanied by a turn of the tide in the psychological contract, which now became more relational in nature. An example of this:

> At the age of 30 you should have the place you wanna live, the family maybe and the company where you would decide to work for a long time.

#### *10.3.2.5 Career aspirations*

The concept of career fields (Iellatchitch, Mayrhofer and Meyer 2003) distinguishes between four typical arenas:

- 'Company world' represents the traditional organisational career.
- 'Free-floating professionalism' can be defined as a specialist career. Individuals work closely with one customer, but only for a limited time, which results in tight coupling but an unstable configuration.
- 'Self-employment' is a career track where individuals work outside large work organisations. Typically, these are either self-employed professionals or entrepreneurs who work in a rather stable and limited field of expertise.
- 'Chronic flexibility' is characterised by frequent job changes. Unlike in Free-Floating Professionalism, however, there is rarely a single domain of expertise.

About half of the respondents (49 per cent) considered 'company world' to be the closest to their own professional preferences. This reflects a preparedness to enter into a long-term commitment to an employer — which raises questions about frequent claims that this generation has professionally nomadic preferences. 'Free-floating

Configuration of actors

stable — unstable

Coupling to organisation: tight — loose

| | stable | unstable |
|---|---|---|
| tight | **Company World**<br>strive for a position of responsibility and influence and a long-term career within one organisation<br>49.5% | **Free-floating professionalism**<br>want to be under contract to one or a few organisations for special and challenging tasks, staying with the same organisation only for a limited time<br>34.1% |
| loose | **Self-employed**<br>seek "traditional" self-employment, i.e. offering a range of quite standardized products and/or services to a relatively stable clientele<br>4.8% | **Chronic Flexibility**<br>aspire to a "freelancer" career with different projects for various clients and ever-changing work contents<br>11.6% |

*Figure 10.1* Desired career fields for one's professional future

professionalism' was chosen by 34 per cent of the respondents, whereas 5 per cent saw themselves as 'self-employed and 12 per cent as freelancers ('chronic flexibility').

## 10.4 Emerging broad themes

The empirical study has some limitations. First, a sample of CEMS-MIM students is a very special sample as compared with the broader populations of business school graduates or graduates of the second cycle of Bologna in more general terms. Second, as a short questionnaire was chosen in order to promote response rates, there was no space to allow coverage of all major issues relevant for this area, but focuses on core issues. Hence, the emerging picture is less differentiated than one would like it to be. Third, while the interview material is quite extensive and content analysis allows broad categorisations, more intensive methods of analysing the available texts could have produced further insight by unearthing latent structures in the text. Fourth, qualitative analyses across different cultures using different languages run into a number of problems currently not satisfactorily solved: for example, when to switch from the original language to the lingua franca of the project (in this case English) or how to compare texts in different languages.

Bearing these limitations in mind, we regard three themes as important beyond the concrete sample analysed in our empirical study and applying, by and large, to younger generations currently entering the workforce.

### 10.4.1 Trusting the system and using it for career crafting

The respondents in our sample place a high emphasis on work as a major domain of their life. For them, participating in the world of work is a way of finding their place in society, and work has meaning in itself. They bring to work some traditional values such as the readiness to strive hard or to be committed to a cause. In particular, members of this generation are willing to integrate themselves into given systems and hierarchies. They do not question the basic assumptions and principles of the economic system; and there is no major disagreement with the objectives of the organisation. While they are not rebels, they constantly monitor their activities and engagement in the light of their own demands. They have subscribed to the 'Project Me': taking a long-term view of their own careers for which they themselves are responsible, they soberly calculate the effects of current activities on their career capital and their future opportunities while constantly searching for opportunities where an investment of their career capital (for example, competencies and networks) may pay off even more. They see the world as full of opportunities on which they can capitalise. Career and development opportunities offered by the organisation are only to a modest degree regarded as a path one has to follow because of organisational demands. Rather, individuals view them as opportunities that they contrast with their own short- and long-term preferences.

Overall, this leads to people crafting their own careers. The younger generations balance considerations of functionality and creativity in this ongoing process of construction, continuously looking inside themselves to monitor developments, looking outside in order to detect developmental paths and looking ahead in time to evaluate current developments in light of the long-term consequences (Inkson 2006). Against the backdrop of substantial self-confidence, they move through the world of work and between work and non-work domains at their own pace and according to their own decisions.

### 10.4.2 Transactional versus relational contracts with organisations

Psychological contracts contain a set of mutual expectations, perceptions and informal obligations governing the relationship between two parties

(Rousseau 1995). In the world of work, psychological contracts provide the basis for relationship dynamics between organisations and their members, including the benchmark against which violations of tacit expectations are measured. Relational psychological contracts emphasise a more long-term view rooted in shared ideals and values, mutual respect and interpersonal support, leading to, among other things, expectations of loyalty from the individual and job security on the side of the organisation. In contrast, transactional psychological contracts emphasise a calculating engagement based on a quid pro quo relationship where the mutual exchange has to be gratifying on a short-term basis. Since the 1990s the dominant model has shifted from relational to transactional. This leads to less emphasis on stability, permanence, predictability, fairness, tradition and mutual respect, and favours self-reliance, flexibility and adaptability.

Individuals in previous age cohorts often regarded such a shift as a loss and somewhat hard to adapt to. Younger generations entering the labour market and growing up under the dominance of the transactional contract have already internalised this type of relationship. They feel at ease with entering a short-term give-and-take relationship. If they possess excellent qualification profiles, they are confident that they have something to offer organisations looking for their contributions. Nevertheless, relationships with organisations are merely 'serial monogamies': the relationship will end rather soon and therefore investments have to pay off over a short time span. Still, members of these generations are fully committed to the organisation during this time. In a sense, they are both distant and passionate: distant in the sense of not committing themselves on a long-term basis to one organisation, passionate in terms of 'temporary passion' for the concrete task, work group or responsibility. It turns out to be more difficult to involve individuals as 'deeply' as in previous times.

The emphasis on transactional contracts is supplemented by a partial swing to, and incorporation of, elements of the relational psychological contract in later stages of life. At the 'age 30 transition' the picture changes towards a relational type of contract. Here, more long-term relationships with less hectic and continuous matching activities will presumably prevail. This second career stage is less a concrete point in time but covers a change in life circumstances and views about the world and about work associated with the establishment of a more long-term private partnership, the possibility of having children or a reduced amount of geographical mobility.

### 10.4.3 Seeking recognition and admiration

In the world of work, employee rewards (the provision of monetary and non-monetary incentives for work), which are often linked to individuals' contributions to the organisational output, are regarded as central to attracting and retaining individuals as well as to enhancing organisational performance (Rynes and Gerhart 2000). Beyond monetary rewards and hierarchical progression and recognition at professional and personal levels, a specific type of recognition is of high value for new generations, namely, admiration. This requires a special place in the social network. At the professional level this is linked to a kind of celebrity culture. To be seen by others as being special in one's professional expertise and contribution and 'at centre stage' is clearly important. To achieve this, something on top of what used to be seen as solid and sufficient has to be attained – for example, successfully taking extraordinary risks, acquiring outstanding qualifications or striving for unusual combinations of competencies. Admiration goes beyond the 'normal' quest for positive feedback from one's environment, which is a traditional driver for individuals and a well-known element of organisational reward systems. These young individuals are exclusive and self-focused ('it's me'), highly competitive and inclined to take top positions and aim at an outstanding degree of visibility within the respective social networks ('global reach'). These results are in line with analyses pointing out attempts by individuals and organisations to establish grandiosity in the world of work (Alvesson and Robertson 2006; Chatterjee and Hambrick 2007).

## 10.5 Implications for research

The findings of our study have two major implications for future research. First, the study highlights the fact that broad concepts such as 'Millennials' or 'Generation Y' are at the same time valuable and somewhat limited. They are valuable in the sense that they identify developments and weave them into a coherent pattern. However, they are also limited in the sense that they do not account for other factors influencing the mindset and behaviour of specific groups within a generation. The respondents in our sample are a good example of this. In terms of age they are typical members of Generation Y. However, their educational socialisation in high-profile business schools and related programmes brings another important factor into the equation. By anticipating the requirements for entering the world of work with a business education background, additional factors such as knowing about the restraints of the labour market or the role of corporate culture play a role. In relation to research, this has empirical as well as theoretical consequences. At the empirical level, more studies looking at sub-groups of this generation are needed. For example, we know next to nothing about how expectations about work and employers differ along cultural and educational dimensions. At the theoretical level, too, much additional work is needed. So far no coherent models exist that systematically integrate social, cultural and educational background variables into the thinking about different generations and that allow stringent empirical research based on these models.

Second, studies such as these are snapshots: they look at the situation of a particular group at a specific point in time. What clearly is missing is a developmental perspective, in a twofold sense. On the one hand, it would have been highly interesting to track the career development of the individuals in our sample and to see how their careers unfolded, whether current perspectives on work, leadership and organisation remained stable or changed, and to what extent the 'age 30 transition' actually took place. On the other hand, it also would be highly interesting to monitor developments across various cohorts of graduates. Will later cohorts have similar views? If not, why? For organisations such monitoring could create a better and more in-depth understanding of relevant segments of the labour market. At the same time, such insights could be valuable inputs for individual career planning and career counseling.

## 10.6 Implications for practice

The findings in this study have a number of potential implications for private sector organisations, many of them linked with employer branding (Schumann and Sartain 2006) and talent management (Collings and Mellahi 2009).

### 10.6.1 Attracting talent

Two major issues for many companies are how to attract and retain individuals who are well educated and can choose between different options for employment; and how to sell and advertise the organisation when trying to attract highly qualified individuals in their early career stages who are in high demand in the labour market. First, it seems that younger generations do not look primarily at the organisation itself when seeking a job. Hence, rather than primarily selling the organisation as a whole, it seems important to highlight how the concrete job and tasks positively influence individuals' career capital, such as their technical expertise, their industry experience, their ability to take future steps and the size and quality of their professional networks. The younger generations look for returns on their investments. Unless organisations are able to make it crystal clear what these returns will be and how individuals can profit from them, it is hard to win them over. For example, being a big global organisation does not constitute in itself a decisive argument for this group. However, if the organisation demonstrates its capacity to emulate a setting characterised by a concrete series of projects and short-term career episodes compatible with different career aspirations rather than being an anonymous environment where each individual is only a small cog in a large wheel, then it improves its chances of seeming attractive to this group. Second, it seems to be important to demonstrate that the organisation is a good corporate citizen and that the concrete job and the tasks linked to it do not enter the moral twilight zone.

### 10.6.2 Retaining talent

At least in the early stages of their employment, the respondents in our sample were constantly monitoring whether they would derive the most for their future career out of their current employment relationship. At the same time, they were highly mobile and ready to change employer when a better deal came up. For organisations, a good starting point is to acknowledge this situation and not implicitly to count on such employees remaining with the organisation in the long run. Therefore, it seems to be wise to enter a relaxed quid pro quo exchange relationship where both sides invest in what they can offer. Viewed from the perspective of work organisations, this can be highly demanding since they cannot take for granted many things that used to be part of the package in previous times, for example a willingness on the part of the employee to go through hard and not immediately rewarding times without ready payback visible on the horizon or the implicit understanding that the first stages of one's career lack many opportunities for shining glory. Yet, if an organisation is able to craft jobs that offer a well-balanced ratio of give and take, it will attract people who are willing to work hard and bring in a strong portfolio of competencies and eager to learn.

### 10.6.3 Leaving an imprint

Although Hall defines 'career' as a 'bundle of socialisation experiences' (Hall 1987, p. 302), the processes considered relevant for a successful career include mainly adult and organisational socialisation. Basically, early career periods are formative years (Bray, Campbell and Grant 1974), when individuals entering the world of work are looking for orientation. Organisational socialisation (van Maanen and Schein 1979; Schein 1984) is one way of leaving an imprint on young adults looking for guidance and orientation within the world of work. For organisations, the task is twofold. First, in their own interest they provide newcomers with an environment where they can bring in what they have learned during their education and where they can further develop their technical and personal competencies. In doing so, organisations are enhancing their own human capital base. Second, if organisations play an active and deliberate socialisation role, they not only contribute to the greater good in general but also remain in good repute when individuals leave them – which is very likely to happen given that these individuals are in the early stages of their careers. Yet organisations are well advised to create friendly rather than potentially hostile future customers or colleagues.

### 10.6.4 Compensation and reward

Given the importance of a balanced quid pro quo relationship, the question of compensation and reward becomes especially important. Three things seem important in guiding organisational practice. First, organisations should provide a sound material basis. Second, intangible benefits are clearly important to members of younger generations, in particular the feeling of being a member of the family, and social recognition and admiration are highly valued. As for recognition, emphasising and enabling work-related personal relationships and pointing out the unique contribution that these employees make towards achieving overall organisational goals seem essential. As for admiration, it can be a double-edged sword. On the negative side, organisations most likely need to be careful about how much they spotlight young employees in order not to create excessively high expectations. In addition, such spotlighting can easily lead to serious internal conflict over the amount and type of acknowledgement received and whether it is fairly distributed. On the positive side, however, such forms of recognition often do not cost very much in monetary terms and are very powerful. Third, and perhaps most important, it is essential that organisations point out the return on investment for individuals, that is, how technical and social competencies, contacts and networks and future career opportunities grow as a result of the current activities, and illustrating these positive affects by reference to previous job holders whose next career steps built on their previous experience.

### 10.6.5 Leadership

Our survey produced three main findings on leadership. First, members of these generations seem to be not sceptical about leadership. Although they set high standards for leadership, they are fully expecting and hoping for guidance and advice. At the same time, organisations also can count on the readiness of these individuals to work hard and devote time, energy and passion to a joint cause. Second, they are feedback seekers. While interpretations of this vary (for example, looking for constant attention from superiors or reducing uncertainty linked with ambitious goal setting), it is obvious that individuals are very open to feedback and ready to take it into account when settling into the world of work. Therefore, making honest, constant and thorough feedback (for example, 360-degree appraisals) an integral part of the prevailing leadership practice increases organisations' chances of influencing these individuals. Third, members of these generations want to make a difference and contribute to something which is important to the organisation and to them. By providing them with such opportunities and building a strong sense of joint mission for the tasks or projects in hand, organisations can trigger high-performance behaviour.

## 10.7 Summary and conclusions

The respondents in our sample clearly voiced their preferences and perceptions about work and its role in their lives. A developmental perspective – that is, what current work does to later opportunities (or the lack of them) – is crucial for this group. While in some areas (such as the importance of tangible rewards and hierarchical advancement) this group looks quite familiar, a few specific characteristics may be signs of a tidal shift linked with a new generation entering the labour market. In particular, they include the combination of individuals working hard and being sympathetic to large organisations and at the same time demanding much from organisations in the early years of their careers and, after internalising a transactional psychological contract, having a different time horizon for the developing relationship with organisations. This has a number of consequences, not only for research but also for organisational practice, including recruitment and leadership as well as questions about organisations' compensation and incentive systems.

# Part IV
# The Employer's Perspective on Managing an Age-Diverse Workforce

In Part III we adopted the perspective of both older and younger workers in order to examine their experiences, motivation, attitudes and preferences. We now examine the issues associated with managing an age-diverse workforce from the perspective of the employer or organisation. We have already established that employers may want to promote age diversity within their workforce. Now we focus on one segment of an age-diverse workforce, namely, older workers, and discuss how these individuals can be encouraged by employers to remain in the workforce.

In Chapter 11, Vanessa Beck discusses the practices that an employer may adopt to retain older workers or to extend working life. In particular, the chapter looks at the impact of flexible working, rewards, training and job design, using evidence from qualitative research.

In Chapter 12, Alan Felstead focuses on one of the areas that has been identified as important in retaining older workers – that of training and learning. In particular, the chapter examines both formal and informal learning in older workers using data from three surveys in the UK.

In Chapter 13, Sarah Harper looks at another specific area of importance in the retention of older workers, that of health. The chapter considers the health issues that may be considered as people age and how these can be addressed by employers.

# 11
# Extending Working Life: The Retention of Older Workers

*Vanessa Beck*

The need to extend working lives has been explored and discussed, showing that a broad range of factors influences whether such an extension can and will occur on a broader scale than is currently the case (Vickerstaff et al. 2008). This chapter explores the various policies and measures that employers can put in place to encourage the extension of working lives. The contextual factors that employers need to consider include: (*a*) the institutional framework; (*b*) changes in the economy; and (*c*) changes in working lives.

Age-discrimination laws and pension systems that form determining influences on the different available pathways into retirement are not necessarily conceived to encourage or reward the extension of working lives. Pathways into retirement, whether this is a direct or a gradual process or follows encounters with disability, unemployment and a range of benefits, therefore require closer examination regarding their potential usefulness for both employees and employers.

The economic context in which transitions occur from employment to retirement or from employment to unemployment, to economic inactivity or to retirement (and sometimes back to employment) has changed considerably. There is an increased use of technology; companies experience more competition and often have more demand for flexible work. At the same time, employers and employees face higher levels of risk partly because of the 2008–9 recession and business cycles with knock-on effects for working conditions. The socio-cultural conception of age has also changed. Stereotypical and discriminatory attitudes to older people are still evident, for example among employers, and there is some evidence that ageist attitudes towards older workers are reinforced in the context of the recession (TAEN 2009). However, highly public discussion of the increased pension age and age discrimination legislation has started raising awareness of the changing demographics of our society.

The institutionalisation of the life course, that is, what people are expected to do in their lives, is less rigid than in the past. Education tends to be extended and marriage or starting a family is often postponed, though an increasing number of people decide against both. Coupled with generally healthier and longer lives, there are less distinct life events associated with certain age groups, making it more difficult to determine when people become 'old'. For some older workers, this results in a will to extend working past state pension age, but others consider this phase a welcome opportunity to enjoy other aspects of their lives.

It is clear that decision-making structures are made up of many layers, from government policy all the way to individual employers and older workers, and that the interrelationship between the various actors and players is a key factor. In this chapter, we consider the role of employers and their influence on extending working lives by utilising aspects of human resource management (HRM) practices available to them. Lyon, Hallier and Glover (1998, p. 63) came to the conclusion that 'the HRM credo represents an added threat to the status, treatment and security of older workers'. They based this statement on a discussion of the challenge that older workers present for human resource management. While HRM aims to invest in employees and thus aspires to retain workers with the employer over the long term, a further aim of HRM is to ensure organisational adaptability, which, according to Lyon, Hallier and Glover (1998) excludes older workers from the core membership of the organisation. Thus, 'HRM not only legitimises existing attitudes, it also provides a seemingly more coherent and, above all, business-focused explanation of the drawback of employing older workers' (1998, p. 59). While many contextual issues such as the Age Regulation Legislation (see Chapter 3), societal awareness of demographic change and, potentially, some attitudes among employers may have changed since this argument gained currency, the general perception remains that employers' attitudes towards older workers are negative and that the systems and practices in place disadvantage older workers.

Against this backdrop, this chapter aims not to extend the question whether HRM has negative consequences for older workers but to investigate, instead, what employers can do to extend working lives. Armstrong-Stassen (2008) has argued that there is more to the debate on extending working lives than the individual preferences and characteristics of older workers, and that there are organisational characteristics and practices that have a significant impact on decision-making processes of both older workers and their employers. The culture of organisations thus significantly influences the HRM approach to older workers. Armstrong-Stassen and Lee (2009) argue, for example, that the age composition of the workforce is influential in determining whether a positive attitude will be taken. While the majority of workers may feel most comfortable working with individuals of their own age, it is in fact age-diverse workforces that are most successful at bringing together the required mix of skills, experience, knowledge and ability. Older workers may feel undervalued or treated unfairly by supervisors if working in a predominantly younger group, but mixing all age groups can counter such perceptions. Bringing about an age-mixed workforce might not be immediately possible, but is a realistic aim for most organisations and could become a necessity given the changing demographics of the workforce overall (see Chapter 2).

The range of functions that make up HRM reinforces the importance of the key questions to be addressed in this chapter: what can employers do to bring about an age-mixed workforce in their company? What changes need to be undertaken to encourage the extension of working lives? And what is the impact of measures and the time frame within which this impact is noticeable? While the latter question will need to be considered in future research, the following sections consider a range of measures, including different flexible working options; training and development; job design; compensation and incentives; and recognition and respect. The main argument advanced throughout is that individual measures on their own are unlikely to bring about much change in working lives. It is the combination of the measures into an overall package and policy towards older workers that will show success in extending the working lives of older workers, to the mutual benefit of these individuals and their employers.

The chapter is based on a review of relevant literature and research undertaken for the Learning and Skills Council in the East Midlands region of the UK, investigating employers' attitudes towards older workers and the use of, or potential for, learning as a means to increase older workers' motivation and therefore encourage them to remain in the labour market for longer (see Beck 2009). The research consisted of 32 semi-structured interviews. These included interviews with the five Sector Skills Councils (SSCs) responsible for the majority of workers in the sectors under investigation, namely: Construction Skills, the Sector Skills Council for Science, Engineering and Manufacturing Technologies (SEMTA), Skills for Health, Skills for Logistics, and SkillSmart Retail. The majority of the interviews were conducted with employers in these five sectors, more specifically HR managers or owners depending on the size of the organisation. It was generally easier to recruit larger employers to participate in the research; but a number of small and medium-size enterprises were also interviewed, the smallest employing three individuals. To establish the context for the older workforce in the East Midlands, short interviews were conducted with public bodies and NGOs that have been active in the region (see also Farmer and Soulsby 2009). Interviews were mainly conducted on the phone between July and September 2008, and were taped and transcribed for analysis. The research found, not unsurprisingly, that training and development are not used strategically, especially for older workers. Nevertheless, the interviews with employers revealed innovative, informal and flexible arrangements between employers and older workers, some of which are outlined in this chapter.

## 11.1 Flexible working options

The opportunity for flexible work schedules, in the form of the reduction of the working week, flexible hours, job sharing or periods of (unpaid) leave, has long been considered an important tool in motivating older workers to remain in employment for longer (Loretto, Vickerstaff and White 2007). There are many opportunities and challenges that flexible working options might bring to different types of employers in different sectors (Beck 2009). While sectors such as health and retail already have a considerable proportion of their workforce working part time, this is not the case for employers in construction or engineering. Employers in these sectors emphasise the importance of teamwork and being present, and argue that part-time work is not traditionally offered. The importance of workplace cultures is highlighted by the following quotation, which reveals a lack of imagination or willingness to rethink procedures in order to accommodate flexible working options.

> It's [part-time work] been debated and it's been put on the back burner again because we just can't see how it would work. Yes, it would be a great benefit, but at the end of the day there's too few of us here with 70 people not to know when we're all in.

As indicated, sectors without a tradition or straightforward use for part-time work might nevertheless find flexible working practices beneficial. In sectors where work is seasonally influenced, such as construction, a good case could be made for periods of leave when there is less work available. While the length of leave and the level of pay during these periods would need to be negotiated, this could be arranged mutually by employers and employees.

Even where flexible working options are available, inequality of access has been found to hamper their usefulness for those who may be in most need of flexibility to accommodate caring responsibilities (Golden 2008). Employers also face problems in that filling vacancies for part-time or shift work can be difficult, which one employer linked to the age of their employees. In the specific context of a sales department, flexibility was crucial to ensure a sale could be completed successfully:

> I think over time your attitude will no doubt change. You become less hungry and less quick to get out of your seat and talk to people, and less willing to go and do a 7 o'clock demonstration at someone's house, because you want to go home and see the kids. You can't blame them for that.

Despite the importance of flexible working options overall, there is evidence (Armstrong-Stassen 2008) to suggest that providing opportunities for flexible work schedules and reduced working hours are more important for those who have changed jobs or even careers (and sector) than for individuals who remain in a career job. In the logistics sector in particular, many picking and sorting jobs in post-rooms were undertaken by part-time older workers who had previously worked in other companies or sectors, similar to the situation in sections of the retail sector.

A crucial question remains whether access to flexible work options is spread evenly across occupations and the hierarchical ladders within them. Leibold and Voelpel (2006, p. 45) might argue that older workers 'will accept "entry" level jobs, as ways into new lines of work or flexible options suited to a preferred lifestyle'; but Macnicol (2008) rightly questions whether the 'McDonaldisation' of old age is really desirable. Employers should therefore be encouraged to offer good-quality, flexible working options to a broader section of the workforce, including older workers. Important aspects of such provisions include pre- and post-retirement options, not only to encourage later retirement but also to offer phased-in retirement, trial retirement and retirement with call-back arrangements. These types of flexibility would address those problems identified with cliff-edge retirement (a situation where an individual is working one day and retired the next) that affect both individual older workers, for example in terms of their fulfilment or social engagement, and the employers' need to retain experience and (tacit) knowledge. For example, organisations often rely on individuals who are already retired if there is a need for specific skills or added labour. However, these informal arrangements often work in favour of the organisation in that they can rely on an available workforce when they need it, whereas for the individual there is little or no guarantee about the regularity of such call-backs.

There is little evidence that phased-in or trial retirements are widely utilised; and, as outlined above, call-back arrangements are often informal and advantage employers more than employees. It is thus questionable whether workplaces send out especially positive messages to their existing workforce with regards to the value placed on older worker and the recognition given to their experience and skills. As Seifert (2008) points out, the changes necessary to make working hours 'age-appropriate' are considerable and unlikely to be implemented at once. Imaginative combinations with various forms of exit strategies and other incentives therefore need to be investigated. Overall, flexible working options on their own are only one factor and can only work to encourage older workers to remain in the labour market as part of an overall positive human resource (HR) strategy towards this group of workers (see Armstrong-Stassen 2008). The following section therefore considers training and development, an important part of the package that employers can implement to retain older workers in the labour market.

## 11.2 Training and development

There is an established relationship between involvement in training and development and overall company performance (see Nikandroua et al. 2008). It is thus important for workers to receive training and development to keep their job skills up to date and to learn new skills, for example in terms of access to new technologies. Moreover, training and development opportunities are an investment in a workplace and furthermore function as a motivating factor for older workers as they are a sign of appreciation of their contribution (Nyhan and Tikkanen 2008). The lack of access to training and development available to older workers has been established in various national contexts including the UK (Beck 2009; Barnes, Smeaton and Taylor 2009), Germany (Frerichs and Naeglele 1997) and across Europe (Fouarge and Schils 2009). Utilising the European Community Household Panel, Fouarge and Schils (2009) have shown that, across Europe, older workers participate less in training than younger workers and that this holds especially true for workers with few or no qualifications (training of older workers is discussed in more detail in Chapter 12).

One reason for the lack of involvement of older workers in training is the belief that investment in the human capital of younger workers is more effective because they will have longer periods in the labour market in which they can provide a return on this investment (see Mayhew, Elliott and Rijkers 2008). This argument can be questioned, especially in the light of the extension of the state pension age in the UK. Although it seems that most companies provide no formal training or development opportunities specifically for older workers, there is evidence that many employers rely heavily on the skills, experience and knowledge of older workers and expect an informal knowledge transfer to younger workers to occur (Beck 2009). To this end, older workers are often asked to work with younger workers or apprentices in the role of trainer, mentor or co-worker. The following quotation from the construction sector suggests that there are further aspects of this role that ensure younger workers are introduced to the sector's and the company's requirements.

> So the old ones are still there teaching the new ones the tricks of the trade that they don't learn at college and the few shortcuts, and making sure they adhere to the rules in health and safety.

It could thus be thought that learning *from* older workers is more common than learning *for* older workers, even though both could be important aspects of retaining older workers (Nyhan and Tikkanen 2008). Not all older individuals would want to work in the role of trainer or mentor or feel comfortable working with younger workers. It is therefore important to educate managers about the effective utilisation of older employees by building on their skills, knowledge and experience. The aforementioned potential improvement in organisational performance via increased access to training and development opportunities and by tailoring job design should be part of a two-way process in which the performance of older workers is evaluated and appraised in an unbiased manner and useful feedback provided. It is thus also necessary to train supervisors and managers in how to reduce age bias in performance appraisals and how to recognise the performance of older workers fairly and accurately (Armstrong-Stassen 2008). As previously indicated, the role of the manager is key in influencing the position of older workers within companies; and it is therefore not surprising that previous research has found a relationship between the development of managers and the performance of organisations (Mabey 2004). There are age-awareness training courses available for managers, but it is unlikely that many companies have engaged in such learning and development for their senior staff members. The economic recession that began in 2008 will put further strain on employers and make it less likely that training and development opportunities are offered.

As Armstrong-Stassen (2008) points out, it is also important that older workers are given the same opportunities as younger employees to be promoted or transferred, as this will encourage motivation among this group of workers. The majority of older workers do not feel that they have equal chances and that they are unlikely to be promoted once they are 55 years or older (Ni Léime, 2009). There are thus clear shortcomings in learning and training opportunities provided by employers. There is a need to ensure that the learning process occurs in two directions, that is, that older workers do not only pass on their skills and experience but that they are also undertaking learning for their own benefit. To ensure such a development, the position of the manager is key. Age-awareness training for managers should ensure that they provide opportunities to older workers and, in addition, is a precondition for other HR practices such as recognising and respecting older workers and ensuring fair and unbiased appraisals. The combination of learning and development opportunities described here would increase the human capital of all those concerned and increase the likelihood of continued participation in paid employment (see Fouarge and Schils 2009). In order to make possible such learning and development for both older workers and their managers, it might be necessary to consider and to continually reassess job design.

## 11.3 Job design

An important latent function of employment is to provide a meaningful occupation; it is therefore important that workers are assigned challenging work (Jahoda 1982). Depending on the specific sectoral and occupational context, employment-based challenges may be physical or mental and may or may not change with length of service and position held. It could be assumed that the majority of workers carry on in jobs they have been working in and that there is therefore little opportunity for new roles for older workers. As the following quotation from an interview with an engineering employer shows, however, there are jobs where a reduction in workload pressure and job demands might be necessary.

> it's the shop floor line worker who's doing repetitive standardised work. That's where the real question will come. A lot of workers are

> saying what's going to happen if I'm older. And I think the answer is basically the longer you're in the role, the easier the job becomes, the smoother the process. What we do is we systematically assess the job based upon what kind of body movements and forces are necessary. So we have a detailed ergonomic assessment of every job broken down into 14 body parts. So we can rate what is the physical demand of the job and obviously we have a detailed scoring system and effectively our approach is to gradually reduce the rating so that there is a wider range of people that could be doing that job.

While it may be difficult to redesign entire jobs (see Buckle et al. 2008) for older workers, this quotation shows that it is possible to reduce the demand on individuals by tinkering with the job role. In a less physical environment, such adjustments may (*a*) be required in less cases and (*b*) be easier to implement. Smith (2008) suggests that it is not merely the physical requirements of the workplace that need addressing but also how the work context can support different types of work styles, and suggests that, for the knowledge workers under investigation in the study, distinct spaces for collaboration, for concentration and for contemplation were required.

In addition to changing existing work environment and roles, new roles are thus also possible, as, for example, the discussion on training and development suggests that older workers are frequently utilised to work with younger workers to pass on experience, knowledge and skills and thus retain these for the future of the organisation. Previous research has shown that an improved compatibility between the worker and the work environment improves the physical, cognitive and emotional health of the workforce (Genaidy et al. 2008). Boyce (2008, p. 179) thus suggests that 'by incorporating trans-generational design in their workplace, employers can improve performance and safety for all ages'.

Addressing job design to improve the match between workers and their work environment would necessitate employers taking a more long-term and strategic approach to the deployment and development of their workforce. Such a position is unlikely to occur unless employers start to act on the emerging societal awareness that the workforce as a whole is ageing. This is especially the case if job design can be effectively implemented only within a holistic and new approach to age management in the workplace. Further important aspects include compensation and a wealth of possible incentives.

## 11.4 Compensation and incentives

Many evaluations of the debate on extending working lives have considered the position of older workers in the labour market according to the push, pull and jump factors that influence individuals' decisions (see Schmid and Hartlapp 2008). The relevance and range of these factors will have been affected by the 2008–9 recession. For example, the general rise in unemployment may act as a push factor while the context of financial insecurity will encourage other older workers to remain in employment to ensure they have an adequate pension. Despite the increased risk following the recession, we are here mainly interested in the pull factors that can influence decisions to extend working lives.

Compensation in the form of incentives to continue employment, improved benefits or improved pension plans can act as important pull factors to encourage older workers to remain in the labour market for longer. Long service has been rewarded by discounts on goods, improved leave entitlement and access to company shares. However, age-discrimination legislation may prohibit age-related rewards such as share schemes based on age. Such rewards need to reflect possible changes in the preferences of older workers. Hedge (2008) suggests, for example, an increased interest in health insurance. One organisation in the construction sector that seemed to have captured a simple but significant 'pull' effect for older workers had instituted a club of long-serving employees, membership of which had come to be perceived as a high-status achievement.

> And once they've done their 25 years they get invited to the Club and they have a 'do' every year. Once they retire they're still allowed to be part of the Club and go to the party and things. There are about 250 members at the minute and it's quite a big thing. People will ask to stay on until they can get into the Club. If they're due to retire before their 25 years, they'll ask if they can extend it, you know, in order to get into the Club.

The institution of the Club in itself is less important than the recognition and social status which goes along with membership and which transcends employment status because even retired workers value this membership. These aspects are discussed in more depth in the next section. Depending on the context in which benefits or rewards may be offered, they may therefore seem to be quite minor offerings that achieve an effect mainly because of the status that both the organisation and individual older workers afford them.

Pensions can act as important pull or push factors as some individuals may have a good pension to look forward to while others may have to continue working for longer to ensure that they can draw an adequate pension. There is evidence to show that countries with generous early retirement systems also have fewer older workers participating in training, which, as indicated above, is linked to extending older workers' involvement in the labour market (Fouarge and Schils 2009). As the retirement routes in the UK tend to be neither flexible nor generous, older workers are more likely to participate in training and work for longer, though on both indicators the Swedish context (flexible but moderately generous) is the most likely to contribute to extending working lives (Fouarge and Schils 2009).

The realisation that there is an appetite among the workforce for more flexible working and retirement options has, however, led to the introduction of a variety of scenarios in which individuals may retire or defer their retirement while drawing or not drawing (some or all of) their pension and while continuing or not continuing to contribute to their pension scheme (CIPD 2008). The flexibility in options aims to increase retention and allow for more choice in retirement options. Gough and Hick (2009) have shown that occupational pension schemes can influence the retention, although not the recruitment, of workers, if seen as part of an overall package offered by the employer.

The new regulations 2006 permit a variety of pathways such as phased retirement and shifting down while drawing down part or all of a pension. Smeaton, Vegeris and Melahat (2009) report that among 50–59-year-olds 12 per cent of men and 9 per cent of women are drawing their pension while working, with the percentage for men in the 60–64-year-old category increasing to 31 per cent drawing their pension in full and 15 per cent drawing their pension in part. Figure 11.1, a vignette of practices in a logistics company, shows how such pathways may be enabled or encouraged by employers.

As the following quotations show, a side effect of the new regulations may be confusion about what employers and individual older workers can and cannot do (TAEN 2009). This problem was particularly pronounced in the health sector, where additional company regulations exist. The perception here was that older workers do not gain from extending their working lives once they have worked a certain number of years because the pension would not increase. When asked about

> The 'Logistics' Company works in international mailing and dispatch. It has a freight works department which operates global exports and imports, a logistics department for storage and distribution, and a UK and international courier service. Of the just under 100 staff, the majority work in the post room processing mail; in logistics, picking, packing and distributing; or as office workers. Almost 30 per cent can be classified as older workers with approximately a third of these past retirement age.
>
> The company makes a point of 'keeping more of an eye' on workers who are past retirement age and speaks to them on an annual basis about how they are feeling and whether they can carry on working. Most people who are over 65 work part time, though most had done other, more involved jobs in the past and mainly in other companies, thus joining 'Logistics' Company only after retirement age. A common entry route into the company is via temping agencies before being taken on directly by the company.
>
> When recruiting, the company looks mainly for experience, not qualifications, thus considering where individuals worked previously, what positions they've held, and whether they're industry-related. Parts of the industry are quite 'incestuous', everybody knows people who've worked at other places together and word-of-mouth information is important.
>
> The company has seen five individuals return to work with them following their decision to retire. Retirement age is thus not a true measure of retirement for the company as most 'go out in dribs and drabs'. Reasons for continuing to work include not being able to afford retirement and feeling they would get bored if they were at home all day.

*Figure 11.1* Logistics Company

incentives for older workers to carry on working, an employer from the health sector made the following statement:

> I don't think there is at the moment. I'm not sure about the pension policy, you know, if you retire and then you come back to work, I'm not familiar with how that would work with regard to your salary so to speak, because it obviously affects your salary.

The potential of older workers thus seems to have been recognised by some companies, especially where the type of work lends itself to various forms of part-time work. There are examples of organisations using compensation and rewards in attempts to retain older workers; but it is questionable whether they are trusted enough to make them effective. The overall trend towards more flexible working scenarios may also lead to some confusion regarding state and occupational pensions and the various options that employers and their older workers can choose from.

## 11.5 Recognition and respect

Underlying the majority of the aforementioned factors or possibilities for employers to take action is the need for recognition of, and respect for, older workers. Leibold and Voelpel (2006, p. 65) question whether organisations know how to 'reengage, retrain and reignite' older workers. The culture of any organisation is difficult to change but age-related stereotypes are likely to influence decision-making processes regarding pay, promotions, assignment and training opportunities, as mentioned above (Hedge 2008). Armstrong-Stassen (2008) argues that the treatment of older workers prior to retirement will influence their decision to remain in the labour market, retire and/or return to work. The importance of 'perceived procedural justice, respect from work-group members, contribution to the organisation and desire to continue working' form a significant positive relationship (Armstrong-Stassen 2008, p. 48). A starting point is obviously to adhere to the age-discrimination legislation, although, as Parry and Tyson (2009) show, there is no necessary conformity in responses to the introduction of the new laws, and implementation will vary considerably by company and sector. Parry and Tyson (2009) also suggest that the business case for age diversity in the workforce is important for many organisations. Yet the adherence to legislation or pursuit of a business case in themselves are not sufficient to address age stereotyping and its consequences, especially if they are part of the culture of an organisation. Leibold and Voelpel (2006, pp. 96–8) thus argue that a new managerial mindset is needed to address the following problems:

- assuming leaders will proactively and effectively implement solutions once ageing workforce threats become crucial;
- inability to relate ageing workforce challenges and solutions to the enterprise's strategic objectives;
- regarding partial or 'quick-fix' solutions as adequate;
- neglecting employee attitudes concerning the sharing of valuable knowledge;
- overestimating technological solutions to 'capture' knowledge; and
- inadequate coordination of ageing workforce solutions.

In addition to complying with the age legislation, there is a need for employers to 'ensure that the accomplishments, experience, knowledge and expertise of older employees are recognised, appreciation is shown when older employees do a good job and they are treated with respect by others in the organisation' (Armstrong-Stassen 2008, p. 48). A first step is to recognise the role older workers play in the company and the potential there is for them to expand this role or create new ones. A simple example of how this can be achieved is provided by Mai (2008), who describes the 'Compass' process established at Siemens in Germany. The company found its older workers' situation to be 'characterised by a lack of orientation and perspective, resulting in de-motivation' (Mai 2008, p. 22). A personnel development measure was devised which included a wide-ranging personal development plan to allow workers to do what they were interested in while ensuring support and feedback to the process. The programme thus provides development opportunities, recognition and new challenges while also delivering potential for innovative developments and a motivated workforce to the company. In the case of Siemens, adjusting the corporate culture is therefore part of good leadership.

A further important aspect of showing recognition and respect to older workers is to acknowledge and appreciate accomplishments and jobs well done. While there is considerable discussion of the role of rewards within organisations (see, for example, Brown and Purcell 2007), there is much less concern about recognition. Petersen and Willig (2004, p. 338) claim that the 'contemporary logic of work is unable to provide adequate forms of recognition', leaving workers of all ages continuously seeking recognition without 'ever having the possibility of receiving proper respect'. While the rhetoric maintaining that 'employees are the most important resource of the company' is common, evidence of its implementation is much harder to come by. Recognition and respect should be extended to all workers and employees, further highlighting that it is important not to single out older workers. The retention of older workers thus needs to be a long-term goal for organisations. This would benefit workers and employees of all ages and would parallel the life-course perspective advocated on the issue of the ageing workforce (Smeaton and Vegeris 2009). Equal benefits would be derived from recognising the experience, knowledge, skill and expertise not only of older workers but of all individuals working for a given company (McCrare, 2005) as this would allow for an accurate assessment of resources and possibilities available. Moreover, as Armstrong-Stassen (2008) points out, recognition and respect are some of the few HR practices that can be provided without adding any considerable financial cost to the organisation, although they do require a considerable reassessment and potential restructuring of approaches and practices. As previously indicated, a key issue is also to ensure that the basic idea of recognition and respect for all employees underlies all HR activities including, but not limited to, those outlined in this chapter.

## 11.6 Summary and conclusions

Notwithstanding the argument that HR in the past may have had detrimental effects on older workers and that employers can be a hindrance rather than a conducive factor in attempting to extend working lives, this chapter has outlined what employers can do to retain older workers. Flexible working options are increasingly discussed and offered, although there are still some sectors and occupations where non-standard working forms are found difficult to accommodate. Training and development are on the agenda and should generally be available for older workers; but this tends to be dependent on a variety of factors including type of work and outlook of employer. It is also important to differentiate between learning *for* and learning *from* older workers, with suggestions that the latter is more likely to occur because of the importance of knowledge retention for organisations. To ensure that older workers are motivated to continue working for longer, job design, in terms of both the physical environment in which the job is undertaken and the content and aim of the roles, need to be considered. Ensuring that a job is challenging and interesting while it can be undertaken in an appropriate environment that suits the individual is key to the worker's health, well-being and interest in work. These can be further improved by offering compensation and incentives or so-called pull factors to encourage workers to remain in employment for longer. These may include financial rewards, the state and occupational pension systems as well as a range of non-monetary rewards that may provide individuals with access to social networks and fulfilment of other latent factors of employment that may continue past retirement. However, there are indications that the attempts to put in place aspects of all these factors have led to widespread confusion among employers regarding what they can and cannot do for or with older workers. The level of changes brought about by the age-discrimination legislation and the Age Positive Campaign (see www.agepositive.gov.uk) is encouraging because they indicate a need for considerable change and a will to implement it. At the same time the volume of change has made it difficult for employers to keep up with the requirements of the legislation and, in addition, take positive steps to make their workforces more mixed in age categories.

Underlying these developments is a need for a change of mindsets among employers and employees alike to make the new working contexts as beneficial to both parties as is possible. While employees might still be reluctant to work longer, there are positive effects of employment as long as there is a chance for some self-determination of what work is undertaken when and how. Employers are increasingly likely to find themselves dependent on older workers, as the pool of available labour shrinks and is dominated by older age groups. Despite a wealth of activities that employers could undertake to encourage the extension of working lives, it seems that many companies are still avoiding the issue and that the potential problems have not yet been fully appreciated. Overall, however, the biggest challenge might be to ensure that employers do not pick and mix individual policies or activities but that they implement coherent policies and approaches that respect and reward older workers.

# 12

# The Importance of 'Teaching Old Dogs New Tricks': Training and Learning Opportunities for Older Workers

*Alan Felstead*

This collection and its contributions have, in large part, been motivated by the changing age profile of those who live and work in the developed world. Populations in these parts of the world are ageing fast (see Chapter 2). For example, in 2007 less than fifth of the European population was aged 65 and over, but by 2032 this age group is predicted to increase to around a quarter (Dunnell 2008; Lutz 2008). In the absence of any other change, this means that the average age of those in employment will rise. The average age of workers will grow even faster if government plans to raise the retirement age and keep workers in employment for longer are successful. Such trends pose training and development issues for managers, who will be facing the future with an ever 'greying' workforce whose experience of formal education is a distant memory. For example, it is estimated that 70 per cent of the UK's 2020 workforce have already left school, college or university (HM Treasury 2006, p. 1).

By highlighting how workplace training and learning opportunities vary across the life course, this chapter offers a response to this heightened interest. In particular, the chapter examines how, according to existing evidence, training varies by age in terms of its incidence and length as well as providing new evidence on how the quality of training and the possibilities for workplace learning also vary by age. The chapter comprises three principal sections. The first reviews existing research evidence, the second outlines the new data sources drawn on for this chapter, and the third presents some new evidence. The chapter's originality stems from the three UK-wide surveys upon which it draws. Two were carried out in collaboration with the National Institute of Adult Continuing Education (NIACE) and the other was funded by the Economic and Social Research Council (ESRC) and a consortium of government funders (Felstead et al. 2005; 2007a; 2007b). The chapter thus presents new evidence and opens up new areas for debate. The chapter concludes that the changing demographic profile of the UK – and those of other advanced industrial nations – means that tackling age inequalities in training and learning will be of crucial importance in enhancing future economic prosperity. Therefore, 'teaching old dogs new tricks', by encouraging older workers to pass on more of their skills to others and convincing them that training and learning is worthwhile, will be crucial for effective management of an ageing workforce.

## 12.1 Reviewing existing evidence

Ageing populations pose a major challenge for governments struggling to cope with the fiscal consequences of demographic change – the increased demand for social services, pensions and benefits funded by a declining proportion of working adults. Extending working lives, encouraging people to delay retirement and increasing the employment rate among older people are important government policy responses (Department of Work and Pensions 2005). There have even been some suggestions that the retirement age in the UK may be raised more quickly and higher than originally planned (*Financial Times* 2009a; 2009b). A European-wide response has been to set a target for increasing the employment rate of those aged 55–64 (European Commission 2003, pp.28–9). Known as one of 'Lisbon targets', the 50 per cent rate has been achieved in the UK and is rising steadily across Europe (see Figure 12.1). The UK's favourable position in this respect is corroborated by other studies which examine the employment rate of older men and women workers, conventionally defined as those between 50 and the state pension age (SPA) (Khan 2009; Dini 2009).

### 12.1.1 What has happened to job quality?

While the increase in the employment rate of older people this has been heralded as a UK success, the question arises as to whether it has been achieved at the cost of a decline in the quality of the working life. After all, older workers may be trapped in poor-quality jobs and employed in precarious positions. People aged over 50, for example, are more likely to be self-employed than those in younger age groups, yet 'there is little [research] on attitudes to, and experiences of, small-business ownership' (Curran and Blackburn 2001, p. 891). Part-time work is also more common among older people, although more so among women than men. They are also over-represented among other forms of flexible labour such as temporary working and working at home (Felstead et al. 2000).

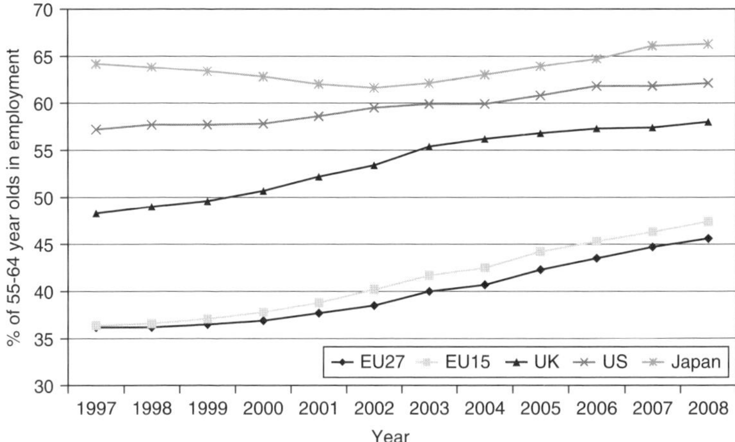


*Figure 12.1* Older workers' employment rates in selected parts of the world, 1997–2008
*Source*: Eurostat.

These flexible types of employment are often referred to as 'bridge jobs' as they can ease the transition from full-time employment to retirement. However, access to high-quality bridge jobs is limited to certain groups. So older men with higher educational qualifications and those previously employed in professional occupations are more likely to be in better-paid flexible jobs. Occupants of these jobs also report high levels of job satisfaction commensurate with the high levels of job autonomy they enjoy. In contrast, women aged over 50 are more commonly employed in part-time jobs, often working for low rates of pay with few training opportunities (Platman 2004; Lissenburg and Smeaton 2003; for a detailed discussion of the interaction between age and gender, see Chapter 5).

As Taylor (2008) argues, the concerns of older workers have received more attention from policymakers in recent times than in the past. He shows how pensions have been reformed, employment programmes changed and legislation introduced in order to enhance the working lives of older workers. There is also tangible evidence that this is having a real effect on the lived experience of older workers. Based on data from a total over 22,000 workers in Britain interviewed in 1986, 1992, 1997, 2001 and 2006, it has been shown that the position of older workers in the labour market has improved since the 1990s, in two ways (Felstead 2009). First, older workers have closed the gap with young workers in areas where they were previously disadvantaged. For example, the skill content of jobs differed significantly between age groups in 1986, with older workers located in much lower-skilled jobs than younger workers. However, by 2006 this disadvantage had disappeared for both sexes, although middle-aged workers still occupied the most-skilled positions. So men and women in their fifties were in jobs in 1986 which, on average, required lower qualifications for entry, were associated with shorter training times and could be learned faster. By 2006, parity or better had been achieved with young workers in the labour market. In fact, older men and women were in higher-skilled jobs than younger workers according to some measures.

Second, older workers have maintained some of the relative advantages they have enjoyed for some time. For example, while all workers have experienced an intensification of work and a decline in autonomy since the 1990s, age differences have been maintained with older workers being under less pressure than either their young or middle-aged counterparts. However, despite closing the skills gap and maintaining some of the labour market advantages of age, the loyalty of older workers to their immediate employers – but not employment in general – has fallen sharply since 1992.

### 12.1.2 What has happened to training and learning?

Other features of labour inequality such as access to training have also lessened over time, albeit more slowly. In the 1990s researchers lamented that, despite the rhetoric of lifelong, learning the UK was 'far from any lifelong learning nirvana [since] young workers have much greater access to training' (Machin and Wilkinson 1995, p. 9). So, for example, in 1997 the proportion of employees aged 16–24 who had received training in the last 13 weeks was more than double that for those aged in the Default Retirement Age (39 per cent versus 17 per cent; Taylor and Urwin 2001). Data for 2008 show that regardless of qualification level those in their fifties and above were less likely to receive training than their younger counterparts (Barham et al. 2009, Figure 4). However, researchers have also pointed out that those aged between 50 and the SPA appear to be catching up. So, while the percentage of older employees who received training in 1992 was less than half of that for the 25–39 age group, by 2002 the ratio had risen to 60 per cent (Urwin 2004, p. 31).

Nevertheless, older workers still remain less likely to receive training. This is a consistent finding, whether 'training' is tightly or loosely defined and whatever country in Europe is examined (Schuller and Watson 2009, pp. 62–9). Furthermore, when older workers do get training, it tends to be shorter. For example, over half of older workers questioned in 2002 reported that the training they undertook in the four weeks before the interview lasted less than one week, compared with around a third of training recipients aged 25–39 and less than a tenth of those aged 16–24 (Urwin 2004, p. 109). In this sense, the intensity as well as the incidence of training varies by age, with older workers being disadvantaged. However, we know little about the relative usefulness or impact that training – or its quality, for short – has on the work experience and whether this, too, differs by age. Furthermore, it is unclear whether the low training incidence among the old 'is a matter of employer resistance or individual unwillingness to train' (McNair 2006, p. 493). Some of the data we present later in this chapter help to address these issues.

In addition to our greater knowledge about the quality of training, recent developments in workplace learning theory suggest that we need to know more about the effectiveness of everyday learning. In-depth studies of a wide variety of jobs – such as those of engineers, accountants, nurses, miners and teachers (Eraut et al. 1999; Fevre, Gorad and Rees 2001; Hodkinson and Hodkinson 2004) – suggest that a great deal of learning goes on at work that is not picked up by standard survey questions. This is mainly because surveys have tended to focus on gathering data on formal training courses, and rather less attention has hitherto been paid to on-the-job learning. This contrast is encapsulated by the respective terms 'learning as acquisition' and 'learning as participation' (Sfard 1998). The former term refers to a conceptualisation that views learning as a product with a visible, identifiable outcome, often accompanied by certification or proof of attendance. The latter, on the other hand, views learning as a process in which learners improve their work performance by carrying out daily work activities via interacting with people, tools and materials.

This conceptual distinction can be used for dividing the empirical literature into two categories. On the one hand, much of the policy-led research takes human capital theory as its frame of reference and implicitly adopts a 'learning as acquisition' perspective. This is evident in the analytical measures used. These include qualification attainment, years spent in formal education and the incidence of training. These indicators are often referred to as 'human capital endowments', and are used to explain why the better endowed are higher paid and vice versa. They are also easy to measure – the number and type of qualifications a person has can be counted, the number of years spent in full-time education can be calculated, and individuals can recall whether or not they took part in a training event in the preceding weeks/months. Such measures are commonly found in national surveys throughout the world with now standard tried and tested question formulations (OECD 1997).

However, case study research on workplace learning tends to adopt a 'learning as participation' approach. This shows that informal learning is often crucial to the effective execution of tasks. While these studies recognise that learning at work is ongoing (Leman 2003), they limit its reach by including only 'significant changes in capability or understanding' and excluding 'the acquisition of further information when it does not contribute to such changes' (Eraut 1997, p. 556). Moreover, these studies highlight the importance of workplace experts in passing on knowledge and expertise to others. Often these experts are those with the most on-the-job experience or those who had acquired more work experience in general (that is, the older members of the workforce) (Pillay et al. 2003).

Given these conceptual and methodological differences, there have only been a handful of attempts to incorporate the lessons of case study research with its emphasis on 'learning as participation' into survey design, which has traditionally been dominated by the 'learning as acquisition' mode of thinking. Nevertheless, the European Working Conditions Survey, for example, now asks workers whether or not their job involves: solving unforeseen problems on their own; learning from others; and learning new things on the job. Despite the limitations of these questions in terms of their relative newness in the series and the absence of a response scale (instead respondents are simply asked to indicate 'yes' or 'no'), the results show that older workers have relatively limited access to these on-the-job learning opportunities. Across Europe such learning opportunities were highest among those aged 25–34 years and lowest among workers in the very youngest (15–24) and oldest (55+) age groups. The least likely group to report access to these learning opportunities was older women workers (Villosio 2008, pp. 49–51). However, we currently know little more than this. The following section aims to address this deficiency by presenting new evidence analysed from an age perspective.

## 12.2 Outlining the new data sources

The new data presented in this chapter come from three data sources – all available for further analysis in the Data Archive at the University of Essex. The first is the 2006 Skills Survey, a UK-wide survey of working individuals aged 20–65. The sample was drawn using clustered random sampling methods to select households within which one respondent was randomly selected. The resulting data set comprises a high-quality, large and representative sample. A total of 7787 respondents participated in the survey. All interviews were conducted in people's homes and lasted for just under one hour, with a response rate of 62 per cent of eligible respondents interviewed. Interviews were completed between March 2006 and March 2007 with three-quarters of the interviews completed in the first six months. Sample weights were computed to take into account the differential probabilities of sample selection according to the number of dwelling units at each issued address, the number of eligible interview respondents, the oversampling of the boost areas and the slight under-representation of certain groups. All of the analyses that follow have been weighted accordingly (for further details see Felstead et al. 2007b).

The second data source is a module of questions inserted into NIACE's Survey on Adult Participation in Learning, which was carried out in 2004. This survey has been carried out in the UK on annual basis since 1999 with occasional batteries of questions on issues of topical interest (see Aldridge and Tuckett 2009). These additional questions aimed to: reveal sources of learning associated with everyday work experience; identify the relative importance of different sources of learning; and trace their workplace correlates (Felstead et al. 2005). The questions formed a module, known as the Learning at Work Survey (LAWS), which comprised part of a weekly omnibus survey carried out by Research Surveys of Great Britain (RSGB). Face-to-face interviews with individuals aged over 16 years were carried out in people's homes during a three-week period in February 2004. The LAWS questions were asked of 1943 employees, who were selected randomly for interview by address. Quotas were imposed on the sample and the results were weighted to produce a representative picture of the UK at the time.

The third source is a survey which, like LAWS, 'piggybacked' on the NIACE Survey on Adult Participation in Learning for 2007. This time, however, a different module of questions was added, designed to capture the features of a 'community of practice'. This is a theoretical concept used in case studies to understand the way in which employees make the transition from novice to old-timer and the trajectory of individuals within particular occupations (Lave and Wenger 1991; Wenger 1998; Fuller and Unwin 1999; 2003). Hence, it is referred to as the Communities of Practice Survey (CoPS). For this survey, 1899 employees were interviewed (see Felstead et al. 2007a). To ensure representativeness, the data reported in this chapter have been weighted to reflect the employee population of the UK.

## 12.3 Presenting new evidence

Frequently analysts have shown that older workers are less likely to receive training than their younger counterparts (McNair 2009;

Urwin 2004; Taylor and Urwin 2001). This is seen as another labour market disadvantage and has led to legislation which promotes equal access to training for workers of all ages. However, it is unclear whether declining participation in training by age is the result of employer unwillingness to train older workers or the reluctance of older workers to take it up. Moreover, the quality of training may differ by age. Previous research, for example, suggests that not all training episodes are intended to raise skill levels by the same amount, and some are not about raising skill levels at all. Instead, some training is designed to enhance employee commitment and has little to do with raising skills, and some aims to ensure conformity with standardised and prescribed ways of working which restrict the skills used at work (Felstead et al. 2009). The quality of training can differ in other respects, too. For example, even where skills are acquired as result of training, they may or may not be important enough for the employer to award a pay rise. The quality of training may also differ according to whether it raises levels of job satisfaction and enjoyment. Focusing exclusively on the incidence and intensity of training – where older workers are at a disadvantage – fails to acknowledge the many ways in which the quality of training episodes may differ, hence creating another source of labour market disadvantage. An important aspect of the 2006 Skills Survey was the addition of a set of questions designed to shed light on these issues.

The results confirm that the incidence of training declines sharply with age for both men and women (see Table 12.1). In general, those who have undertaken training rate its impact on their work performance as beneficial and well worthwhile. However, its quality in these terms declines to some degree with age. For example, men and women in their fifties who receive training are a little less likely than their younger counterparts to say that it improved their skills and working practices. More notably, the training they receive is far less likely to result in a pay rise or add to their enjoyment at work. So older workers are less likely to participate in training, and even when they do it is likely to be of a slightly poorer quality.

It is commonly assumed that employers are reluctant to train older workers because the pay-offs can only be reaped over a relatively short time period, older workers are more resistant to new ideas and have little new to learn at their time of life. On this basis, we would expect the reasons for and consequences of not receiving training to vary with age. However, employer reluctance to offer training in the face of employee demand for it was reported by, if anything, a slightly higher proportion of younger workers. This suggests that employer reluctance

*Table 12.1* Training and its quality by age and gender, 2006

| | **Training incidence**[1] **(%)** | **Quality (%)** | | | |
|---|---|---|---|---|---|
| | | **Has raised skills used at work a little or a lot**[2] | **Has improved working practices**[3] | **Pay increased following training**[4] | **Enjoy job more**[5] |
| | 1 | 2 | 3 | 4 | 5 |
| Men's age Groups | | | | | |
| 20–34 | 68.8 | 93.2 | 89.4 | 30.0 | 60.4 |
| 35–49 | 71.4 | 91.1 | 86.2 | 13.3 | 57.1 |
| 50–65 | 55.1 | 85.7 | 80.0 | 9.0 | 52.0 |
| Women's age Groups | | | | | |
| 20–34 | 72.3 | 92.4 | 88.4 | 24.9 | 64.7 |
| 35–49 | 69.1 | 92.0 | 85.9 | 15.3 | 63.0 |
| 50–65 | 60.8 | 90.1 | 85.2 | 8.4 | 57.7 |

*Notes*: [1]Respondents were asked: 'In the last year (that is since [Month] 2005), have you done any of these types of training or education connected with your *current* job?' The card listed a number of options. The table presents the proportion of the employee sample reporting at least one of these activities.
[2]In this column, we report the percentage of trainees who responded 'a lot' or 'a little' to the question: 'Would you say that this training or education has improved your skills ...' (the other alternative response was 'not at all') and confirmed that they 'are able to make use of these skill improvements in your current job.'
[3]In this column, we report the percentage of trainees who agreed with the statement: 'The training has helped me improve the way I work in my job.'
[4]Those in receipt of training were asked whether they agreed with the statement: 'I received a pay increase as a result of my training.'
[5]Respondents were asked: 'Still thinking about the training you received over the last year in your current job, which of the following statements apply?'. Among the list was the following statement: 'The training has made me enjoy my job more.'
*Source*: Own calculations from the 2006 Skills Survey.

to offer training hinders the training prospects of the young more than the old (see Table 12.2). However, attitudes towards training do vary with age, as expected. For example, around two-thirds of older men and women said that they 'did not want any training', compared with between a third and two-fifths of their younger counterparts. Similarly, the perceived drawbacks of not receiving training – in terms of the requirements of the job and the enhancement of the prospect of promotion – also fell with age. Smaller proportions of older workers also thought that the lack of training made it difficult for them to keep pace with changes in the job, and few thought it hindered their

*Table 12.2* Reasons for and consequences of the lack of training by age and gender, 2006

| | **Reasons given (%)** | | | | **Consequences (%)** | |
|---|---|---|---|---|---|---|
| | **Wanted but not given**[1] | **Did not want**[2] | **Did not need**[3] | **No pay-off**[4] | **Failing to keep up to date**[5] | **Damaging to career**[6] |
| Men' age Groups | | | | | | |
| 20–34 | 24.9 | 37.1 | 69.4 | 51.6 | 23.0 | 10.9 |
| 35–49 | 17.7 | 50.9 | 69.5 | 55.6 | 26.1 | 12.8 |
| 50–65 | 17.4 | 62.4 | 74.7 | 65.5 | 22.6 | 6.2 |
| Women's age Groups | | | | | | |
| 20–34 | 16.4 | 41.9 | 58.5 | 41.5 | 24.5 | 6.1 |
| 35–49 | 14.8 | 56.0 | 70.3 | 55.7 | 20.1 | 8.0 |
| 50–65 | 9.4 | 65.6 | 72.8 | 61.8 | 16.6 | 4.4 |

*Notes*: [1]Respondents were asked: 'You have said that you have not received any training over the last year in your current job. Which of the following statements apply?' Respondents were asked whether they agreed or disagreed with the statements presented. For this column, we report the percentage who agreed with the statement: 'My employer was not willing to provide additional training, even though I wanted it.'

[2]In this column, we report the percentage who agreed with the statement: 'I did not want any training.'

[3]In this column, we report the percentage who agreed with the statement: 'I did not need any additional training for my current job.'

[4]In this column, we report the percentage who agreed with the statement: 'Training would not help me get a better job in my organisation.'

[5]Respondents who undertook no training during the year before interview were asked: 'Was there any time over the last year in your current job when training would have been useful for keeping up to date with the skills required?' The table presents the results of those who said 'yes'.

[6]These respondents were also asked whether they agreed or disagreed with the statement that: 'Lack of training damaged my career opportunities'.

*Source*: Own calculations from the 2006 Skills Survey.

career opportunities. The reported need for training also declined with age – approximately three-quarters (72.8 per cent) of older women workers reported that they did not receive training because it was not needed for their current job, compared with three-fifths (58.5 per cent) of those aged 20–34. From this we can conclude that employers do not appear to be overly resistant to providing training for older workers. However, older workers not in receipt of training rate the benefits of training lower than their younger counterparts, and even when they do receive training they consider it to be less beneficial to them than do their younger counterparts (see Table 12.2).

Few data sets are capable of providing insights into the different ways in which people learn to do their jobs better. The main reason for this is a concentration on formal episodes of learning typified by off-the-job training courses as well as the use of the term 'training' in questionnaires which tends to focus respondents' minds on these formal events (Campanelli et al. 1994). However, there have been recent attempts to correct this neglect. One example comes from a Norwegian telephone survey of 1502 employees carried out in 1999 (Skule 2004). Its starting point was dissatisfaction with the orthodoxy of capturing 'learning as acquisition' through measures such as participation rates, training hours, the financial cost and level of qualification awarded. Instead, it focused on identifying the conditions associated with 'learning-intensive' jobs. These jobs were defined according to the subjective judgement of the occupants, the length of specific learning required to do the job well and the durability of the skills learnt. The Learning at Work Survey (LAWS) carried out in 2004 across the UK is another example of an attempt to provide quantitative evidence for the 'learning as participation' approach, but so far these results have not been examined from an age perspective.

A major innovation of LAWS was the collection of data on how individual employees rated various activities in terms of their helpfulness in enhancing work capabilities. Respondents were given a list of activities (that can be conducted in, during and out of work) and were asked to what extent each had helped them to learn to do their job better. Respondents were asked to choose a response from a five-point rating scale. This is in accord with the 'learning as participation' approach and its emphasis on process *and* outputs. However, the activities themselves reflected both approaches. The 'learning as acquisition' approach and its emphasis on filling the human mind with materials that are delivered, conveyed or facilitated by another was captured by asking respondents about the usefulness of five activities. These were: training received; qualifications studied; abilities acquired outside of work; work-related reading undertaken; and the internet as a source of information. The 'learning as participation' approach, on the other hand, gives a greater emphasis to taking part in activities, the fluidity of actions, the dialectical nature of the process of learning and the importance of the workplace as well as the classroom as a site of learning (Cunningham 2004). In order to assess and map the relative learning potential of these activities, the survey asked respondents to rate the usefulness of the following five activities in helping them to improve their work performance: doing the job; being shown by others how do things; reflecting on one's own performance; watching and listening to others; and using trial and error on the job.

Over half reported that simply doing the job had helped them learn most about how to improve (Felstead et al. 2005). Almost nine out of ten respondents said that their job required them to learn new things and pass on tips to colleagues, and a similar proportion agreed that they had picked up most of their skills through on-the-job experience. However, not all work activities proved to be as helpful. The use of the internet, for example, to download materials, participate in e-learning and seek out information was regarded as being of no help at all to almost half the sample. Despite the emphasis placed on training course attendance and the acquisition of qualifications, both were lowly rated by respondents in terms of their helpfulness in improving work performance. Activities more closely associated with the workplace, such as doing the job, being shown things, engaging in self-reflection and keeping one's eyes and ears open (that is, facets associated with 'learning as participation'), were reckoned to provide more helpful insights into how to do the job better. All of these factors were rated as more helpful sources of learning than attending training courses or acquiring qualifications.

Similar patterns were found for the young, middle-aged and older employees. However, the latter were far less likely (both absolutely and statistically speaking) than younger employees to rate all of the sources of learning helpful in improving work performance (see Table 12.3). For example, older employees rated activities such as watching, listening, reflecting and doing the job – all given emphasis by the 'learning as participation' approach – as less helpful in learning to do their jobs better than their younger counterparts did. This evidence suggests that, in addition to getting less formal training and high 'quality' training in particular, older employees are also less likely to benefit from the many other ways in which people learn at work.

The importance of organisational and managerial support for learning has received increased attention in recent years (for example, Eraut et al. 1999). For example, managers can provide helpful advice on job improvements, identify the limits of those in their charge and offer promotion counselling. LAWS therefore asked respondents whether their jobs were designed to promote learning and to rate the helpfulness of their manager (where they had one) in each of these roles. The evidence reveals that the jobs of older workers were less likely to be constructed to help their incumbents to learn or to pass on the benefits of their experience to others (see Table 12.4). Furthermore, line managers were less helpful to older workers in offering advice on how to learn and were

*Table 12.3* Learning sources for improved job performance by age

| **Sources of learning**[1] | **Helpfulness rating**[2] | | |
|---|---|---|---|
| | **17–34-year-olds** | **35–49-year-olds** | **50-year-olds and over** |
| (a) Learning as acquisition | | | |
| Training courses paid for by your employer or yourself | 2.54 | 2.48 | 2.25 |
| Drawing on the skills you picked up while studying for a qualification | 2.26 | 2.30 | 2.08 |
| Using skills and abilities acquired outside of work | 2.28 | 2.20 | 2.17 |
| Reading books, manuals and work-related magazines | 2.04 | 2.16 | 2.11 |
| Using the Internet | 1.36 | 1.30 | 0.90 |
| Learning as acquisition index[3] | 2.12 | 2.10 | 1.92 |
| (b) Learning as participation | | | |
| Doing your job on a regular basis | 3.29 | 3.34 | 3.23 |
| Being shown by others how to do certain activities or tasks | 2.91 | 2.74 | 2.50 |
| Reflecting on your performance | 2.75 | 2.70 | 2.61 |
| Watching and listening to others while they carry out their work | 2.74 | 2.54 | 2.27 |
| Using trial and error on the job | 2.17 | 2.01 | 1.67 |
| Learning as participation index | 2.80 | 2.68 | 2.45 |

*Notes*: [1]This table is based on the responses given to the question: 'To what extent have the following activities helped you learn to do your job better?' At this point in the survey, respondents were asked to respond to each of the activities read out by the interviewer (listed in the left-hand column of the table) by selecting the most appropriate response from the scale shown to them on a computer screen.

[2]As a summary of the responses given, scores were allocated according to the helpfulness rating attached to each activity. A score of 4 was given to respondents who reported a factor as 'a great deal of help', 3 to 'quite a lot of help', 2 to 'of some help', 1 to 'a little help' and 0 to activities considered as 'of no help at all'.

[3]In order to summarise the data further, the sources of learning are grouped according to two approaches – acquisition and participation (see text). Each is composed of five activities with scores ranging from 4 to 0 and divided by five to produce an index. The findings for those 50 and over are compared with the two other age categories.

*Source*: Own calculations from the Learning at Work Survey 2004.

less likely to give advice on possible career moves. Yet line managers were particularly good at recognising the extent of the abilities of those under their charge and especially the superior abilities of their older workers (see Table 12.5).

In these circumstances, it is somewhat surprising that the organisation of work and line management did not make more of older employees'

*Table 12.4* Learning requirements of jobs by age

| **Learning requirements**[1] | **Agreement/disagreement rating**[2] | | |
|---|---|---|---|
| | **17–34-year-olds** | **35–49-year-olds** | **50-year-olds and over** |
| My job requires that I keep learning new things | 1.06 | 1.10 | 0.97 |
| My job requires that I help my colleagues learn new things | 0.95 | 0.97 | 0.88 |
| My supervisor or manager could do my job if I were away | 0.59 | 0.42 | 0.33 |

*Notes*: [1]Respondents were asked to indicate how much they agreed or disagreed with a number of statements relating to the learning and skills requirements of the job they currently held. The statements were read out by the interviewer (reproduced in left-hand column in table) and the respondent was asked to select a response from one of four options displayed on a computer screen (shown in first row of table).
[2]As a summary, scores of +2, +1, – 1 and –2 were allocated according to the response given with positives indicating levels of agreement and negatives levels of disagreement with each statement. The table shows average scores for each question.
*Source*: Own calculations from the Learning at Work Survey 2004.

*Table 12.5* Line management facilitation of learning and development by age

| **Source of managerial facilitation**[1] | **Helpfulness rating**[2] | | |
|---|---|---|---|
| | **17–34-year-olds** | **35–49-year-olds** | **50-year-olds and over** |
| Recognising the extent of your abilities | 2.57 | 2.65 | 2.71 |
| Helping you learn to do your job better | 2.40 | 2.30 | 2.02 |
| Giving you advice on promotion | 2.01 | 2.01 | 1.82 |

*Notes*: [1]Respondents were asked: 'How helpful is your supervisor or manager in [a number of situations]'. These included those listed in the left-hand column. Respondents were asked to choose one of five options listed on a screen shown to them as each situation was read out by the interviewer. The responses were: 'a great deal of help' (scored as 4); 'quite a lot of help' (scored as 3); 'of some help' (scored as 2); 'a little help' (scored as 1); and 'of no help at all' (scored as 0).
[2]The scores were used to create a Helpfulness Rating shown in the right-hand column of the table.
*Source*: Own calculations from the Learning at Work Survey 2004.

accumulated experience and recognised abilities. From other evidence (collected by the Community of Practice Survey, the third survey reported here), it is clear that older employees are willing to pass on their experiences to new colleagues, even though they stand to learn far less in

*Table 12.6* Sharing knowledge at work, by age

| **Aspects of knowledge sharing at work**[1] | **Percentage strongly agreeing with statement** | | |
|---|---|---|---|
| | **17–34 year olds** | **35–49 year olds** | **50-years old and over** |
| I feel obliged to help newer colleagues | 19.8 | 25.5 | 26.6 |
| On the whole I'm left to my own devices | 11.3 | 16.9 | 20.4 |
| I frequently learn new things from colleagues | 17.0 | 16.9 | 13.3 |
| I sort out work problems on my own | 8.2 | 11.4 | 12.2 |
| I keep what I know about how to do the job to myself | 2.6 | 2.1 | 1.4 |

*Note*: [1]This table is based on the responses given to the question: 'I am now going to read out a number of statements about your job. For each one I read out, please tell me how much you agree or disagree with it, taking your answer from the screen'. Then, they are offered a series of statements as listed in the left-hand column of the table.
*Source*: Own calculations from the Communities of Practice Survey 2007.

return. For example, employees aged 50 and over were twice as likely to strongly agree that they feel obliged to help out new colleagues (26.6 per cent) as to strongly agree with the statement that 'I frequently learn new things from colleagues' (13.3 per cent). However, a roughly equal proportion of employees aged 17–34 – around a fifth – reported themselves as givers and receivers of such work knowledge. However, older employees were more likely than other age groups to problem-solve alone and to be left to their own devices with the attendant danger that not all of their valuable skills were being passed onto others (see Table 12.6).

## 12.4 Summary and conclusions

The looming demographic crisis has heightened interest in extending the working lives of citizens across the developed world. As a consequence, researchers have found policymakers keen to know more about a number of issues. These include: what discourages people from staying in work longer and what might encourage them to stay longer or delay their retirement (see Chapter 11); how and in what ways older workers differ from their younger colleagues; and what aspects of work older workers value most. The distribution of training opportunities and how this varies by age has also figured in many studies. This chapter has reviewed these studies and, by drawing on three new data sets, it has added to the evidence available on the training and learning opportunities of older workers.

In two respects, the position of older workers in the labour market has improved since the 1990s. First, older workers have closed the skills gap with young workers. Second, they have maintained some of the relative advantages they have enjoyed for some time. For example, while all workers have experienced an intensification of work and a decline in autonomy since the 1990s, age differences have been maintained with older workers under relatively less pressure than either their young or middle-aged counterparts (Felstead 2009). However, older workers remain disadvantaged with regard to training and development opportunities. They are less likely to receive episodes of formal training, and its duration tends to be shorter than that received by younger workers. Moreover, the training older workers receive tends to be of a lower quality than that received by their younger counterparts. However, the motivation to learn is weaker among older workers' with the lack of training regarded as having more limited consequences for them than for those aged under 50.

These disadvantages extend to other, less formal ways in which people learn at work, such as watching, listening, reflecting and doing the job. Older workers benefit less from these forms of learning than their younger counterparts. Furthermore, line managers and the organisation of work are less effective at facilitating the learning of older workers and allowing them to mentor others. In spite of this, older workers are the most willing 'teachers' in the workplace, and line managers recognise the abilities of older workers better than they do other age groups.

Two clear messages for managing a 'greying' workforce emerge from this chapter. First, older workers need to have stronger incentives to press for formal training; at the moment such incentives are relatively weak. The prospect of longer working lives may go some way to encourage more older workers to press for greater access to high-quality training opportunities to make their longer working lives more rewarding. For the same reason, informal sources of learning may become more important for older workers. Second, managers need to do more to tap into the skills and experience of older workers by enhancing their 'teaching' role in the workplace. At present, older workers are willing to pass their skills on, but it is not clear that this willingness has been fully exploited. In these two respects, managers of older workers and older workers themselves both need to change, but, as is well known, 'teaching old dogs new tricks' is difficult to do well. However, it is a challenge – like it or not – that employers in the UK and other advanced economies will have to confront. Only time will tell how successful they have been in dealing with this aspect of managing an ever 'greying' workforce.

# 13
# Health and Well-Being in Older Workers: Capacity Change with Age

*Sarah Harper*

> *Ageing is a very dynamic process. You can be too old for a job at 30 and too young for a job at 45. It is a continuous process.*
>
> (Hallet 1997, p. 28)

This chapter will consider health and well-being among older workers and in particular the evidence for capacity change with age. Perhaps the most significant implication for older workers and their employers is the potential change in work capacity with age. While this is by no means universal, it is widely recognised that physical, mental and social capabilities may undergo some degree of change (TUC 2006; Scottish Executive 2005). This raises a variety of concerns, particularly in the area of the health and safety of older workers. However, the extent to which potential change in work capacity with age affects health and safety depends to an extent upon the nature of the work. For example, those involved in sedentary clerical work may be less affected than those who are involved in work of a very physical nature. In addition, while a series of changes have been noted to generally occur across the life course, it is now widely recognised that very few capacity changes are directly related to decline arising from chronological age alone. Most have a strong environmental component, and can be modified or reduced. Indeed, with the exception of sensory deterioration, which does seem to occur along a more or less fixed chronological continuum, albeit one that is also subject to some environmental modification, most so-called age-related decline is in fact closely linked to environment and behaviour. Furthermore, considerable adaptations can be made to the workplace to compensate for any decline in capacity. It is now generally accepted that chronological age is no longer a sufficient reason to exclude older workers from the workforce, as most capacity change, particularly in early old age, can be mitigated by good ergonomic design (Benjamin and Wilson 2005).

## 13.1 Manual occupations

Capacity changes specifically affecting manual work are those arising from decline in cardiovascular and aerobic function, and pertaining to the musculoskeletal system. There are, however, significant individual differences with respect to aerobic and cardiovascular function arising from highly variable lifestyle habits and previous working habits. As Ilmarinen (2001) showed, an unfit 45-year-old can have lower aerobic and cardiovascular function than a fit work colleague aged 65 years.

Because of declines in cardiovascular and aerobic function older manual workers may experience a decreased ability to do heavy work, decreased ability to work in certain environments, such as those with intense heat or cold, reduced capacity for shift work, and a need for greater recovery time from exertion. Appropriate workplace modifications thus include changes in work design or use of equipment for lifting, restrictions on the amount of lifting/heavy physical tasks and an increase number of breaks (Aittomaki et al. 2005; Benjamin and Wilson 2005; Kowalski-Trakofler, Steiner and Schwerha 2005; Ilmarinen 2005)

There is also strong evidence linking certain work-related risk factors with the occurrence of musculoskeletal disorders (MSD) of the lower back and upper extremities. The connection between occupational factors and the occurrence of different kinds of MSD – frequent bending and twisting, heavy physical work, repetition, forceful exertions, non-neutral body postures and whole-body vibration – has been well documented (Keyserling 2000a; 2000b; Burdorf and Sorock 1997; Buckle 1997).

In addition, a wide range of work-related psychosocial factors have been found to be linked to MSDs. Institute of Medicine (IOM) (2001) point out, high job demands and high job stress are work-related psychosocial factors that are associated with the occurrence of upper-extremity disorders. These include rapid work pace, monotonous work, low job satisfaction, low decision latitude and control, job stress, low social support at work, high psychological demands and beliefs about level of dangerousness of work (Hoogendoorn et al. 2002; Toomingas et al. 1997; Hemingway et al. 1997; Bongers et al. 1993). There is also a strong association between psychosocial factors, MSDs and sickness absence due to MSD (Walker-Bone and Cooper 2005).

However, the evidence remains inconclusive regarding the *actual* level of association between certain non-work psychosocial factors and MSD. According to the Ontario Universities Back Pain Study, low-back pain, for example, seems to be a function of both the physical demands of the job and a number of workers' perceptions. Both physical and psychosocial factors were associated with the reporting of low-back pain and therefore both of these factors should be addressed in the design and modification of work. Physical risk factors included peak lumbar shear force, peak load handled, and cumulative lumbar disc compression. Significant psychosocial factors were high perceived physical load, low opinion of the workplace social environment, perception of lack of control of the job, high co-worker support, high job satisfaction, and perceived over-education (Kerr et al. 2001). Drawing on the US National Interview Health Survey, Kovar and La Croix (1987) report that because of age-related changes in physical capacity older people are less able to perform tasks characterised by high physical demand. Maintaining physical fitness is key here (Kowalski-Trakofler, Steiner and Schwerha 2005). Appropriate workplace modifications include reducing extreme joint movement, excessive force and highly repetitive tasks, and increasing physical fitness through physical training.

1 Some manual occupations demand high levels of sensory ability or place high levels of environmentally generated strain on certain senses, in particular vision and hearing. Certain manual occupations have higher numbers of people exposed to noise – for example, agriculture, mining, construction, manufacturing, transport, and jobs that involve exposure to loud machinery. Dement et al. (2005), for example found almost 60 per cent of workers in a Department of Energy nuclear site had some hearing impairment, and this was exacerbated by age, smoking, duration of work and exposure. Palmer et al. (2002) concluded that the risk of severe hearing difficulty and persistent tinnitus rose proportionally with the number of years in the same working environment. This was more prevalent among men than women, but that may be because more men work in noisier industries. Prevalence of tinnitus increased among manual workers (Quaranta, Assennato and Sallustio 1996). Daniell et al. (2006) showed that in the US, despite 20 years of hearing regulation, most companies did not do much to reduce noise levels. However, neither did employees use the protection they were offered. In the US the National Institute for Occupational Safety and Health recommends hearing-loss prevention programmes for

all workplaces with hazardous noise levels. In the UK the Health and Safety Executive (HSE) recommends that employers start screening employees before exposure – that is, at entry or change of job (HSE 2005) annually for the first two years, thereafter every two or three years.

In terms of vision, older manual workers may experience a reduction in ability to distinguish light and dark and an increase in recognised vision defects – long and short sightedness, astigmatism and eye tiredness (Schneck and Haegstrom-Portnoy 2003). Appropriate modifications include appropriate lighting, anti-glare computer screens and other appropriate technology, appropriate text/font size on computers and in documents/signage, and sufficient rest periods. In addition, regular vision testing is essential (Schneck and Haegerstrom-Portnoy 2003; Ball 2003; Benjamin and Wilson 2005).

Other sensory impairments of older manual workers include greater susceptibility to dermatitis, reduced by the provision of protective gloves, greater susceptibility to the effects of harmful ultraviolet (UVA and UVB) light (for outdoor workers), and reduced thermoregulation. Recognising dehydration in older workers can also be a problem arising from lower thirst levels (Marszalek 2000), and workers in a hot environment may be at risk.

Eliminating slips, trips and falls that occur as a result of impaired balance through sensory impairment, in some cases coupled with musculoskeletal decline, should be a primary workplace objective. Appropriate modifications include improved lighting, even surfaces, clean non-slip surfaces and the removal of objects from floors and in paths and walkways (Benjamin and Wilson 2005; Gauchard et al. 2001; Ohio BWC 2005.) In particular, untidy workplaces, slippery surfaces and poor lighting can contribute to the risk of falls (PPHSA 2006). In addition, uneven floor surfaces, inappropriate footwear and poor carrying techniques can contribute to falls, as can temporal constraints related to urgency (Gauchard et al, 2001). In more than 50 per cent of falls, ground surfaces were found to be defective (Fothergill, O'Driscoll and Hashemi 1995). In particular, Mackey and Robinovitch (2006) found that older women were less able to recover balance because of declines in speed and strength.

The decline in functional and postural balance which may occur with age has been identified as an issue for several occupations including construction workers, nursing staff and home-care workers (Punakallio 2003). However, while older workers have more slips, trips and falls than younger ones, workplace hazards were found to be the same for all ages (Kemmlert and Lundholm 2001). Osteoporosis, increased reaction time and decreased flexibility can also contribute to a higher frequency in falls in older workers (Ohio BWC 2005). Similarly, drugs to treat high blood pressure can affect balance (Ohio BWC 2001).

## 13.2 Clerical, professional and managerial occupations

Many of the above issues also pertain to those employed in clerical, professional and managerial occupations. Declines in the senses are of particular importance here, especially vision and hearing. As earlier discussed, sensory decline is related to age, though in general loss of sensory abilities can be compensated for.

Decline in hearing is typically associated less with a noisy work environment than with individual capacity decline. However, there is evidence that embarrassment prevents employees from reporting workplace hearing problems. As the National Academy on an Aging Society (2004) pointed out, declines in hearing ability may influence decisions on labour-force participation and retirement. In addition, psychosocial changes occur and have effects beyond the hearing loss itself. When people cannot hear well they withdraw from social interactions, and there can also be a reduction in participation in the labour force. As a consequence, social isolation, loneliness and loss of social networks can occur. Nusbaum (1999) suggested that sensory decline may be mistaken for *intellectual* decline and can lead to depression and social isolation, while Gates (2009) suggested that, if left untreated, age-related hearing loss can contribute to isolation, depression and possibly dementia. Indeed, auditory decline may be responsible for some older adults' difficulty with speech recognition and comprehension (Arlinger 2003; Schneider, Daneman and Murphy 2005). The modifications recommended for office workers are in line with those for manual workers.

Given the age range in the early twenty-first century cohorts of workers, there is low probability of severe cognitive decline and dementia. Clearly, cognitive capacity is of particular importance for the performance of professional or managerial occupations, where symptoms of dementia are therefore more likely to be picked up. There is conflicting evidence as to whether the biological processes cause decline in function (Rabbit and Lowe 2000), or whether the accumulation of knowledge and skill actually leads to an increase in job-related performance with age (Westerholm and Kilborn 1997; Rabasca 2000). Additionally, the risk of dementia may decrease with more cognitive and socially challenging working conditions (Seidler et al. 2004; Evans et al. 1997). This raises the question whether people with different labour patterns and occupations have an increased risk of dementia.

'Crystallised' intelligence depends on experience, education and learning, and increases with age, whereas 'fluid' intelligence is more about the ability to solve new problems based on current information, and is therefore about more immediate reactions. There is some evidence that on average older people in the working population perform less well on tests of fluid intelligence (Salthouse 1991a). However, the implications of this for job performance are not clear. Decline in working memory (Salthouse 1991) and in information processing (Smith and Brewer 1995), particularly in terms of speed (Fisk and Warr 1996), may be of particular importance. There is evidence of changes in the learning process (Kubeck et al. 1996), though it is generally agreed that many of these may be overcome by changes in the education process itself, in particular through giving the older worker more time (Kubeck et al. 1996; Rogers 1996). Even in modern technological tasks older workers were able to compensate, so that experienced users of technology may show some age-related slowing in learning rate but minimal age difference in test performance following retraining (Charness et al. 2001).

The general conclusion remains that for the majority of the older working population any capacity decline with age can be compensated for within the workplace so that the effect on job performance itself can be reduced to near zero. In addition, research has consistently found that loss in capacity is compensated for by increase in experience, and that this may be underestimated (Baltes 1991; Warr 2001). As a consequence, the problem-solving ability of older workers is likely to exceed that of younger workers, and in knowledge-based occupations, older workers are likely to be more effective than younger ones. This is not the case in those occupations where new knowledge has entered the job requirement, such as new technological occupations. In addition, low levels of education in early life can act as surrogate factors for late-life cognitive decline, and high levels of education will compensate for these (Winn and Bittner 2005). Similarly, the decline in intellectual functioning among older workers may be compensated for by complex work (Mulatu and Oates 1999).

In conclusion, there is a mismatch in the relationship between cognitive performance and job performance which reveals a negligible age-related loss in performance (Waldman and Avolio 1986; McEvoy and Cascio 1989; Tulving and Craik 2000) and between the apparent declines in cognitive performance with age in laboratory research. This may be due to a lack of rigorous studies, but is also clearly due to the confounding influence of education (Schooler 1987), and the ability of older workers to compensate within a familiar working environment. Key here is suitable on-the-job training and education (Caudron 2000; Lankard 1995).

Older workers experience higher rates of depression than other groups. Emotional strain at work and age were associated with increased odds of depression among US nurses (Muntaner et al. 2006). For older workers, especially those of low socio-economic standing who are nearing retirement, involuntary exclusion from the workforce may be a contributor to ongoing mental health problems. There are elevated risk factors for adverse psychosocial health outcomes from workplace stress and conditions (Pikhart et al. 2004; Godin et al. 2005; Weyers et al. 2006).

There is a substantial literature on diabetes and work (National Academy on an Aging Society 2004; King, Aubert and Herman 1998). Those with diabetes have increased requirements for regular hours, avoidance of shift work and frequent breaks. In addition, they may require a clean private place in which to inject or test blood, and need to eat in the workplace. There is some evidence that diabetes contributes to cognitive deterioration over and above that accounted for by age (Spirduso and Asplund 1995).

Of particular concern to health and safety is the potential change in reaction times. Reaction times are not a purely psychomotor function but depend additionally on cognitive factors. Reaction times tend to increase with age, but there is much variability, depending on the type of task. Sight and light recognition can be impaired as visual reaction times decline with age. This is important with respect to driving or operating machinery (3M 2006). Dynamic visual acuity (DVA) – the ability to resolve details of a moving target – decreases with age, starting around age 45 (Shinar and Schieber 1991). Time-dependent decision making may also compromise older workers' performance. However, if time is sufficient and the task is familiar, performance should not be compromised. Greater complexity needs more time (Haight 2003). Ability to coordinate multiple tasks declines with age, although age-related differences in multiple-task performance decreased with practice. Adjustments need therefore to be made in task design (Sit and Fisk 1999). Decision quality seems not to be affected by age. In their study of younger and older drivers, Walker et al. (1997) found that decision speed was slower for older participants, but age did not affect the quality of decisions. The role of experience must also be factored in here, and we must remember that occupational risk is higher for younger workers than for older workers partly because of young people's lack of experience.

Salthouse (2004) challenged the assumption that, although there are declines in speed, reasoning and memory, there is significant variation between persons. He found age-related cognitive decline to be cumulative across the lifespan, but added that cognitive ability was not the only contributor to successful cognitive functioning, others being motivation and persistence.

As well as the general evidence reported above in manual workers, there are musculoskeletal factors which affect office-based workers. Back pain and neck pain are common, intermittent symptoms in old age, and are associated with general poor physical health (Hartvigsen, Christensen and Frederiksen 2004). Absence from work due to back pain has been found to be strongly inversely related to employment grade; and effects of psychosocial work characteristics, such as control, have been found to differ by grade and gender in both magnitude and direction, thus indicating that the psychosocial work environment represents a potentially reversible cause of ill health (Hemingway et al. 1997). Both physical and psychosocial factors were associated with the reporting of low-back pain and so both of these factors should be addressed in the design and modification of work. Physical risk factors included peak lumbar shear force, peak load handled, and cumulative lumbar disc compression.

Significant psychosocial factors were high perceived physical load, low opinion of the workplace social environment, perception of lack of control of the job, high co-worker support, high job satisfaction, and perceived over-education (Kerr et al. 2001). Existing evidence seems to suggest reducing the occurrence of work-related MSDs by applying a combination of measures, including targeting the psychosocial work environment and not just the ergonomics (Waters 2004).

Gender as a risk factor has not been well researched, and there are conflicting reports. Burdorf and Sorock (1997) found there is no significant association, whereas Gluck, Olenick and Hadler (1998) found a higher rate of claims for back injuries from women in white-collar jobs and from men in blue-collar jobs, yet claims were equal for service occupations. Clearly, gender as a risk factor warrants further study (Dempsey, Berdorf and Webster 1997).

While there is evidence of changes in manual dexterity with age (Pirkl 1995), there has been little systematic investigation of age patterns in psychomotor abilities and ergonomic implications.

## 13.3 Occupations with long working hours and shift work, and high levels of intrinsically stressful work

Occupations with long working hours and shift work, and high levels of intrinsically stressful work involve work which is psychologically, mentally or physically challenging and demanding. The work may require intense, prolonged concentration, with serious consequences if errors are made. Examples of this category are air traffic control, emergency services, health care, prison services, social work and teaching. Workers in such safety-critical occupations include oil, gas and coal operational workers, pharmacists, nurses and medical practitioners, and transport and machinery operators.

Safety-critical workers are those whose action or inaction, arising from ill health, may lead directly to a serious incident. The health of these workers in relation to their on-the-job attentiveness and vigilance is critical. There are two types of safety-critical worker: High Level Safety Critical Worker (Category 1) and Safety Critical Worker (Category 2). Tasks are in Category 1 if a serious incident could result from sudden incapacity or collapse; tasks are in Category 2 if sudden incapacity does not affect the safety of the worker or others. Non-safety-critical workers are those whose health and fitness does not directly affect the safety of themselves or others. Beyond all the factors identified above, these occupations also have an increased incidence of cardiovascular disorders, gastrointestinal problems, sickness absence and substance abuse. Safety-critical workers (Categories 1 and 2), in particular, require a comprehensive physical and psychological assessment to detect conditions that may affect safe working ability, for example heart disease, diabetes, epilepsy, sleep disorders, alcohol and drug dependence, psychiatric disorders and eye and ear problems. These groups are particularly affected by fatigue and shift work.

Whatever its origin, fatigue has predictable effects, such as slowed reaction time, lapses of attention to critical details, errors of omission, compromised problem solving, reduced motivation, and decreased vigour for successful completion of required tasks (Gravenstein, Cooper and Orkin 1990). Thus, fatigue reduces productivity; tired workers accomplish less, especially if their tasks demand accuracy.

> No amount of training, motivation, or professionalism will allow a person to overcome the performance deficits associated with fatigue, sleep loss, and the sleepiness associated with circadian variations in alertness.
>
> (Institute of Medicine 2004)

Fatigue is a well-recognised problem (Shinar and Schieber 1991; Haight 2003) and is of particular importance for critical-safety workers such as drivers and signal operators. Fatigue is closely linked to job design, work load and environment, insufficient rest and time of day.

Fatigue is also linked to shift work. One of the work characteristics most relevant to older workers is shift work. It is well documented that shift work is deleterious to general health. For example, shift work can be more difficult to cope with (Monk 2005). There is a reduction in the amplitude of circadian rhythms, the phases of the circadian rhythm occur earlier and ability to withstand abrupt phase changes is reduced. Similarly, older workers can have problems with sleep quality after night shifts (Kowalski-Trakofler, Steiner and Schwerha 2005). Bonnefond et al. (2006) found that age was related to subjective sleepiness, amount of sleep and psychomotor vigilance. The authors also looked at the relationship of age, sleep or wakefulness, performance and shift work. Age was related only to shift-related changes in the amount of sleep, night shifts being associated with shorter sleep and decreased performance. Shift workers aged over 40 seem to sleep worse after a night shift than after a morning shift. Physical exercise has also been shown to increase sleep length and improve alertness at night (Härmä et al. 2006; Härmä and Ilmarinen 1999).

Rouch et al. (2005) found that cognitive function tends to be impaired by prolonged exposure to shift work. Older workers (aged 35–49, 50–8) experienced more performance lapses than the youngest group (aged 25–34). However, as Härmä and Ilmarinen (1999) point out, the redesigning of shift patterns can help.

Härmä and Ilmarinen (1999) view shift work-related health and safety issues in an ageing workforce as a major challenge for employers. Based on compensation data, Oregon's hospital employees on night shifts were at greater risk of occupational injury than day shift workers (Horwitz and McCall 2004). There were also errors leading to dangers for others. Suzuki et al. (2005), for example, found statistically significant associations between drug administration errors and age and night/irregular shift work, between needlestick injuries and age (see also Levtak 2005), and between incorrect operation of medical equipment and tiredness. The Oklahoma Nurses Association (ONA 2005) found increased odds of reporting errors associated with long shifts, especially in shifts of more than 12 hours. Serious medical errors were made by interns working 24-hour shifts. These reduced when shifts were shorter (Landrigan et al. 2004). A Scottish study in 2003 found that older nurses worked fewer weekends and shorter shifts. Managers recognised the greater difficulty of coping with a 12.5-hour longer day, and were also more likely to work days than nights (Wise 2003). Scott et al. (2006) showed that longer working hours increased risk of errors and decreased vigilance.

Shift workers thus report adverse health effects such as fatigue, reduced sleep quality, gastrointestinal disorders and increased heart disease risk factors (Nicholson and D'Auria 1999). Rodrigues, Fischer and Brito (2001) found shift work to be responsible for a wide range of stressors. Some of this affected home and family life. Gibbs et al. (2005) found that shift work presents a greater health and safety risk precisely because of the additional hazards of working in an offshore environment. This can lead to loss of alertness and reduced performance. The authors suggest that risk may be reduced by attempts to resynchronise circadian rhythms during days off. This could reduce the sleep loss and fatigue that can build up through working night shifts over an extended period. Parkes and Swash (2000) found that a higher proportion of fatal and severe accidents and injuries occurred when work extended beyond the normal 12-hour shift. Night shifts showed higher rates of fatalities and serious injuries. Long tours of duty (more than two weeks) increased the number of fatalities and severe injuries relative to injuries requiring a three-day layoff. Gibbs et al. (2005) in an extensive report for the UK HSE found a 14-night shift caused the least desynchronisation of circadian rhythms. However, they also advised that further interdisciplinary analyses of the relationships between performance and circadian status, adaptation and sleep parameters were essential before any conclusions could be drawn.

Studies have found that shift work has a significant effect on cognitive function. Short-term effects – changes in alertness and efficiency – have been noted in workers whose circadian rhythms are disturbed. Memory may also be affected. Using a variety of neurological tests, Rouch et al. (2005, p. 1282) found:

> Current male shift-workers had lower cognitive performance than never exposed workers. In the same population, memory performance tended to decrease with increasing shift-work duration. Among former shift-workers, the cognitive performance of the participant having stopped shift work more than 4 years ago seemed to be increased, suggesting a possible reversibility of effects.

However, another (smaller) study by Petru et al. (2005) found no negative effects on either cognitive or psychomotor performance; nor was there an increased risk of accidents. Härmä et al.'s (2006) study, unique in that it was an intervention study specifically designed for older workers, showed that a fast forward-rotating shift system improved psychomotor performance and alertness on the night shift and general well-being. The hormone melatonin decreases with age and may be related to poorer sleep and disrupted circadian rhythms (Karasek 2004; Hertoghe 2005). This has important implications for shift work. Most industries now have clear guidelines for shift work management. These include reduction in shift duration, reduction in continuous working time, limiting consecutive shifts and resting between shifts.

It is recognised that shift work appeared to increase fatigue in older workers because of the greater disturbance of circadian rhythms among older adults (Sit and Fisk 1999). However, lifestyle also contributes to fatigue, and younger workers may suffer a greater incidence of fatigue because of their lifestyles. It is clear that this is an area where more research is required, as it could have major implications in some occupations. Specific measures to reduce fatigue include adequate rest breaks taken in a suitable environment, providing facilities for and encouraging naps, and fatigue education.

In conclusion, older workers find shift work more difficult to cope with; and there is some evidence that errors increase after shift work more frequently among older than among younger workers. Shift work has a significant effect on cognitive function, and this appears to be increased in later life linked to an increased disturbance in circadian rhythms with age. This may lead to short-term effects on alertness, efficiency and memory, though the evidence is not conclusive. There is clearly a need for more research on the relationships among ageing, shift work and fatigue.

## 13.4 Summary and conclusions

It is clear that much of the decline in capacity noted here can be compensated for by modifications to the environment. Mental functional capacities such as precision and speed of perception may decrease or weaken with age, but these are more than compensated for by improvements in language use and the ability to process complex information. Motivation to learn is not age dependent, but depends on the organisation of incidence and opportunity for learning (Ilmarinen and Rantanen 1999). Wisdom and work experience increase with age. Even if more time is needed to adapt to and to learn new technologies, older workers are extremely reliable and bring with them other abilities that contribute to productivity. 'Tacit' knowledge will disappear from the workforce together with a vast reservoir of technical knowledge when older workers leave, unless there is a means for it to be passed on to younger colleagues. A similar case is made in the Future of Retirement Study by Harper and Leeson (2006), who point out that 'corporate DNA' is being removed from employers across the globe, particularly in response to early retirement schemes.

A key approach to tackling potential mental and physical decline with age is the concept of 'workability', which has also been extended to 'employability'. This means more than the ability to work; it is a much more holistic notion which embraces the interrelationships between the job itself and personal factors such as physical and mental health, motivation, skills, and the work environment, including not only the specific demands of the job but other factors.

The concept of workability emerged from studies in Finland in the 1990s, spearheaded by Ilmarinen (1998; see also Ilmarinen, Tuomi and Kockars 1997). From the early 1970s there had been early retirement programmes and a series of measures and legislation to reduce the age at which an unemployment pension could be claimed. The emphasis was on creating opportunities for younger people in the labour market – but, as it turned out, they did not necessarily take jobs in place of older people. In the 1990s in Finland, with one of Europe's most rapidly ageing populations and a negatively increasing dependency ratio, the economic downturn led to the need for a solution to the problem of unemployment in the 45 plus age group, in particular those aged 55–64. The workability programme was launched in 1998 and has been (and continues to be) taken up by many countries such as Australia, the US and Canada.

While there is no one definition of workability, Ilmarinen (2001) describes individual workability as 'a process of human resources in relation to work'. This process of workability is not static but changes during the life course of an individual. But changes also occur in the nature of work itself. When new technology or new methods of working are introduced, they affect the workability of an individual. Not every individual will be able to accommodate change at the same speed. Ageing workers have often been made the scapegoat for this mismatch of human resources and changing work demands.

The promotion of workability entails action on the part of both the individual and the workplace. Ilmarinen and Rantanen (1999) identify four different aspects: adjustments to the psychosocial work environment, adjustments to the physical environment, health and lifestyle promotion and the updating of skills. While workability promotion is a concept that applies to all ages, in the case of older workers this needs to be tailored to the effect of age on workability. Increasing and diversifying competence is one aspect of promoting workability. For the individual, examples might include training in new technologies, improved ergonomics, flexible working hours and health promotion. For the worksite, they might include implementation of good age-management strategies with appropriate training of supervisors, exercise programmes, and age-awareness and inclusion programmes. The physical and mental changes that occur with ageing can be compensated for if the workability approach is implemented. In practice any declines in aerobic capacity, cardiovascular function, skeletomuscular strength and endurance and dexterity can be accommodated and do not then pose problems for productivity or health and safety and do not affect people's ability to do their jobs (Shephard 1999; 2000). Ilmarinen suggests that workers should maintain normal age-related fitness levels and that physical workload should decline in parallel with the decline in physical capacity. There is, however, much variability at the individual level, which illustrates the need for individual assessment of workability.

The concept of workability has been refined in other cultural settings. In the UK, for example, the work of Ross and Harper 2009; Harper and Ross 2010 with oil workers developed the workability index to include work performance factors such as intrinsic job motivation, perceived competence and skill utilisation, in an attempt to include more psychological measures of well-being and capacity.

The concept of workability promotion covers precisely the adjustments needed to increase workability and ultimately greater employability. The focus shifts away from what workers cannot do towards what they can. The well-being of individuals and their quality of life are as important as their productivity and quality of work. This leads to greater employability. Employability refers to the relation of workability to society and the actions that need to be taken to raise levels of employment. It includes employment, education, labour market exit policies, social and health services and the prevention of age discrimination (Ilmarinen 2001). This concept has been endorsed by both the Faculty of Occupational Medicine of the Royal College of Physicians and the OECD (2006).

As the Global Commission on International Migration (2005) highlights, global ageing will intensify the world skills shortage and could generate severe competition on the global labour market. European countries in particular have relied heavily on immigrant labour to compensate as their own labour markets contract across a spectrum of occupations: health care, manufacturing, services, retail and IT. However, given the dramatic ageing forecast for transitional and developing economies, it is clear that OECD countries will need to look to the large skills base they already have within their own economies, and retain experienced older workers in their fifties and sixties.

# Part V
# Managing an Age-Diverse Workforce Across National Contexts

So far, we have discussed the nature and impact of age diversity mainly within the single national contexts of the UK, the US and Australia. We have not considered the impact of national context on the management of age diversity; and yet it makes sense that the characteristics of particular counties, such as the legislative environment, business system or culture, might affect how age diversity is managed. This final section of the book therefore compares age diversity in different national contexts.

In Chapter 14, Michael Muller-Camen and colleagues compare age management in the United Kingdom and Germany. These two countries are both within the European Union and so subject to the same EU Directive on age, and yet they have very different business systems and legislative environments.

In Chapter 15, Masa Higo and Jungui Lee compare the United States and Japan in order to investigate why it is that these two countries have different levels of older-worker participation in the workforce.

# 14

# The Impact of National Context on Managing Age Diversity: The Cases of the UK and Germany

*Michael Müller-Camen, Matt Flynn and Heike Schroeder*

## 14.1 Introduction

This chapter discusses the impact of global and European Union (EU) wide pressures on age management in the United Kingdom (UK) and Germany. Following Walker (1999), 'age management' refers to the overall management of an ageing workforce. Although employers have been advised to take younger workers into consideration when framing age-management policies (Employers Forum on Age 2006; Low Pay Commission 2004; Snape and Redman 2003), EU policies have been focused primarily on raising older people's economic activity (European Commission 2004). Accordingly, this research mainly concerns organisational initiatives to encourage older workers to remain in or re-enter work. Our focus on older workers is not meant to deny any discrimination experienced by younger workers, but focuses on how employers are reacting to government initiatives emanating from EU initiatives to bring older people into work.

Germany and Britain are representatives of two different business systems (inclusive corporatist versus arm's-length institutional), varieties of capitalism (coordinated market economy versus liberal market economy) and welfare regimes (conservative versus liberal). The aim of this chapter is to examine the extent to which these different institutional contexts have an impact on age management. The comparative assessment of policies and practices in the two countries is based on an analysis of the available empirical literature as well as on a secondary analysis of case studies and a number of expert interviews. In the next section we analyse current change pressures and then in the following section consider the impact on the British and German institutional contexts. Finally, we contrast and compare age-management practices at the organisational level in the two countries.

## 14.2 Age management, national institutions and change

It is widely assumed that globalisation, demographic developments and the viability of social security systems will have a significant impact on age management (Muller-Camen et al. 2011). Given the universal nature of these influences on the management of an ageing workforce, it is not surprising that a number of research projects conducted across Europe have come up with recommendations for age-management strategies. However, these often do not differentiate substantially between EU countries. For example, Naegele and Walker (2006) recommend that employers take an incremental approach to age management, starting with policies aimed at overcoming age barriers faced by older workers and moving gradually to comprehensive approaches which are holistic, aimed at prevention rather than redress, and address age issues faced by younger as well as older workers. Their study draws from the experience of organisations in 11 EU countries. Although the differences in age practices of organisations of different sizes and sectors are covered, the report does not highlight international variations.

There is a widespread assumption that the current model of youth-centric human resource management (HRM), characterised by direct or indirect discrimination against older workers (Snape and Redman 2003, Loretto and White 2006), is no longer viable (Schroder, Hofacker and Muller-Camen 2008; Walker, 1999) (see Figure 14.1). The alternative proposed is age-positive HRM (Department of Work and Pensions 2005), which is holistic, intergenerational and life-phase oriented.

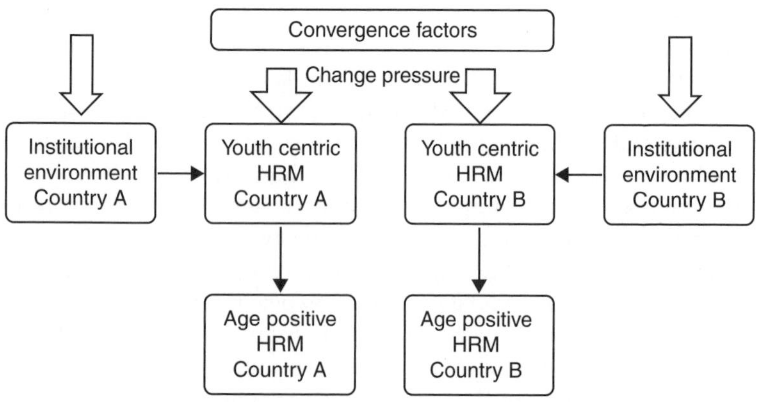


*Figure 14.1* Institutional characteristics for age management in UK and Germany

It contains practical measures such as lifelong learning; systematic change of positions; job design; active health and safety management; and flexible working options that enable people of different ages to work. In addition, it foresees the active recruitment and retention of older workers (Flynn and McNair 2007; Naegele and Walker 2006). However, at least to a certain extent, this literature seems to neglect the impact of divergent national institutions that filter the convergence pressures discussed above and thus may lead to the development of country-specific age-management practices.

Cross-cultural comparative research suggests that national institutional frameworks result in different human resource (HR) practices (Muller-Camen et al. 2004). Therefore, it can be assumed that organisational age-diversity policies and practices differ between business systems (Whitley 1999) and varieties of capitalism (Hall and Soskice 2001). Furthermore, given that the institutional context is in flux, as anti-age discrimination laws are being introduced and societal expectations of age-related HR practices are changing, a comparative analysis is also of theoretical interest, as comparative institutionalism assumes that national institutional environments are stable (Boyer and Hollingsworth 1997; Whitley 2005). However, whereas there is some macro-level economic and social policy research that compares countries (see, for example, Ebbinghaus 2006; Maltby et al. 2003), the age-management literature rarely considers international differences at the workplace level (for exceptions, see Brooke and Taylor 2005; Chiu et al. 2001). For example, the extension of working life may fit traditional practices in welfare systems where early retirement has never been widely practised, but its adoption may be institutionally more contested (Sanders and Tuschke 2007) in an institutional environment where early retirement has traditionally been widely practised.

This chapter compares and contrasts developments in a liberal market economy, the UK, and a coordinated market economy, Germany. As the two countries represent different economic and welfare models, we would expect different reactions to the challenges of globalisation, demographics and new legislation. As Table 14.1 indicates, the institutional framework for age management differs between Britain and Germany in terms of pension systems, incentives for retirement, the importance of external labour markets, employment security and industrial relations.

In order to contrast and compare HR policies and practices towards older workers and the impact of the national institutional environment

*Table 14.1* Institutional framework for age management

| 'Liberal market' UK economy | 'Coordinated market' German economy |
|---|---|
| Variety of occupational and private pensions | Dominance of state pension |
| Incentives for employment after pension age | Social security system provides incentives for early retirement |
| Importance of external labour markets | Strong internal labour markets in most large organisations |
| Low employment security | Relatively high employment security, but insider–outsider labour market |
| Relatively weak trade unions | Collective bargaining and co-determination |

on them in Britain and Germany, we review the available literature, undertake a secondary analysis of existing data sets and provide insights from a number of expert interviews conducted in both countries. There is currently no systematic comparison of age-diversity policies and practices at the workplace level in Germany and the UK. However, various research projects covering several European countries have produced case studies of workforce practices. The publicly available case studies from two that were recently conducted are be used for secondary analysis. One of these is the Eurofound database (http://www.eurofound.europa.eu/areas/populationandsociety/ageingworkforce.htm), whose collection is still ongoing. It contains about 200 case studies of organisations known for best practices in the area of age management and diversity from 27 countries. Twenty-one of these two- to three-page-long case studies are about German organisations and 20 cover British organisations. In addition, we analysed five UK and six German case studies from the RESPECT project (Lindley and Duell 2006). For this project, cases were again selected on the basis of best practice in age management and variation in terms of sector, occupation and qualification level (Lindley and Duell 2006, p. 9). In addition to the literature and this secondary analysis, the chapter is built on a number of expert interviews. Between autumn 2007 and spring 2008, six interviews were conducted with the government, pressure groups, trade unions and employer organisations in the UK, and 11 interviews in Germany with representatives from the government, an HR organisation, employer associations and trade unions, as well as members of research institutes and universities working in this area (for more details see Muller-Camen et al. 2011). The next section gives an overview of the institutional environments affecting age management in Britain and Germany that emerged from this data.

## 14.3 The institutional environment for age management in Britain and Germany

The employment rates of older workers in the UK have been higher than those in other European countries in recent decades, although lower than those some other developed economies such as the United States and Japan (OECD 2006). However, given the substantial skill shortages that the UK faces and problems in financing the welfare system, and an expectation that demographic developments will increase these pressures, the government is interested in increasing employment rates further, and aims to bring one million older people back into work (DWP 2005). As one UK informant noted, while the older-worker participation rate (particularly that of older men) has steadily increased since the turn of the millennium, the rise is consistent with increased participation of other workforce groups such as young workers, working parents, and people with disabilities. While employers are aware of government initiatives to increase older-worker participation, it was thought by both employer and union informants that economic conditions were the main reason for an increase in older-worker participation. In fact, it was noted that, even when faced with skills and labour shortages, UK employers are often unable to see older people as a potential resource.

> Some employers are [able to see older people as a potential resource], but not the majority. The majority wouldn't immediately think, I must look at hiring a different age group and that's going to solve my problem, in the first instance.
>
> (UK Employers' Forum on Age, EFA)

A major plank of the government's approach to this is to demonstrate the 'business case' for employers to eradicate ageism from the workplace by showing the organisational benefits of employing older workers (DWP 2001a). However, firms' receptiveness to the business case argument is mixed and highly dependent on short-term economic conditions (Duncan 2003). Furthermore, employers tend to be much less willing to recruit older applicants than to retain their existing older staff (McNair, Flynn and Dutton 2007). As one UK informant noted,

> I think that's because the employer only counts experience that's gained in my workplace.
>
> (UK Trades Union Congress, TUC)

In contrast to the UK, employment rates of older people in Germany have been relatively low over recent decades. This is explained by key characteristics of the German welfare system, which could be described as the polar opposite to those of the UK, namely, strong incentives for early exit from work, a low importance of lifetime education, a high rigidity of unemployment and an inflexible, highly regulated labour market (Hofäcker and Pollnerová 2006). More specifically, in contrast to the UK, strong labour market boundaries, the predominance of internal labour markets and the unavailability of vocational training for older employees make it much more difficult for unemployed older people to find jobs (Buchholz 2006). Nevertheless, those older people employed in large firms have a very high level of job security (Muller 1999). This is less a result of employment laws than of collective bargaining agreements, many of which stipulate that after a certain length of time in a job no ordinary dismissal of a long-serving employee is allowed (George, 2000).

In order to deal with the structural labour market problems the German economy has faced since the 1980s, generous early retirement schemes were introduced to cushion the impact of organisational restructuring and to alleviate youth unemployment (George 2000; Trampusch 2003). The rationale was well summarised by the German government expert we interviewed, who referred to a discussion some years ago between employer and trade union representatives at the German unemployment agency about whether a campaign to promote the employment of older workers should be prolonged.

> ... and then the labour market situation worsened and the employers asked the trade unionists: Whom should we fire? Would you like the young? Or would you prefer that we fire the old ones and they replied: Perhaps take again the older ones, as they are socially better protected and particularly as there will be a demographic change – we have to give the young people a chance.
>
> (German government: Ministry of Labour)

In some industries the combined efforts of companies, partners in the community and the state led to the development of early-retirement pathways that allowed employees to retire at the age of 55 with only minor financial penalties for their pensions (Trampusch 2003). However, growing problems with the financial sustainability of the German social security system and an anticipation of future skill shortages arising from demographic developments have led to a change of state policies and have also changed the attitudes of the social partners. This issue we now discuss in relation to both the UK and Germany.

### 14.3.1 Changing legislation

In both countries the growing financial problems of the social security system have led to legal changes that increased the pressure on older workers to continue their active participation in the labour market. In the UK, the basic state retirement pension has become even less generous than it already was (Golsch, Haardt and Jenkins 2006), there have been changes to unemployment and disability benefits, and the pension scheme in the public sector has changed. However, whereas one can argue that these changes are in line with the liberal UK welfare regime, there have been much more systemic changes in Germany (Lamping and Rüb 2004). This is not surprising given the very high financial costs of early retirement for the German social security system. Starting in the early 1990s, consecutive reforms of the pension system (Lamping and Rüb 2004), unemployment benefits and the social security system in general (Frerichs and Sporket 2007) shifted the costs of early retirement from the state to employers and individuals and thus made this pathway much less attractive. One outcome of these changes has been that the average age from which retirement pensions may be drawn in Germany increased from 60.8 years in 1996 to 62.3 years in 2005 (Brussig and Wojtkowski 2006, p.11). The average pension age is likely to increase further with a 2007 law that foresees a gradual increase of the state pension age from 65 to 67 between 2012 and 2029. That said, however, the UK average age of retirement has also steadily increased. In 2009 the average retirement age for men was 64.5 (just below the state pension age, SPA) and 62.4 for women (well above the SPA), up from their lowest points in 1994 for men (63 years) and in 1984 for women (60.7 years) (Office for National Statistics 2009).

Governments in both countries have been more reluctant to use the law to reduce age discrimination at the workplace than they have to reform their social security systems. In the UK, although in the 1990s there was already substantial evidence of discrimination against older workers (Taylor and Walker 1998), Conservative and Labour governments alike have followed a voluntarist approach and have tried to influence employers by making a business case in favour of employing older people (Duncan 2003; Taylor 2004). During interviews with UK experts, it was noted that the impetus for the new age-discrimination regulations came from the European Union. Although the Labour Party had made a manifesto commitment to legislate on age discrimination, it adopted the voluntarist approach taken by its predecessor when it came to office in 1997.

> So, Labour in opposition was pro age-discrimination law but as a rights issue and then decided in government in its first term not to legislate.
>
> (Age Concern England, ACE)

The impact of awareness campaigns has been limited, and research suggests that discriminatory employer behaviour towards older workers has not much changed, at least with regard to recruitment (McNair et al. 2004). Only as a result of the EU anti-discrimination Directive of 2000, which required Member States to transpose anti-discrimination standards into national law, was a national law proscribing age discrimination passed in 2006. The draft legislation triggered a substantial public debate (and a European Court of Justice legal petition from the Age Concern group Heyday), with the most contentious issue being whether there should be a default retirement age of 65 (Sargeant 2005).

Meanwhile, the implementation of the EU directive in German law, which began with a draft bill in 2001, was even more controversial than in the UK, for at least three reasons First, instead of covering just age, all grounds for discrimination listed by the EU were dealt with by one comprehensive law. Second, the first draft legislation by the then coalition Social Democratic–Green Government went beyond the minimum standards demanded by the EU. Third, equality is one of the few areas of labour law where UK standards have been higher, and German standards lower, than those prescribed by the EU. According to legal experts, the 2006 General Act on Equal Treatment (Allgemeines Gleichbehandlungsgesetz, AGG) is not meeting the requirements of the Directive and thus there may be many legal challenges. The main reason for this is that several labour laws are still in effect that treat age as a legitimate criterion for differentiation between employees (Schmidt 2008). For example, age is still a selection criterion for any dismissal for economic reasons (Skidmore 2004). However, in practice the impact of the law on HR practices is not comparable with what has been suggested for the UK. German employers and particularly HR managers were critical of the law before its introduction because the law was considered to increase the bureaucratic burden, especially in recruitment and promotion processes (DGFP 2006). This view is similar to the one expressed by the UK employer group, the Confederation of British Industry (CBI), but not the HR managers' Chartered Institute of Personnel and Development (CIPD). German experts, however, stated that the regulation so far has only had a small effect on HR processes. It is also interesting to note that the anti-discrimination law does not play a role in the German age-management discourse. Overall, the impact of EU-driven age regulations on HRM is felt much less in Germany than in the UK.

One reason for the differences between the two countries' experiences with the implementation of age-discrimination regulations, as cited by UK and German informants, was the difference in their legal systems. It was noted in the expert interviews that the scope and application of the new regulations in the UK is still uncertain, as the courts have issued only a few opinions about the law. Accordingly, the high level of uncertainty in the UK is leading employers to err on the side of caution in order to comply with the law. Some informants, for example, noted that the new regulations have been used by the government to encourage employers to accept the business case for age diversity (see Chapter 2).

> I think employers have become much more risk averse and I think that [is] a symptom of the way that the regulations were sold. I guess with all regulation that comes in there is a balance between exultation and penalty.
>
> (The Age and Employment Network, TAEN)

Experts also cited the relatively weak employment protection in Britain, as compared with that in other European countries, as an explanation for the greater effects of the anti-discrimination regulations on British workplaces than on workplaces in other European countries.

> People are far more likely to use discrimination law when they're unhappy with a situation at work and employers therefore have to deal with that as a much higher risk than perhaps employers in other European countries.
>
> (EFA)

Differences between the German and the British industrial relations structures might therefore mediate the relative effect of the age-discrimination regulations in the two countries. While the strong German industrial relations structures might buffer the effect of the regulations as conflicts are dealt with internally, the lack of a similarly strong system in Britain might lead employers to fear that employees call on external tribunals to solve age discrimination-related cases.

### 14.3.2 Active labour market policies, awareness and research

In addition to legal changes, the British government as well as the German government used other means to increase the employment rate of older workers. Among these are active labour market measures and awareness campaigns. To start with active labour market policies, in both countries specific schemes targeting older workers were introduced only after 2000. In the UK the 'New Deal 50 plus' programme was introduced, which combines support for job-seeking with in-work income support and training. It is an extension of the New Deal programme which initially targeted workers aged under 25 and is open only to those who have been unemployed for six months. This has proved particularly challenging for older workers, who find a return to work after long-term unemployment difficult. The UK government has also introduced tax credits specifically targeted at low-income workers who are over 50 years old in order to offset loss of income support. Work-Based Learning for Adults also falls into this category (Frerichs and Taylor 2005). German equivalents are the 2002 Job-AQTIV Law that promotes vocational training for older workers and foresees wage subsidies. Together with the so-called Hartz labour market reforms implemented in 2003 that reduced the maximum duration of unemployment benefits, the German government has adopted a carrot and stick approach that is similar to policies in the UK (Frerichs and Taylor 2005).

As for awareness campaigns, both governments became active at the turn of the twenty-first century. The UK government published a Code of Practice in Age Diversity and the later updated Age Diversity at Work (DWP 2001a), and an Age Positive website (www.agepositive.gov.uk). Meanwhile, in Germany the Federal Employment Agency launched the '50 plus – they can do it' image campaign in 2006. Also noteworthy is the 1999–2003 Demotrans project which aimed to heighten awareness and present solutions to help firms cope with demographic developments. Whereas in the UK there seems to be at least some cohesion among the various legal, labour market and awareness campaigns, Frerichs and Sporket (2007) argue that the German government has no explicit or integrated 'older worker policy'. Instead, different ministries are involved and some of the interventions, and legal measures contradict each other – a point that was also supported by the expert interviews.

### 14.3.3 Social partners and the age lobby

Under the coordinated German system, employers' associations and trade unions are much more influential than in the UK. Whereas up to the 1990s the German government, employers and trade unions promoted early retirement as a means to solve labour market problems, the emphasis has since shifted to keeping older workers in employment (Frerichs and Sporket 2007). Despite this paradigm shift, recent collective bargaining agreements still support early retirement pathways. For example, in the 2005 agreement on demography in the German Steel Industry, it was explicitly agreed to lobby the government on the extensions of the part-time retirement law beyond 2009. Nevertheless, over recent years the federation of German employers' associations (Bundesvereinigung Deutscher Arbeitgeberverbände, BDA) and the German trade union congress (Deutscher Gewerkschaftsbund, DGB) have initiated research projects that examined best practice in age management and on this basis have drafted guidelines for employees or works councillors on how to deal with an ageing workforce (BDA 2004; DBG 2005). The major difference between these two interest groups appears to be that employers favour a voluntary, awareness-raising approach, whereas trade unions are interested in regulations supporting the retention of older workers in collective bargaining agreements at the industry or the regional level, and works agreements at the workplace level (Frerichs and Sporket 2007). In Germany, most collective bargaining agreements contain measures which increase employment security and protect salaries in the cases of restructuring related to age and tenure (Bispinck 2005). In contrast, the 2007 Collective Agreement on Managing Demographic Change in the iron and steel industry of northern Germany, which foresees a mandatory analysis of the age structure and the implementation of measures based on it, is still unique. Favourable economic conditions, a rapidly ageing workforce (without changes, the average employee age will increase to 53 in 2015) and a very determined trade union have led to an agreement that combines policies for younger employees, older employees and early retirement options.

In the UK, the main ideological divide on the issue of age lies between the employers' organisation, the CBI, on the one hand, and the TUC and CIPD on the other. The CBI has seen age regulations as a cost imposition on employers, particularly with regard to mandatory retirement, which is described as a way for employers to dismiss underperforming older employers with dignity (CBI 2003). It also sees government intervention as largely redundant, given that employers are responding to economic factors by changing their approaches to managing older workers (CBI 2006).

> They've seen it as basically a regulatory agenda and they've been there to fight off regulation rather than engage in a dialogue about how you manage an ageing workforce.
>
> (ACE)

Partly in order to counteract the CBI's opposition to the government's age-diversity agenda, Age Concern established a lobbying organisation of (primarily large) employers to champion age-neutral approaches to HR. The Employer's Forum on Age became an independent organisation in 2002, in part because employer constituents felt Age Concern's policies on work overemphasised older workers' interests.

After discussing the institutional environment and the position of key national actors, we now compare and contrast policies and practices towards older workers at the organisational level.

## 14.4 Organisational policies and practices towards older workers

### 14.4.1 Current practices in the UK

The academic literature suggests that discrimination against older workers is still widespread in the UK (Duncan 2003; McNair and Flynn 2005; Sargeant 2005; Snape and Redman 2003; Taylor 2004). For example, although there are fewer specific age limits, there are often 'inferred preferences' in relation to age; older employees tend to receive lower ratings in performance appraisals; they have less access to training and development opportunities; and they are more likely to be passed over for promotion and selected for redundancy. UK informants talked about the double approach employers take to performance-managing older workers. On the one hand, managers are loath to identify deficiencies in older workers' performance, and are often inclined to allow poor performers to 'coast' into retirement.

> I am sure that what you have now are people who really aren't quite up to their job. If they are in mid-career they are more likely to be managed out of their job, if they are two years away from retirement age the manager is more likely just to not make a fuss.
>
> (ACE)

Managers therefore believe that overlooking poor performance provides older workers with a certain amount of job security. However, it was also noted that employers who, implicitly or explicitly, allow people to coast into retirement may find other ways to release poor performers while avoiding the process of formal dismissal.

> I think that is going to be, realistically, pretty difficult to shift as a culture because it is just so much hassle for a manager and distressing for all involved to manage someone out through a competency process or through engineering a redundancy or whatever.
>
> (ACE)

Further, employees with declining importance often miss out on training opportunities that would enable them to improve their performance, and in turn, job security. Informants did not feel that employers' approaches to performance managing older workers were motivated solely by ageism but rather reflected weaknesses in the performance-management process. Line managers frequently lack faith in appraisals, regardless of the ages of staff, and therefore do not feel it is worth the hassle to conduct uncomfortable conversations with poor performers who are close to retirement.

Incentives for good performance may also be linked with benefits that are perceived to be attractive to younger rather than older workers.

> A line manager might need to be aware that, as we discussed a little bit earlier, that more senior people may not have the same expectation or demands. They might have automatically absorbed from the culture or what they've seen before, no point in asking. I've finished. I've got to the end of the line in my career. The last time I got promoted was ... I should know it all now. Where can I go to from here?
>
> (CIPD)

The impact of age-awareness campaigns in promoting age-friendly workplaces is limited, as 'age management' is barely on the agenda of senior managers, and stereotypes about old workers' abilities are still widespread among employers, management and younger employees (Brooke and Taylor 2005; Loretto and White 2006). Age management is still perceived as primarily an issue which is relevant only to the HR department of an organisation. However, other parts of organisations are beginning to take an interest in the issue. Functions which were mentioned included finance, which has an interest in minimising pension and retirement costs; legal, which has a stake in managing the organisation's approach to the new age-discrimination regulations; and marketing, which is interested in matching employees' and customers' age profiles.

UK informants felt that the relatively low level of influence HR directors exert in UK organisations contributes to the limited importance of age management as a business issue. Nevertheless, according to the 2004 Workplace and Employment Relations Survey (WERS), 96 per cent of all workplaces with 100 or more employees in the UK have formal written equal opportunities policies or policies on managing diversity. Although the grounds of discrimination most commonly covered were sex, race and disability, age was also important, with 68 per cent of policies including it. However, only a minority of workplaces with more than ten employees that had an equal opportunity policy monitored or reviewed recruitment and selection, promotion or relative pay rates with reference to age (Kersley et al. 2005). More recently evidence suggests that there had been little improvement in these figures in advance of the age-discrimination regulations (Metcalf and Meadows 2006).

A 2005 survey of HR managers found that age measures adopted by about half of the organisations surveyed are in addition to an age-diversity policy, a ban on age factors in recruitment, a review of service-related benefits and a flexible working policy covering all workers (Parry and Tyson 2006). However, it is questioned whether formal policies are implemented by junior and middle managers on the ground (McNair and Flynn 2005; McVittie, McKinlay and Widdicombe 2003). UK informants felt that line managers' neglect of age-management issues reflect the relatively low importance British employers attach to HR issues. Line managers have few incentives, especially short-term ones, to ensure that age-diversity policies are implemented.

> Most line and operating managers, especially once you get out of the HR Department, have very short-term business objectives and they have the HR staff piled in on top of them but their performance is not usually judged about how well do they manage their human resources, it is did they meet their sales targets. Obviously you need your people working for you in order to meet your objectives but the first question is did you meet your objectives? Did you meet your business objectives?
>
> (TAEN)

It was thought that middle managers could play an important role in disseminating HR policies, including those on age. Middle managers were described by the CIPD informant as the 'marzipan layer' of an organisation which could improve the lines of communications between HR departments and line managers.

So far we have painted a relatively homogeneous picture. However, age policies differ according to sector, size and labour market conditions (McNair and Flynn 2005, p. 21). Already for some years the retail sector has taken a positive stance in employing older workers, although this is mainly limited to large employers, and largely restricted to front-line jobs (McNair and Flynn 2005). Nevertheless, targeting older employees for very low-level vulnerable positions might only reinforce ageist stereotypes (Taylor and Walker 2003).

### 14.4.2 Current practices in Germany

As in the UK, academic observers in Germany found widespread discrimination against old employees (Becker, Bobritchev and Henseler 2004; Naegele and Krämer 2001, p. 71; Rump 2003). More than half of German firms have no employees over the age of 50. Training focuses on young employees; and older employees have a much lower participation rate, although the level of qualification explains this at least to some extent (Bellmann and Leber 2003). An informant of the German trade union organisation, the DGB, emphasised that 'qualification beats age' when it comes to employing older people, whereby highly skilled older individuals tend not to be disadvantaged vis-à-vis their younger counterparts. Lowly qualified individuals, regardless of their age, suffer from a clear disadvantage. In particular, the jobs of those with low qualifications are narrowly designed, do not provide enough challenges and thus lead to extended phases of non-learning, as is also shown by Morschhäuser's (2006) case studies. Furthermore, increasing work demands have increased stress and led to workplaces where employees cannot 'grow old' (Buck und Dworschack 2003, pp. 36–8). Experience is often not valued. This, however, appears to depend on the hierarchical level, where the experience of top management employees is valued much more highly than the experience and tacit knowledge of production and middle-management workers. An expert representing the German Association for Personnel Managers (Deutsche Gesellschaft für Personalführung, DGFP) mentioned that former senior managers often remain integrated in their organisations through consulting roles.

In Germany, older applicants have a much smaller chance of being hired than younger ones (Büsch, Dahl and Dittrich 2004). In 2003 only 17 per cent of all newly recruited employees were aged 45 or older (Vogler-Ludwig 2005, p. 12). Survey evidence also suggests that

10 per cent of all firms employing 20 or more workers agree with the statement that they generally do not recruit older applicants (Brussig 2005). Given the widespread discrimination against older workers suggested by the literature cited above, one wonders whether German firms have any formal policies to support this group of employees. The representative 2002 survey by the Institute for Labour Market and Employment Research (Institut für Arbeitsmarkt und Berufsforschung, IAB) of HR policies specifically designed for old workers suggests that mixed-age work groups have been implemented by only one third of medium- and large-sized (with 500 plus employees) organisations. Also, training courses specifically designed for older employees are offered only in 4 per cent of these organisations. Only 13 per cent of the survey participants reported efforts to adapt job content and performance measurement to the potentially changed situation of older workers (Bellmann et al. 2003). The informant from the DGFP pointed out that, although age diversity is of high strategic importance to HR managers in the biggest German companies, organisations lag behind on the implementation of corresponding HR measures. The expert from Dortmund University emphasised:

> Most bigger companies in Germany now do something about the issue of demographic change. They have a working group or a strategy, but you never know what they do exactly. ... Certain issues or topics are picked up by personnel managers and they take a look at another company, or they deal with age management that might be quite interesting. So they also take this subject and try to do something about that and we can observe that in Germany at the moment.
>
> (Dortmund University)

Even though unemployed older workers have a disadvantage vis-à-vis younger and highly skilled individuals, most old employees enjoy a relatively high level of employment protection, which means that it is almost impossible to dismiss them and only generous company or state monetary incentives can entice them to leave employment before retirement age. For the implementation of early retirement policies, employers need and currently also receive support from employee representatives at the plant and company levels, as well as from trade unions at the industry level (Aleksandrowicz 2005). The same point was also emphasised by an expert from the DGB, who mentioned that trade unions have a different perspective on the usefulness of early retirement options. One of the most important early retirement tools is *Altersteilzeit* (part-time employment prior to retirement), which aims to facilitate the transition to retirement by allowing employees to reduce their working hours with generous compensation of some of the lost earnings. However, instead of a gradual shift into retirement by working 50 per cent throughout the *Altersteilzeit*, most employees (and employers) use the block model, which envisages a few years of full-time work by employees followed by the same number of years in inactivity though they remain officially part of the workforce before entering retirement. The German government, however, has abolished this model and started to phase it out in 2010, although the minister in charge has suggested that a revised version should be introduced. However, an expert from the DGFP mentioned that firms are currently looking for alternative early retirement options that will be company-financed. The informant from Dortmund University added that some companies discuss the option of lifetime working accounts, which enables organisations to exploit employees while they are young and still deemed productive, and to retire them early in a cost-neutral way. According to him, the 'deficit model', which assumes that older employees are less productive than younger ones, therefore still exists in the perception of many employers.

At this point it is worth noting differences between industries in the treatment of old employees. Whereas the IT and software industry is known for its youth-centric HR style, many medium-size manufacturing firms have successfully integrated old and young workers and created an age-diverse employment structure (Köchling et al. 2000). Although the IAB survey suggests that the incidence of formal age-management practices declines with firm size, this also applies to early retirement. For example, whereas the part-time early retirement option is used by 86 per cent of firms with 500 or more employees, only 8 per cent of those with between 8 and 19 employees use it. According to the Bertelsmann Foundation expert, there are three explanations for this. Early retirement is expensive, it is too difficult for small firms to administer, and there is much less pressure from works councils, which often do not exist in small German firms, to introduce early retirement.

### 14.4.3 Differences between British and German practices

The national literature cited above makes it difficult to assess the relative degree of age discrimination and the incidence of policies that foster the employment of older people in Britain and Germany. Nevertheless, there is at least some comparative data on employment rates, action programmes covering older workers, training and flexible working. To start with employment rates, since the 1980s those of older workers have been much lower in Germany than in the UK. However, in both countries the trend of decreasing labour market participation rates has been stopped and has been reversed in recent years (see Tables 14.2 and 14.3). Noteworthy is a steep increase in employment for men aged 55–64 in Germany between 2003 and 2008 from 47.1 per cent to 61.7 per cent. The German experts consulted had no definitive explanation for this very strong increase, but speculated that it may be due to a combination of changes in the social security law, fewer opportunities for early retirement, skill shortages in some areas and demographic developments.

UK informants generally felt that economic growth and skill shortages in some sectors and regions are the main causes of increased older activity among older people in this period.

> The reason why UK employment of over-50s has increased in the last decade, first and most important is probably the state of the economy. Obviously the economy has been growing and labour market demands have been growing and it has also been stable.
>
> (ACE)

*Table 14.2* The employed percentage of men aged 55–64 in Germany, the UK and the EU-15 countries, 2003–8

| | 2003 | 2004 | 2005 | 2006 | 2007 | 2008 |
|---|---|---|---|---|---|---|
| Germany | 47.1 | 50.7 | 53.6 | 56.5 | 59.4 | 61.7 |
| UK | 64.9 | 65.4 | 65.7 | 66.0 | 66.1 | 67.7 |
| **EU 15** | 51.8 | 52.5 | 53.4 | 54.4 | 55.1 | 56.0 |

*Source*: OECD (2009).

*Table 14.3* The employed percentage of women aged 55–64 in Germany, the UK and the EU-15 countries, 2003–8

| | 2003 | 2004 | 2005 | 2006 | 2007 | 2008 |
|---|---|---|---|---|---|---|
| Germany | 30.9 | 33.0 | 37.6 | 40.3 | 43.4 | 46.0 |
| UK | 46.3 | 47.3 | 48.1 | 49.0 | 49.0 | 49.0 |
| **EU 15** | 32.0 | 33.2 | 35.5 | 36.7 | 38.0 | 39.9 |

*Source*: OECD (2009).

> I mean you will get different responses to labour market needs and maybe at different skill levels as well and more activity going on in the areas where skills are very scarce and difficult to recruit. An employer might lean over backwards a bit more to retain them.
>
> (CIPD)

One informant noted that employers are finding that their expected labour pool (young, single applicants) is drying up, and they are compelled to look for other sources of labour, such as working parents, immigrants, ex-offenders and older workers. Because employers have experience of their own staff, and know their competencies and experience, retained older workers are often seen (as one UK informant put it) as the 'best of the worst' potential applicants. This, however, may not be the case with regard to recruiting older job seekers, who may be more vulnerable to ageist stereotypes. The same point was made by one of the German experts, suggesting that there are no differences between the two countries in this respect.

Comparative data from the OECD suggests that, with respect to participation in job- and career-related training, German older workers are more disadvantaged than UK workers. According to 1999 OECD data reported by Hofäcker and Pollnerová (2006, p. 46), the participation rate of younger people (25–9 years old) in Germany is 3.32 times higher than for older people (50–4), whereas in the UK the equivalent 'age discrimination quota' figure is only 1.55.

Employer surveys (for example, Metcalf and Meadows 2006) indicate that very few organisations set explicit age limits on access to training. However, as some informants noted, older workers may be more reluctant to participate in training than their younger colleagues, particularly if they left school early.

> There is definitely an issue about people who left school at 14 and have never been in touch with education. [It's] about one job for life and if you've not been in a culture of retraining and moving on over the years.
>
> (ACE)

Employers may collude with reluctant older workers who avoid training participation. It was also thought that employers need to tailor training more towards older workers' needs and motivations in order to raise participation rates.

> So it's an answerable question because although they are primed to do that it will then depend on the individual's belief in themselves to be able to go back to work, which is very important, and then also the level of training and how it is actually delivered. One thing we come across, and this is nothing new, it's been brought out quite often, is how you train different age groups or how you train different individuals.
>
> (DWP)

More directly, comparable data emerges from the British and German best-practice case studies developed by the pan-European Eurofound and RESPECT research projects (see section 14.2). In terms of policies and practices reported by these cases, the German organisations covered emphasise on work organisation, work design, ergonomics and health, possibly partly because about half of the examples are manufacturing firms. Interestingly, it is reported that three of the German firms included, Bosch, KSB and Deutsche Bank, still use early retirement. Whereas ergonomics, well-being and health are also popular measures among the UK cases, job design and work organisation are not. Instead, awareness raising, flexible retirement and flexible working policies are emphasised. Three other differences are worth pointing out. First, about half of the UK organisations are from the public sector, whereas in the German sample this is true for at most a quarter. Second, several of the German case studies mention that the introduction of age-management measures, particularly those in the area of work organisation, took place within public or state-funded applied research projects. Third, whereas some UK organisations covered reported that unions were formally consulted, several of the German cases reported that members of the works council took part in the steering committee that developed and/or implemented age-diversity measures. This involvement goes beyond the law. One of our experts even suggested that in Germany most innovative age-management practices have been initiated by works councils. Although other experts did not confirm this, they at least suggested that organisations with strong employee representatives are more likely to practice age management, partly because they have no alternative in the face of a rapidly ageing workforce.

Not only the measures but also the change drivers reported by the British and German best-practice cases differ. In the UK cases, the age-management drivers most frequently reported are a general emphasis on equal employment and diversity, skills shortages and the likely impact of the 2006 age-discrimination legislation. Although some of these drivers were also mentioned by German case-study firms, the basic driver seems to be fundamentally different. Most of the German cases perceive themselves to be good employers, to offer employment stability and to have a very low level of labour turnover despite stable or declining employment levels. None of them mentioned the German anti-discrimination legislation, which was already discussed when the case studies were conducted, but instead pointed to legislation that increased the retirement age and made early retirement less financially viable. Given the very restrictive German dismissal law, these firms therefore have to deal with a rapidly ageing workforce. Thus, the means adopted are less about making the organisation more attractive for older people but more about finding ways to cope with this problem. This includes, for example, lifetime working-hours accounts, in which employees can save overtime for early retirement. Interestingly, some of the local government organisations as well as large formerly state-owned utility firms in the UK sample that in the past relied extensively on early retirement mentioned the need to move away from such a culture as a motivation for change, and in some ways they resemble the majority of German cases. Given this pressure and the direct impact of government policies, it is probably not a surprise that about half of the UK cases come from the public sector.

## 14.5 Summary and conclusions

Institutional theory often assumes long-term stability and neglects change. The example of demographic change and its impact on national institutions such as discrimination and social security legislation suggests that institutional environments can sometimes change quickly. This leads to changes at the organisational level. However, although supra-national pressures for convergence are strong, they result in similar but not identical changes at the national level. Consequently, although some parallel developments can be observed at the organisational level in the UK and Germany, the management of older workers at the organisational level differs, and changes are path-dependent. This is particularly shown in the following areas of trade union influence, government intervention and the impact of the law.

First, trade union influence on the development of age-management policies, both in the UK and in Germany, has been double-edged. On the one hand, trade unions have supported the perpetuation of early retirement options, both to preserve the 'intergenerational contract' between older and younger workers and to protect older employees' 'right to retire'. On the other hand, trade unions have also lobbied for HR policies which support older workers staying in employment until retirement age. This is especially so in sectors (such as the German steel sector, mentioned above) where the membership base has exerted pressure on the union to do so. Given the predominance of a tripartite approach at the industry or national level in Germany, as well as a greater influence of employee representatives at the workplace level, German unions may be more successful in pressing for the adoption of age-management practices.

Second, the effect of government or state initiatives that aim to encourage older workers' labour market participation differs. Both the UK and Germany have adopted age-discrimination regulations. However, feedback from national informants in both countries indicates that the regulations have had a greater impact on employer behaviour in the UK than in Germany. In the absence of case law, UK employers seem to be uncertain about the scope and application of the new regulations and therefore adopt a stricter approach to the legislation than their counterparts in Germany. Risk aversion may therefore play a greater role in HR policy in the UK than in Germany. Both the UK and the German governments have carried out employer outreach publicity campaigns aimed at demonstrating the 'business case' for age-diversity policies. In the UK, government has had somewhat greater success in changing employer attitudes. This appears to be largely the result of what one informant described as the 'carrot and stick' approach. The 'carrot' is the potential of extending working life for older workers to remedy skills and labour shortages faced by employers, especially in the south of England. The 'stick' is the greater sensitivity shown by UK employers than their German counterparts with regard to the age-discrimination regulations.

Third, the longevity of early retirement incentives in Germany will also constitute a strong pull factor that still leads older workers in the country to exit the workforce early. In contrast, the British government has phased out state-financed early labour market exit options. Instead it offers modest incentives for older workers to stay in work longer. These include, for example, tax credits and the augmentation of state pension entitlements for those individuals who postpone their labour market exit.

However, these pull factors are only half of the story of older workers' attitudes towards work and retirement. Push factors, employer actions which lead employees to premature retirement, are also important. Institutional ageism has been identified in both countries but is manifested in different ways. In Germany, for example, the internal labour market system on the one hand creates job security but on the other hand might also constitute a disincentive for lifelong learning and skill updating. Age-based pay structures can lead to perceptions that older workers are less value for money than their younger colleagues. As a result, employers may view older workers as less productive employees, creating an incentive for early retirement programmes. On the other hand, short-term economic pressures may lead employers in Britain to view older employees only as a 'reserve army', reducing pressure for long-term approaches to increasing economic activity among older workers.

# 15
# Working Longer in National Contexts: Comparing Japan and the United States

*Masa Higo and Jungui Lee*

This chapter aims to contribute to our understanding of age-diversity management by clarifying the importance of identifying older workers within their national contexts. While receiving relatively little attention outside cross-national comparative literature, national contexts are powerful determinants of individuals' labour market behaviours over the course of their working lives (Freeman 2007). Particularly for older workers, national contexts powerfully shape opportunities and decisions at the workplace and in the labour market, including those related to retirement and continued employment beyond conventional retirement ages (Walker 2005).

This chapter focuses on the national contexts of Japan and the United States. These two national contexts exemplify substantially different models of age management in the workforce at large, and older workers' labour market behaviours and prospects in particular. Both Japan and the US today are among the largest and most mature economies in the world. In management and policy literature, much has been said about the ageing of the population and of the workforce of these two countries. As will be discussed later, however, labour-force participation rates among older workers, particularly men, are substantially higher in Japan than in the US. That is, workers, men in particular, in Japan's national context remain in the workforce longer than do those in the US national context.

This chapter aims to illustrate the importance of the national contexts by discussing how their differences account for the gap in older people's labour-force participation rates. Some factors distinctive to Japan's national context contribute to the tendency for workers in Japan to remain in the workforce longer than those in the US.

National contexts comprise a wide range of broad structural conditions surrounding individuals' working lives over time. Such structural conditions, largely external to individual workers' control, are often taken for granted by individual workers (Freeman 2007). This chapter focuses on three main components of the two countries' national contexts: (*a*) demography, (*b*) national labour market institutions, and (*c*) public policies. This chapter discusses, for the first component, how Japan and the US differ from one another in the level of demographic pressure to increase the aggregate hours of labour supplied by older workers. For the second, we discuss differences in national labour market institutions constraining or enabling workers' continued employment in later life. For the third, we examine differences in the role of government intervention in the labour market aiming to promote older workers' participation beyond conventional retirement age. The goal of this chapter is to clarify how these differences in national context help to explain why workers in Japan remain in the labour force longer than those in the US. The discussion presented in this chapter may be useful generally for understanding how national contexts contribute to promoting and constraining age diversity in the workforce on a national level.

This chapter first establishes that workers in Japan remain in the workforce longer than those in the US by presenting recent data on both countries' older worker labour-force participation rates. Second, the chapter describes the differences between the two countries in each of the three components of the national contexts. It also explains how each of the differences helps to explain the gap between the labour-force participation rates of Japanese older workers and their US counterparts. The chapter concludes by summarising its main argument for the importance of national contexts in managing age diversity in the workplace. It also briefly introduce Esping-Andersen's (1990) and Holliday's (2000) theoretical models of the role of public policy in moderating the labour market, which facilitates our understanding of national contextual differences between Japan and the US.

## 15.1 Older worker labour force participation

Older workers both in Japan and the US remain in the labour force longer than those in most other industrialised countries today (OECD 2009b). In 2008 the labour-force participation rate for those aged 60 and older (including men and women) was 30.2 per cent for Japan and 25.8 per cent for the United States. These figures are much higher than those for the United Kingdom (16.7 per cent), Germany (10.4 per cent, Italy (7.6 per cent), and France (5.7 per cent) in the same year. Of all 30 OECD countries, Japan stands out as the only large-scale industrialised country with a mature economy today with a substantially higher labour-force participation rate among older workers (age 60 and older) than the United States. As of 2008, for the older worker labour-force participation rate, Japan ranked third and the US ranked seventh among OECD countries (OECD 2009b).

In most industrialised countries today, the age groups 60–4 and 65–9 are particularly important in connection with components of national contexts that affect labour market behaviours among older people (Hardy 2006; Schulz and Binstock 2008). Labour-force participation rates among each of these two age groups are higher for Japan than for the US. As Figure 15.1 shows, in 2008 the labour-force participation rate of the 60–4 age group was 59.8 per cent for Japan and 54.1 per cent for the US. For the 65–9 age group in the same year, the rates of both countries are lower but remain substantially higher for Japan (37.4 per cent) than for the US (30.7 per cent) (ILO 2009).

The gap between the labour-force participation rates for workers aged 60 and older in Japan and the US is much greater when just males are compared than when male and female workers are grouped together (ILO 2009). As Figure 15.1 shows, for the 60–4 age group the participation rate for males in 2008 was 76.4 percent for Japan and 59.9 percent for the US For the 65–9 age group in the same year, the participation

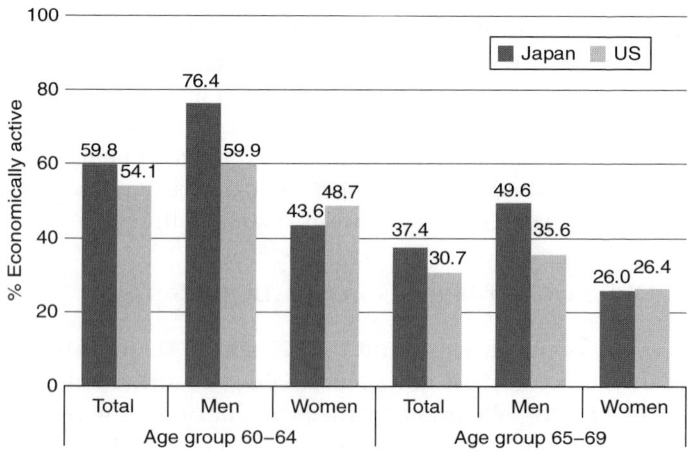


*Figure 15.1* Japan and the US compared: percentage of economically active population by gender and age group, 2008
*Source*: Based on data drawn from ILO (2009).

rates in both countries were lower, but again remained substantially higher for Japanese males (49.6 per cent) than for US males (35.6 per cent). For these age groups, nearly one half of Japanese males were still in the labour force whereas in the US the level was well below one half (OECD 2009b).

In Japan a larger fraction of older workers in the labour force are employed on part-time or temporary contractual bases (non-regular employment) than in the US (Higo and Yamada 2009; Williamson and Higo 2009). As will be discussed later, in the national context of Japan part-time and temporary employment opportunities, as opposed to full-time, permanent or regular employment, are more available for older workers than in the US (Japan Institute for Labour Policy and Training 2009; OECD 2004).

## 15.2 Demography: ageing of the population and the workforce

One of the clearest differences found between the national contexts of Japan and the US is in the levels of demographic pressure on the countries' workforces and national economic conditions. Differences in this component of the national contexts help to explain why workers in Japan remain in the workforce longer than those in the US. Whereas both Japan and the US have experienced ageing of the population and of the workforce, the impacts of current and projected demographic changes are substantially greater for Japan than for the US. In contrast to the US, over the next few decades Japan is projected to experience depopulation, with a shrinking of the workforce size and a decline in national economic productivity. The demographic pressures to retain older workers in the labour force are greater for Japan and for the US These greater demographic pressures for Japan have generated a greater need for the country to retain workers in the labour force as long as possible (Williamson and Higo 2009).

Currently, Japan has the oldest population of all 30 OECD countries, including the US, in terms of both the median age of the total population and the percentage of the total population that is aged 65 and older. As at 2008, the median age of the population was 44.7 for Japan and 36.5 for the US, which made Japan the oldest and the US the 23rd oldest of all OECD countries (United Nations 2009). In 2008 the percentage of the population aged 65 and older was 22.8 per cent for Japan and 12.9 per cent for the US. This percentage for Japan is the highest of all OECD countries, followed by Germany (20.4 per cent) and Italy (20.3 per cent). Unlike Japan, the US is younger than many OECD countries; the average percentage for all OECD countries is 14.6 per cent (OECD 2009b).

Over the past several decades, Japan has also experienced much faster demographic changes than the US. It is projected that it will take the US about 69 years (from 1944 to 2013) for the percentage of the population aged 65 and older to rise from 7 per cent to 14 per cent of the total population. By contrast, in Japan not only has this demographic change already happened but it occurred in only 26 years, from 1970 to 1996 – much faster than the projection for the US (United Nations 2009). Including the US, most industrialised countries today have had many decades to adjust to changing age structures. For instance, it took 115 years in France (from 1865 to 1980) for the population aged 65 and older to rise from 7 per cent to 14 per cent of the total population, and 85 years in Sweden (from 1890 to1975) (United Nations 2009).

Increases in life expectancy, decreases in the childbirth rate and a combination of these demographic factors are the main drivers for population ageing (Lloyd-Sherlock 2010). The estimated average life expectancy at birth of the Japanese in 2007 was 82.02 years, an extension of 20.75 years since 1950. That of the US in 2007 was 78.0 years, an extension of 9.8 years over the same period (United Nations 2009). While the total fertility rate in 2008 was 2.09 for the US, the corresponding figure for Japan was significantly lower at 1.32. In Japan, if the fertility rate were to remain the same as in 2008, about 32.3 per cent of the population would be over 65 years of age by 2050, more than double the 1995 figure of 14.6 per cent (Ministry of Health, Labour, and Welfare MHLW 2009).

Such a low rate of childbirth is projected to lead to depopulation in Japan. The total population of Japan reached its peak of 127.74 million in 2006. On the assumption that the current fertility rate continues and there are no major change in immigration policies, Japan's total population is projected to decline to 121.14 million by 2025 and to 108.25 million by 2050 (National Institute of Population and Social Security Research 2007). By contrast, the US population is ageing, but it is certainly not shrinking, at least over the next few decades. As of 2008, the US total population was 303.83 million, and it is projected to increase to 357.45 million by 2025 and to 429.01 million by 2050 (US Census Bureau 2009).

The decline of Japan's total population will directly shrink the size of the country's workforce and dramatically weaken the country's capacity in the ever more competitive global economy of the twenty-first century

(OECD 2004). Japan anticipates a significant labour-force shortage in the decades ahead, as indicated by the trends of the old-age dependency ratio, which crudely indicates the number of workers potentially available to support the elderly population (Higo 2006; Schulz and Binstock 2008). Old-age dependency ratios discussed in this context are calculated by dividing the population aged 65 and older by the working population (age 20–64) based on the median variant projection (OECD 2007). Over the next few decades, the increase in the old-age dependency ratio, which translates into a decrease in the working population in relation to the size of the elderly population, is projected to be far greater for Japan than for the US. From 2000 to 2050, the ratio is projected to increase from 32.2 per cent to 94.9 per cent in Japan – meaning there would be approximately just one working person for every elder person in the population. During the same period, the dependency ratio of the US is projected to increase much more moderately, from 23.5 per cent to 50.3 per cent (OECD 2009b).

The increase in the old-age dependency ratio in Japan is projected to reflect a continual decrease in the size of the country's workforce over future decades. As Figure 15.2 shows, Japan's workforce size had been growing by an average of 0.91 per cent a year between 1980 and 2000; the workforce size is, however, projected to shrink by an average of

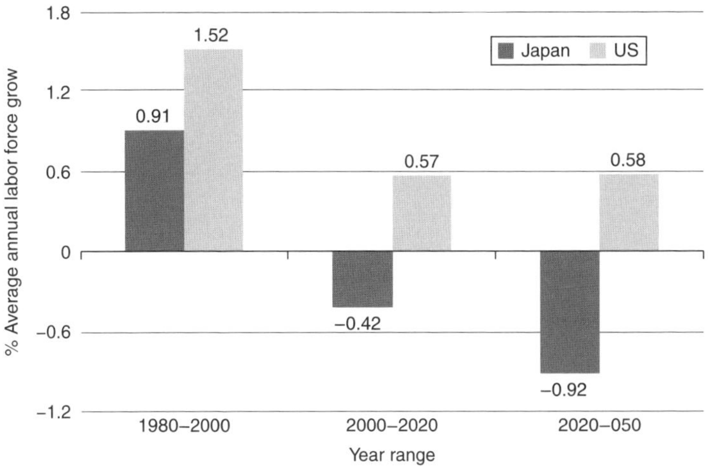


*Figure 15.2* Japan and the US compared: trend of average annual labour force growth, 1980–2050
*Source*: Based on data drawn from OECD (2008) and MALW (2008).

0.42 per cent a year between 2000 and 2020. Between 2020 and 2050 this continuing decline in Japan's workforce size is projected to be even more problematic, shrinking at an average rate of 0.92 per cent per year. By contrast, the size of the US national workforce is projected to increase by an average of 0.57 per cent a year between 2000 and 2020, and by 0.58 per cent a year between 2020 and 2050 (MHLW 2009; OECD 2004).

## 15.3 National labour market institutions: age-barriers and employment security in later life

Institutionalised rules and practices characterising a country's paid labour market – its national labour market institutions – powerfully constrain workers' labour market behaviour options and decisions (Freeman 2007; Walker 2005). The differences between the national labour market institutions in Japan and the US are the second factor that helps to explain why workers in Japan tend to remain in the labour force longer than those in the US. As discussed below, to date workers in Japan have experienced greater institutional employment security, particularly in later life, than have those in the US. The institution of 'lifetime employment' – one of the most foundational employment institutions in Japan – contributes partly to the difference in later-life employment security (Ono 2007).

The lifetime employment institution has been one of the most prevalent employment institutions characterising Japan's workforce and labour market throughout the country's post-war history (Gordon 1998; OECD 2004). Under this institution, typically workers are hired and retained with the same employers, or within the employers' networks, until retirement (Lincoln, Gerlach and Ahmadjian 1996). The lifetime employment institution consists in essence of 'regular employees', namely, those employed on the basis of full-time and presumably indefinite contracts, who typically stay with the same employers until retirement (Ono 2007). In Japan such human resource management practices and labour market behaviours were solidly institutionalised across industrial sectors and in most occupations during the time of the post-war reconstruction, when employers and workers needed to be mutually engaged for a long duration for the country's economic development (Gordon 1998). Under this institution, workers as 'lifetime employees' were generally assured of long-term, secure employment and regular wage increases through seniority-based wage systems. Simultaneously, this institution assured employers of a stable workforce supply as a result of the long-term corporate loyalty of workers, particularly full-time male employees (Bauman 2005; Takayama 2002). Partly because of this institution, Japan's workforce is characterised by a lower level of job mobility and a greater level of employment security than the US workforce. That is, generally, workers in Japan are more likely than those in the US to stay with the same employers over the course of their working lives and to experience a lesser degree of risk of firing and lay-offs (Dore 2004; OECD 2004).

Roughly since the 1990s, the lifetime employment institution has been in steady decline (Kato 2001). In 1988 the share of those employed on the basis of full-time and presumably indefinite contracts – the core workforce of the institution – accounted for about 82 per cent of the total economically active population in the country; by 2009, however, the figure had dropped to some 65 per cent (MHLW 2009). However, older employees currently under the lifetime employment institution still benefit from the institutionalised long-term employment and employment security until retirement (Genba 2005). In downsizing, most employers in Japan first freeze the hiring of new, younger employees. Job retention rates of already employed workers have not shown substantial change since the 1990s (Higo and Yamada 2009; Ono 2007).

By contrast, in the US today the lifetime employment institution has either substantially declined or has been historically absent from most industries (James 1994). Partly because of the prevalence of at-will employment and the practice of flexible employment and management, the workforce of the US is characterised by a combination of a greater level of job mobility and a lower level of employment security (OECD 2007; Schulz and Binstock 2008). A major implication of this characteristic of the US national context for employment in later life is that, generally, as workers in the US grow older they are more likely to experience age barriers to continued employment beyond a conventional retirement age both in the individual workplace and in the labour market at large (Hardy 2006).

In the US, the 1968 Age Discrimination in Employment Act (ADEA) has prohibited employers from discharging, refusing to hire, or otherwise discriminating against on the basis of age any individual who is at least 40 years old. Despite this legislation, some employers continue to make hiring and firing decisions based on inaccurate and stigmatising stereotypes of older people in the workforce and in the labour market (Nelson 2004). At the workplace, older workers tend to receive fewer opportunities than younger workers for retraining, promotion, and retaining jobs. When seeking employment, older adults tend to confront age barriers to hiring (Schulz and Binstock 2008).

For instance, the average duration of unemployment was about 16 weeks for younger people (aged 20–34), whereas the figure for the older counterpart (aged 45–65) was substantially longer at 24 weeks (US Department of Labor 2008)

Another major reason for employers' reluctance to retain older workers and to hire older job seekers in the US is the tendency for older workers' pension benefits and health insurance to be more costly than that of younger workers (Munnell and Sass 2008). These benefits are typically determined largely by the age and health ratings of a company's workforce. For instance, annual average medical claim costs were US$7622 for employees aged 60–4, whereas the corresponding figure for those aged 25–9 was US$2148 (Towers 2009).

In Japan's labour market, there is no anti-age discrimination legislation equivalent to ADEA in the US (Williamson and Higo 2009). In addition, the lifetime employment institution in Japan typically entails *mandatory retirement corporate policies*, which is a form of age discrimination since it forces workers to leave the workplace, regardless of their will, solely because of their age (Lazear 1979; Macnicol 2006). This aspect of Japan's national context may seem at first glance to be less protective of workers in old age. However, as discussed below, the prevalence of the lifetime employment institution in Japan in effect contributes to the employment security of older workers more than do the labour market institutions of the US.

Currently, the employment security provided by the lifetime employment institution substantially covers workers at least up to age 65. As of 2008, more than 90 per cent of employers in Japan practised mandatory retirement corporate policies. Most of those employers still set 60 as the age criterion for mandatory retirement. By law, however, they are obliged to make an effort to re-employ these workers within the same workplaces or within the employers' networks at least until the workers reach age 65 (MHLW 2009). Thus, the lifetime employment institution in Japan secures employment for a substantial portion of workers in the country's workforce at least up to age 65. Furthermore, health insurance in Japan provides universal coverage financed not only by co-payments of employers and employees but also by national and local government subsidies. Thus, provision of health insurance does not provide as much of a disincentive for employers to hire or retain older workers as it does in the US (Higo 2006). These characteristics of the workforce and labour market in the Japanese national context contribute partly to protecting workers from age barriers to continued employment in later life at least until age 65.

Overall, the national employment institutions in Japan aim directly at protecting long-term employment security for those who are already employed (Williamson and Higo 2009). The main goal of ADEA in the US, by contrast, can be understood primarily as promoting social equity through the equal distribution of new employment opportunities across age groups including older workers.

## 15.4 Public policies: government facilitations of working beyond retirement age

The third national contextual difference between the labour markets of Japan and the US can be found in the role of their governments. Prolonging the working lives of older workers beyond conventional retirement ages has been a substantially more imperative national agenda for Japan than for the US (Williamson and Higo 2009). With a number of administrative and legislative initiatives and public policy measures, the Japanese government has intervened in the labour market mainly in two ways: by promoting employment security in later life for those who are currently employed, and by assisting older job seekers in finding employment opportunities. As discussed below, in both areas the Japanese government's effort and results to date are substantially greater than those of the US government.

One of the main policy measures that the Japanese government has implemented roughly since the 1990s is to provide a set of financial incentives and assistance for employers to retain their older employees beyond mandatory retirement age at least until age 65. While the current law – the 2006 amendment of the Law Concerning Stabilization of Employment of Older Persons (Law No. 68 of 25 May 1971) – obliges employers to make efforts to retain their older employees until age 65, the government acknowledges the mounting pressure facing many employers to reduce human resource costs in today's competitive economy (Higo and Yamada 2009). Thus, in exchange for such legal obligations, the current law allows employers to change workers' employment conditions including wages, employment status and job contents when they reach mandatory retirement age. Under this policy arrangement, employers in Japan typically terminate employment of those who have reached mandatory retirement age, and rehire them in temporary or part-time positions with reduced wages and responsibilities (Seike and Yamada 2004). Since 1995, the government has also provided the Employment Continuation Benefit for the Aged, which is a de facto subsidy programme aiming to compensate workers aged

60–4 who experience a wage reduction of more than 25 per cent after reaching the mandatory retirement age set by their workplaces. In financial year 2007, the government spent about US$1.4 billion on this programme (National Institute of Population and Social Security Research 2007).

By contrast, in the US such an age-based financial subsidy programme aiming to secure the continued employment of older people who are already employed is virtually absent. This is because, unlike the current policy climate in Japan, ADEA has made it unlawful in the first place for employers to 'reduce compensation, terms, wages, conditions, or privileges of employment, because of such individual's age' (US Equal Employment Opportunity Commission 2008, Section 623 (a)-(1)). As a financial incentive for employers to continue to employ older employees at least up to age 65, the Japanese policy contributes to relieving employers of some of the financial pressures associated with paying otherwise high wages to many of these workers (Higo and Yamada 2009).

The second area of Japanese government intervention is to help older job seekers find employment opportunities through a number of public active labour market programmes. One of the main active labour market programmes for older job seekers in Japan is the Silver Human Resource Center (SHRC). Operated since the early 1980s, each chapter of this programme is fully subsidised by the national and municipal governments and provides local residents aged 60 and older with opportunities primarily for such non-regular employment as temporary, contract, part-time, or other forms of paid work. Through this programme, registered members may also access free training and education aiming to increase their employability, including job skills training, lectures, counselling services for job matching and job interview preparation. Such job training and education are provided with the cooperation of a variety of business owners' associations and other public employment security institutions (National Silver Human Resource Center (NSHRC) 2008). The US equivalent of the Japanese SHRC programme is the Senior Community Service Employment Programme (SCSEP), which Congress authorised under Title V of the Older Americans Act of 1965. Similar to the Japanese programme, the SCSEP of the US provides subsidised, part-time and community service work opportunities. The US programme targets those who are aged 55 and over, are currently low-income and are expected to suffer as a result of their poor employment prospects (SCSEP 2007).

The active labour market programmes of Japan and the US share common policy objectives. Nonetheless, the scale of the Japanese SHRC programme is clearly greater than that of the US SCSEP programme; in both input and outcome the Japanese programme is far more extensive than the US counterpart. The total annual spending for the Japanese programme in financial year 2007 was approximately US$3.2 billion, which was far more than the approximately US$436 million spent for the US programme. The growing enrolment number for the Japanese programme was at 778,468 by 2008, while the US programme had only 61,000 members in the same year, even though the US is more than twice the size of Japan in total population (NSHRC 2008; SCSEP 2007). The output of the Japanese programme, too, is substantially greater than that of the US programme; as of financial year 2006, the employment rate through the programme (measured as the percentage of programme participants who remained employed three months after initial programme participation) was about 84 per cent for the Japanese programme and only about 32 per cent for the US programme (NSHRC 2008; SCSEP 2007). By this measure, the Japanese programme is about 2.6 times as effective as its US counterpart in bringing older job seekers into the workforce. Mainly because of the low rates of participation and of employment through the programme, in 2005 the US Office of Management and Budget (2008) assessed the performance results and programme accountability of the SCESP of the US and found it to be ineffective.

The goal of prolonging the working lives of older workers as a way to mitigate projected workforce shortages is more explicit in the Japanese SHRC programme than in the US SCESP programme. As of 2007, for the Japanese programme 66 per cent of the total enrolment were men (NSHRC 2008), but for the US programme only 29 per cent were men (SCSEP 2007). The greater percentage of men than women in the Japanese programme may reflect a stronger policy goal to assist men – the core members among the country's older workforce – in remaining economically productive as long as possible. In the case of the US programme, on the contrary, the percentage of older women enrolled in the programme is much greater than the percentage of older men. Given this discrepancy, the primary objective of the US programme seems not to be to prolong the working lives of older workers. Rather, it may best be understood as a public anti-poverty programme designed to reduce poverty levels among single older citizens, many of whom are women and who are often regarded as one of the most economically vulnerable categories of people in the US today (Williamson and Higo 2009).

## 15.5 Summary and conclusions

Both employers and public policymakers in most industrialised countries today have been challenged to bring more older workers into the workforce and to retain them beyond the conventional retirement age. Crucial to addressing these goals is to understand the impact of national context on managing age diversity in a country's workforce. Placing older workers within their national contexts helps to clarify how broad demographic, institutional and administrative conditions shape the past and current conditions and the future prospects of older workers within a country.

This chapter has discussed the case of older workers in the national contexts of Japan and the US. While the populations and the workforces in both countries are ageing, the national contexts of these two countries substantially differ from one another in at least three respects: the levels of demographic pressure, national labour market institutions and the roles of the government in facilitating longer working lives. In each of these three respects, Japan's national context contributes to the tendency of workers in the country to remain in the workforce longer than those in the US

First, current and projected demographic trends in Japan put the country under greater pressure than the US faces to prolong the working lives of older workers. Unlike the US, due largely to the drastic demographic changes projected for the decades ahead, Japan anticipates a decline in the workforce and in national economic vitality in coming years. Prolonging the working lives of older workers aims not only to provide older workers with opportunities to remain economically active but also to sustain the country's economic vitality in the decades ahead.

Second, as a foundational labour market institution of Japan, the lifetime employment institution contributes partly to older workers having longer working lives than those in the US. In many industrialised countries today, the institution of lifetime employment has substantially declined or been virtually non-existent, and it is in decline even in Japan. However, to date this institution still plays a key role in Japan's labour market by providing older workers with employment security at least up to their mid-60s. Most employees in the US today do not have to contend with corporate rules that mandate retirement based on their age. However, because of persistent institutional ageism in the workplace and labour market in the US, many workers are likely to face more age barriers to employment in later life than Japanese workers do under the lifetime employment institution.

Finally, the Japanese government's more active intervention in the ageing workforce situation generates an important national contextual difference between Japan and the US. The unprecedented workforce shortage and the decline in national economic capability in the twenty-first-century global economy have rendered increasing older worker labour force participation a top national policy priority in Japan (Williamson and Higo 2009). Thus, the Japanese government has been spurred to intervene more aggressively in the country's workforce and paid labour market with a variety of policy measures designed to increase the labour supply of older workers. The level of government intervention in Japan is clearly greater than that in the US. By contrast, despite the growing public notion of crises associated with population ageing, as Rix (2004) argues, prolonging the working lives of older workers has never been a major public policy in the US

In effect, such national contextual differences in terms of the role of the government resonate closely with the differences in the two countries' theoretical models of the role of public policy in moderating the labour market. In the theoretical literature, the case of the US represents the 'liberal-residual' model, in which public policy generally uses arm's length interventions in the labour market. Based largely on a market-oriented, laissez-faire approach, the government in this model prioritises the demands of the labour market (such as employers' needs) over social equity and rights of workers (such as prohibition of age barriers to older workers) (Esping-Andersen 1990). By contrast, the case of Japan is understood as a form of the 'productivist' model, in which the government intervenes in the labour market more actively and thoroughly than would a government of the market-oriented, liberal-residual model (Holliday 2000). The main goal of public policy in the productivist model is to continually pursue economic/industrial growth by a variety of facilitative measures designed to integrate and retain as many workers in the country's workforce as possible. As discussed in this chapter, the Japanese government is substantially more committed than the US government to promoting employment among older workers. This national contextual difference between Japan and the US clearly supports the broad theoretical distinction between the liberal-residual and productivist models of public policy.

The discussions presented in this chapter by no means argue that Japan has managed to achieve greater age diversity in the workforce and thus a more effective and competitive national workforce than the US. This chapter suggests, rather, that older workers in Japan are more likely than those in the US to be integrated into the workforce, and that this tendency is attributable largely to the differences between three national contextual factors in Japan and the US. The variations in older workers' labour market behaviours within these different national contexts also contribute to our theoretical understanding of the different ways in which public policy affects the labour market at large in the liberal-residual and productivist models.

Nonetheless, it is important to note that our understanding of the differences between the national contexts surrounding older workers and between the theoretical models of the role of public policy in Japan and the US remains subject to change. While Japan is projected to remain one of the most aged countries in the industrialized world over the next few decades, the lifetime employment institution in Japan – a key institutional factor providing employment security for older workers in the country's workforce – has been in decline roughly since the turn of the millennium (Higo and Yamada 2009). Furthermore, challenged by today's unprecedented economic downturn on a global scale, the Japanese government's commitment to support employment in later life may not remain as firm as it has been over the last few decades. Present and future Japanese experiences with age management in the workforce may yield significant lessons not only for the US but also for those ageing countries that anticipate similar challenges and dilemmas in making their workforces more competitive well into the twenty-first century global economy.

# References

3M (Australia) (2006). *Reaction Times*, available at: http://www.3m.com/intl/AU/reflective/reactiontime.html (accessed 31 March 2010).

ABN AMRO Management Services v Hogben (2009). UKEAT/0266/09/DM.

Adams, S. J. (2000). 'Generation X: How understanding this population to better safety programs', *Professional Safety*, 45, 26–30.

Adamson, S. J., Doherty, N. and Viney, C. (1998). 'The meanings of career revisited: Implications for theory and practice', *British Journal of Management*, 9, 4, 251–9.

Age Concern (2006). *Ready for the Scrapheap' Looking for Work after 50,* (London, England: Age Concern).

Age Positive (2001). available at: http://web.archive.org/web/*/http://www.agepositive.gov.uk.

Age UK v Secretary of State for Business, Innovation & Skills (2009). EWHC 2336.

Ainsworth, S. (2002). 'The feminine advantage: a discursive analysis of the invisibility of older women workers', *Gender, Work and Organization*, 9, 5, 579–601.

Ainsworth, S. and Hardy, C. (2007). 'The construction of the older worker: privilege, paradox and policy', *Discourse & Communication*, 1, 3, 267–85.

Aittomaki, A., Lahelma, E., Roos, E., Leino-Arjas, P. and Martikainen, P. (2005). 'Gender differences in the association of age with physical workload and functioning', *Occup Environ Med*, 62, 2, 95–100.

Aldridge, F. and Tuckett, A. (2009). *Narrowing Participation: The NIACE Survey on Adult Participation in Learning 2009,* available at: http://shop.niace.org.uk/narrowing-participation.html (accessed 20 September 2010).

Aleksandrowicz, P. (2005). 'The interplay of retirement policy and externalisation strategies towards older workers in Polish and German enterprises', Paper presented at 7th Conference of the European Sociological Association, Research Network Ageing in Europe, Poland: Torun.

Alkers, L. (2006). 'Managing an Ageing UK Workforce', *British Journal of Administrative Management*, 15, 12–13.

Allen, T. D., Russell, J. E. A., Poteet, M. L. and Dobbins, G. H. (1999). 'Learning and development factors related to perceptions of job content and hierarchical plateauing', *Journal of Organisational Behavior*, 20, 7, 1113–37.

Alsop, R. (2008). *The Trophy Kids Grow Up: How the Millennial Generation is Shaking up the Workplace* (San Francisco: Jossey-Bass).

Alvesson, M. and Robertson, M. (2006). 'The best and the brightest: The construction, significance and effects of elite identities in consulting firms', *Organization*, 13, 2, 195–225.

Amabile, T. M. (1993). 'Motivational synergy: Toward new conceptualizations of intrinsic and extrinsic motivation in the workplace', *Human Resource Management Review*, 3, 3, 185–201.

Appelbaum, S. H. and Finestone, D. (1994). 'Revisiting career plateauing: Same old problems – Avant-garde solutions', *Journal of Managerial Psychology*, 9, 5, 12–21.

Appelbaum, S., Serena, M. and Shapiro, B. (2005). 'Generation X and the Boomers: An analysis of realities and myths', *Management Research News*, 28, 1, 1–33.

Arlinger, S. (2003). 'Negative consequences of uncorrected hearing loss – A review', *International Journal Audiol*, 42, Suppl.2:2, S17–S20.

Armstrong-Stassen, M. and Cameron, S. (2005). 'Factors related to the career satisfaction of older managerial and professional women', *Career Development International,* 10, 3, 203–15.

Armstrong-Stassen, M. M. and Templer, A. (2006). 'The response of Canadian public and private sector human resource professionals to the challenge of the aging workforce', *Public Personnel Management*, 35, 247–60.

Armstrong-Stassen, M. (2008). 'Organisational practices and the post-retirement employment experience of older workers', *Human Resource Management Journal*, 18, 1, 36–53.

Armstrong-Stassen, M. and Lee, S. H. (2009). 'The effect of relational age on older Canadian employees' perceptions of human resource practices and sense of worth to the organization', *The International Journal of Human Resource Management,* 20, 8, 1753–69.

Armstrong-Stassen, M. and Ursel, N. D. (2009). 'Perceived organizational support, career satisfaction and the retention of older workers', *Journal of Occupational and Organizational Psychology*, 82, 201–20.

Arnold, J. (1997). *Managing Careers into the 21st Century* (London: Paul Chapman Publishing).

Arthur, M. B. (1994). 'The boundaryless career: A new perspective for organizational inquiry', *Journal of Organizational Behavior*, 15, 295–306.

Arthur, M. B., Khapova, S. N. and Wilderom, C. P. M. (2005). 'Career success in a boundaryless career world', *Journal of Organizational Behavior*, 26, 177–202.

Arthur, M. B. and Kram, K. E. (1989). 'Reciprocity at work: The separate, yet inseparable possibilities for individual and organisational development', in M. B. Arthur, D. T. Hall and B. S. Lawrence (eds). *Handbook of Career Theory* (New York: Cambridge University Press), pp. 292–312.

Arthur, M. B. and Rousseau, D. B. (1996). *The Boundaryless Career. A New Employment Principle for a New Organizational Era* (Oxford: Oxford University Press).

Australian Labor Party (2009). *Nation Building Stimulus Plan*, available at: http://www.economicstimulusplan.gov.au/pages/default.aspx.

Axinn, W., Pearce, J. and Ghimire, D. (1999). 'Innovations in life history calendar applications', *Social Science Research*, 28, 243.

Baethge, M. (1992). 'Changes in work and education as constituting factors of social identity. Theoretical and political implications', in T. Halvorsen and O. J. Olsen (eds). *Det kvalifiserte samfunn?* (Oslo: Ad Notam Gyldendal).

Ball, K. K. (2003). 'Real-world evaluation of visual function', *Ophthalmology Clinics of North America*, 16, 2, 289–98.

Baltes, P. R. (1991). 'The many faces of human ageing: Toward a psychological culture of old age', *Psychological Medicine*, 21, 4, 837–57.

Baltes, P. B. and Baltes, M. M. (1990). *Psychological Perspectives on Successful Aging: The Model of Selective Optimization with Compensation* (New York: Cambridge University Press).

Bamforth, N., Malik, M. and O'Cinneide, C. (2008). *Discrimination Law: Theory and Context* (London: Sweet and Maxwell).

Banks, J. and Tetlow, G. (2008). 'Extending Working Lives', in J. Banks, E. Breeze, C. Lessof et al. (eds). *In the 21st Century: Older People in England: The 2006 English Longitudinal Study of Ageing (Wave 3)* (London: Institute for Fiscal Studies).

Barham, C., Walling, A., Clancy, G., Hicks, S. and Conn, S. (2009). 'Young people and the labour market', *Economic and Labour Market Trends*, 3, 4, 17–29.

Barnes, H., Smeaton, D. and Taylor, R. (2009). *An Ageing Workforce: The Employer's Perspective* (Brighton: Institute for Employment Studies).

Barnett, R. C. and Hyde, J. S. (2001). 'Women, men, work, and family: An expansionist theory', *American Psychologist*, 56, 781–96.

Baruch, Y. (2006). 'Career development in organisations and beyond: Balancing traditional and contemporary viewpoints', *Human Resource Management Review*, 16, 2, 125–38.

Baruch, Y. and Rosenstein, E. (1992). 'Career planning and managing in high tech organisations', *International Journal of Human Resource Management*, 3, 3, 477–96.

Baum, S. K. and Boxley, R. L. (1983). 'Age identification in the elderly', *The Gerontologist*, 23, 5, 532–7.

Bauman, Z. (2005). *Work, Consumerism and the New Poor*, 2nd edn (New York: Open University Press).

BDA (2004). *Ältere Mitarbeiter im Betrieb: Ein Leitfaden für Unternehmer* (Berlin: BDA).

Beck, V. (2009). *Older Workers – Older Learners, The Perspectives of Employers in the East Midlands* (Leicester: Learning and Skills Council).

Becker, F. G., Bobritchev, R. and Henseler, N. (2004). *Ältere Arbeitnehmer und alternde Belegschaften: Eine empirische Studie bei den größten 100 deutschen Unternehmen. Diskussionspapier 529 der Fakultät für Wirtschaftswissenschaften* (Bielefeld: Universität Bielefeld).

Bedeian, A. G., Farris, G. R. and Kacmar, K. M. (1992). 'Age, tenure, and job satisfaction: A tale of two perspectives', *Journal of Vocational Behavior*, 40, 1, 33–48.

Beehr, T. A. and Bennett, M. M. (2009). 'Examining retirement from a multi-level perspective', in K. S. Schultz and G. A. Adams (eds). *Aging and Work in the 21st Century* (New Jersey: Lawrence Erlbaum Associates).

Bellmann, L., Hilpert, M., Kistler, E. and Wahse, J. (2003). *'Herausforderungen des demographischen Wandels für den Arbeitsmarkt und die Betriebe'*, *Mitteilungen aus der Arbeitsmarkt- und Berufsforschung*, 2, 133–49.

Bellmann, L., Leber, U. (2003). *'Individuelles und betriebliches Engagement in der beruflichen Weiterbildung'* In: BWP, 3, 14–8.

Benjamin, K. and Wilson, S. (2005). *Facts and Misconceptions about Age, Health Status and Employability HSL/2005/20*, (Buxton, UK: Health and Safety Laboratory).

Biggs, S. (2004). 'Age, gender, narratives, and masquerades', *Journal of Aging Studies*, 18, 1, 45–58.

Birkelund, G. E., Gooderham, P. N. and Nordhaug, O. (2000). 'Fremtidige næringslivsledere: kjønn, jobbpreferanser og karrierepreferanser'. [Future business leaders: Gender, job preferences and career preferences], *Tidsskrift for samfunnsforskning*, 41, 594–619.

Bispinck, R. (2005). *'Tarifliche Senioritätsregelungen: Eine Analyse von tariflichen Regelungen in ausgewählten Tarifbereichen', Elemente qualitativer Tarifpolitik*, 59.

Blanden, J., Gregg, P. and Machin, S. (2005). 'Educational inequality and intergenerational mobility', in S. Machin and A. Vignoles (eds). *What's the Good of Education?* (New Jersey: Princeton University Press).

Bokum, N. t., Flanagan, T., Sands, R. and Steinau-Steinruck, R. v. (2009). *Age Discrimination in Europe* (London: Kluwer).

Bond, J. T., Thompson, C., Galinsky, E. and Prottas, D. (2003). *Highlights of the National Study of the Changing Workforce* (New York: Families and Work Institute).

Bongers, P. M., de Winter, C. R., Kompier, M. A. and Hildebrand, V. H. (1993). 'Psychosocial factors at work and musculoskeletal disease', *Scand J Work Environ Health*, 19, 5, 297–312.

Bonnefond, A., Härmä, M., Hakola, T., Sallinen, M., Kandolin, I. and Virkkala, J. (2006). 'Interaction of age with shift-related sleep-wakefulness, sleepiness, performance, and social life', *Experimental Aging Research*, 32, 2, 185–208.

Bornmann, L. and Enders, J. (2004). 'Social origin and gender of doctoral degree holders. Impact of particularistic attributes in access to and in later career attainment after achieving the doctoral degree in Germany', *Scientometrics*, 61, 19–41.

Bourdieu, P. (1993). *Sociology in Question* (London: Sage).

Bourdieu, P. (1977). *Outline of a Theory of Practice* (Cambridge: Cambridge University Press).

Bown-Wilson, D. and Parry, E. (2009). 'Career plateauing in older workers', in S. G. Baugh and S. E. Sullivan (eds). *Maintaining Focus, Energy and Options over the Career* (Charlotte, North Carolina: Information Age Publishing, Inc).

Boyce, R. (2008). 'An ergonomic approach to the aging workforce, utilizing this valuable resource to best advantage by integrating ergonomics, health promotion and employee assistance programs', *Journal of Workplace Behavioural Health*, 23, 1, 179–99.

Boyer, R. and Hollingsworth, J. R. (1997). 'From national embeddedness to spatial and institutional nestedness', in J. R. Hollingsworth and R. Boyer (eds). *Contemporary Capitalism: The Embeddedness of Institutions* (Cambridge: Cambridge University Press).

Boyes, L. and McCormick, J. (2005). *A Coming of Age* (York: Joseph Rowtree Foundation).

Bradford, F. (1993). Understanding Generation X. *Marketing Research,* 5, 2, 54–5.

Bray, D. W., Campbell, R. J. and Grant, D. L. (1974). *Formative Years in Business* (New York: Wiley).

Briscoe, J. P. and Hall, D. T. (2006). 'The interplay of boundaryless and protean careers: Combinations and implications, *Journal of Vocational Behavior*, 69, 4–18.

Brooke, L. and Taylor, P. (2005). 'Older workers and employment: Managing age Relations', *Ageing and Society*, 25, 415–29.

Brown, D. and Purcell, J. (2007). 'Reward management: On the line', *Compensation Benefits Review*, 39, 28, 28–34.

Brussig, M. (2005). *Die 'Nachfrageseite des Arbeitsmarketes': Betriebe und die Beschäftigung Älterer im Lichte des IAB-Betriebspanels 2002,* Altersübergangs-Report 2005–2.

Brussig, M. and Wojtkowski, S. (2006). *Durchschnittliches Renteneintrittsalter steigt weiter, Altersübergangsreport 2006–2*, available at: http://www.iaq.uni-due.de/auem-report/2006/2006-02/auem2006-02.pdf.

Bryson, M. C. and Siddiqui, M. M. (1969). 'Some criteria for aging', *Journal of the American Statistical Association*, 64, 1472–83.

Buchholz, S. (2006). 'Men's late careers and career exits in West Germany', in H. Blossfeld, S. Buchholz and D. Hofäcker (eds). *Globalization, Uncertainty and Late Careers in Society* (London/New York: Routledge).

Buck, H. and Dworschack, B. (2003). *Ageing and Work in Germany: Challenges and Solutions*, available at: http://www.demotrans.de/documents/BR_DE_BR15.pdf#page=27.

Buckle, P. W. (1997). 'Fortnightly review: Work factors and upper limb disorders', *BMJ*, 315, 7119, 1360–3.

Buckle, P., Woods, V., Oztug, O. and Stubbs, D. (2008). *Workplace Design for the Older Worker* (Surrey: Sparc. project, University of Surrey).

Bultena, G. L. and Powers, E. A. (1978). 'Denial of aging: Age identification and reference group orientations', *Journal of Gerontology*, 33, 5, 748–54.

Burdorf, A. and Sorock, G. (1997). 'Positive and negative evidence of risk factors for back disorders', *Scandinavian Journal of Work, Environment & Health*, 23, 4, 243–56.

Burke, M. (2004). *Generational Differences*, Survey Report. Alexandria, VA: Society for Human Resource Management.

Burtless, G. and Quinn, J. (2001). 'Retirement trends and policies to encourage work among older Americans'. In P. Budetti, R. Burkhauser, J. Gregory and H.A. Hunt. *Ensuring Health and Income Security for an Ageing Workforce*. (Kalamazoo, MI: Upjohn Institute), pp. 375–416.

Busch, V., Dahl, S.A. and Dittrich, D. (2004). *Age Discrimination in Hiring Decisions: A Comparison of Germany and Norway* unpublished.

Business Week. (7 November 2005). *India: Desperately Seeking Talent*, available at: http://www.businessweek.com/magazine/content/05_45/b3958050.htm.

Cabinet Office (2000). *Winning the Generation Game Improving Opportunities for People Aged 50–65 in Work and Community Activity; A Performance and Innovation Unit Report*.

Campanelli, P., Channell, J., McAuley, L., Renouf, A. and Thomas, R. (1994). *Training: an Exploration of the Word and the Concept with an Analysis of the Implications for Survey Design* (London: Employment Department).

Carlson, D. S. and Rotondo, D. M. (2001). 'Differences in promotion stress across career stage and orientation', *Human Resource Management*, 40, 2, 99–110.

Carstensen, L. L. and Hartel, C. R. (2006). *When I'm 64* (Washington DC: National Academics Press).

Caudron, S. (2000). 'Learners speak out', *Journal of Training and Development*, 54, 4, 52–7.

CBI (2003), *CBI Response to Equality and Diversity*, available at: http://www.cbi.org.uk/ndbs/positiondoc.nsf/1f08ec61711f29768025672a0055f7a8/864466BF6F0359CB80256DE400372734/$file/employoffrespage301003.pdf.

CBI (2006). *Age Discrimination Laws will Cement Changes Already Underway in UK Workplaces*, available at: www.cbi.org.uk (accessed 31 March 2010).

Cann, P. and Dean M. (2009). *Unequal Ageing: The Untold Story of Exclusion in Old Age* (University of Bristol: Policy Press).

Cennamo, L. and Gardner, D. (2008). 'Generational differences in work values, outcomes and person-organisation values fit', *Journal of Managerial Psychology*, 23, 8, 891–906.

Charness, N., Kelley, C. L., Bosman, E. A. and Mottram, M. (2001). 'Word-processing training and retraining effects of adult age, experience, and interface', *Psychology and Aging*, 16, 1, 110–27.

Chartered Management Institute (2008). *Generation Y: Unlocking the Talent of Young Managers* (London: Chartered Management Institute).

Chatterjee, A. and Hambrick, D. C. (2007). 'It's all about me: Narcissistic chief executive officers and their effects on company strategy and performance', *Administrative Science Quarterly*, 52, 351–86.

Chen, P. and Choi, Y. (2008). 'Generational differences in work values: A study of hospital management', *International Journal of Contemporary Hospitality Management*, 20, 6, 595–615.

Chiu, W. C. K., Chan, A. W., Snape, E. and Redman, T. (2001). 'Age stereotypes and discriminatory attitudes towards older workers: An east-west comparison', *Human Relations*, 54, 5, 629–61.

Chiu, W., Chan, A., Snape, E. and Redman, T. (2001). 'Age stereotypes and discriminatory attitudes towards older workers: An east-west comparison', *Human Relations*, 54, 629–61.

CIPD (2007). *Age and Recruitment, State of Play: Summer 2007* (London: Chartered Institute of Personnel and Development).

CIPD (2008). *An Ageing Workforce, The Role of Total Reward* (London: Chartered Institute of Personnel and Development).

Claes, R. and Heymans, M. (2008). 'HR professionals' views on work motivation and retention of older workers: a focus group study', *Career Development International*, 13, 2, 95.

Clarius. (January 2010), *Clarius Skills*, available at: Indexhttp://www.clarius.com.au/PDF/Clarius%20Skills%20Index_December%202009%20Quarter.pdf.

Clarke, L. H. and Griffin, M. (2008). 'Visible and invisible ageing: beauty work as a response to ageism', *Ageing & Society*, 28, 5, 653–74.

Clarke, M. (2008). 'Plodders, pragmatists, visionaries and opportunists: Career patterns and employability', *Career Development International*, 14, 1, 8–28.

Cleveland, J. N. and Lim, A. S. (2007). 'Employee age and performance in organizations', in K. S. Schultz and G. A. Adams (eds). *Aging and Work in the 21st Century* (Mahwah, NJ: Lawrence Erlbaum Associates), p. 109.

Cleveland, J. N. and Shore, L. (1992). 'Self-and supervisory perspectives in age and work attitudes and performance', *Journal of Applied Psychology*, 77, 469–84.

Collings, D. G. and Mellahi, K. (2009). 'Strategic talent management: A review and research agenda', *Human Resource Management Review*, 19, 304–13.

Collins, C. (2006). *Not Ready for the Scrapheap' Looking for Work after 50* (London, England: Age Concern).

Compact Oxford English Dictionary, *http://www.askoxford.com/concise_oed/progression?view=uk*, accessed 20 February 2006.

Conway, N. and Bringer, R. B. (2005). *Understanding Psychological Contracts at Work: A Critical Evaluation of Theory and Research* (Oxford, New York: Oxford University Press).

Corley, T. (1999). 'Becoming an employer of choice for Generation X: The elements of the deal', *Journal of Career Planning and Employment*, 59, 4, 21–6.

Correll, S. J. (2001). 'Gender and the career choice process: The role of biased self-assessments', *American Journal of Sociology*, 106, 1691–730.

Cox, G. (2004). *Productive Ageing: A Study of Ageing and Labour Markets in the North West* (UK: North West Development Agency).

Cox, T. (1994). *Cultural Diversity in Organizations: Theory, Research and Practice* (San Francisco: Berrett-Koeler).

Cox, T. and Blake, S. S. (1991). 'Cultural diversity: Implications for organisational competitiveness', *The Executive*, 5, 45–57.

Crompton, R. and Lyonette, C. (2005). 'The new gender essentialism – domestic and family choices and their relation to attitudes', *The British Journal of Sociology*, 56, 601–20.

Cunningham, I. (2004). 'Back to reality?', *People Management*, 10, 7, 36–8.

Curran, J. and Blackburn, R. A. (2001). 'Older people and the enterprise society: Age and self-employment propensities', *Work, Employment and Society*, 15, 4, 889–902.

Czaja, S. (1995). 'Aging and work performance', *Review of Public Personnel Administration*, 15, 2, 46.

Daniell, W. E., Swan, S. S., McDaniel, M. M., Camp, J. E., Cohen, M. A. and Stebbins, J. G. (2006). 'Noise exposure and hearing loss prevention programmes after 20 years of regulations in the United States', *Occup Environ Med*, 63, 5, 343–51.

DBG (2005). *Umdenken erforderlich! Vorbeugung sichert Beschäftigung bis zum Rentenalter* (Berlin: DGB).

DDI (January 2010). *Leadership In China: Keeping Pace with a Growing Economy, (2005)*, available at: http://www.ddiworld.com/pdf/leadershipinchina_rr_ddi.pdf.

De Cieri, H. and Olekalns, M. (2001). *Workforce Diversity in Australia: Challenges and Strategies for Diversity Management* (Australia: Monash University).

De Cieri, H. (2008). *Human Resource Management in Australia: Strategy, People Performance* (North Ryde: McGraw-Hill).

DeFillippi, R. J. and Arthur, M. B. (1996). 'Boundaryless contexts and careers: A competency-based perspective', in M. B. Arthur and D. M. Rousseau (eds). *The Boundaryless Career: A New Employment Principle for a New Organisational Era* (New York: Oxford University Press), pp. 116–31.

Deloitte (n.d.). *The Talent Crisis in Global Manufacturing: Strategies to Attract and Engage Generation Y*, available at: http://www.deloitte.com/assets/Dcom-Croatia/Local%20Assets/Documents/hr_Managing%20talent%20crisis%20in%20global%20manufacturing.pdf.

DeLong, T. J. (1982). 'Re-examining the career anchor model', *Personnel*, 59, 3, 50–61.

Dement, J., Ringen, K., Welch, L., Bingham, E. and Quinn. P. (2005). 'Surveillance of hearing loss among older construction and trade workers at Department of Energy nuclear sites', *American Journal of Industrial Medicine*, 48, 5, 348–58.

Dempsey, P. G., Burdorf, A. and Webster, B. S. (1997). 'The influence of personal variables on work-related low-back disorders and implications for future research', *Journal of Occupational and Environmental Medicine*, 39, 8, 748–59.

Denecker, J. C., Joshi, A. and Martocchio, J. J. (2008). 'Towards a theoretical framework linking generational memories to attitudes and behaviours', *Human Resource Management Review*, 18, 180–7.

Department of Work and Pensions (2005). *Five-Year Strategy: Opportunity and Security Throughout Life* (London: DWP).

Derr, C. B. and Laurent, A. (1989). 'The internal and external career: a theoretical and cross-cultural perspective', in M. B. Arthur, D. T. Hall and B. S. Lawrence (eds). *Handbook of Career Theory* (Cambridge, UK: Cambridge University Press).

DfEE (1999). *Age Diversity in Employment: A Code of Practice* (London: DfEE Publications).

DGFP (2006). *Personalblitzlicht: Befragungsergebnisse der DGFP e.V. zum Theme, Allgemeines Gleichbehandlungsgesetz,* Praxispapier 8 /2006.

Dini, E. (2009). 'Older workers in the UK: Variations in economic activity status by socio-demographic characteristics, household and caring commitments', *Population Trends*, 137, 11–24.

D'Netto, B. and Sohal, A. S. (1999). 'Human Resource Practices and Workforce Diversity: An Empirical Assessment', *International Journal of Manpower*, 20, 530–47.

Doherty, N. and Tyson, S. (2002). 'The management of high potential – UK Perspectives', in C. B. Derr, S. Rousillon and F. Bournois (eds). *Cross-Cultural Approaches to Leadership Development* (Wesport, USA: Greenwood Press).

Dore, R. (2004). *Stock Market Capitalism: Welfare Capitalism, Japan and Germany versus the Anglo-Saxons* (London, UK: Oxford University Press).

Dries, N., Pepermans, R. and De Kerpel, E. (2008), 'Exploring four generations' beliefs about career is "satisfied" the new "successful"?', *Journal of Managerial Psychology*, 23, 907–28.

DTI/DWP (2002). *Equality and Diversity: The Way Ahead,* (October, London: The Stationary Office).

DTI (2003). *Equality and Diversity: Age Matters* Age Consultation. Available at: http://webarchive.nationalarchives.gov.uk/+/http://www.berr.gov.uk/files/file24331.pdf (retrieved 31 March 2010).

DTI (2006). *Objective Justification* (London: DTI).

Duncan, C. (2003). 'Assessing anti-ageism routes to older worker re-engagement', *Work, Employment and Society*, 17, 1, 101–20.

Duncan, C. and Loretto, W. (2004). 'Never the right Age? Gender and age-based discrimination in employment', *Gender, Work and Organisation*, 11, 1, 95–115.

Dunnell, K. (2008). 'Ageing and mortality in the UK: National statistician's annual article on the population', *Population Trends*, 134, Winter, 6–23.

DWP (2001). *Evaluation of the Code of Practice on Age Diversity in Employment: Final Report* (October, London: DWP/National Opinion Polls).

DWP (2001a). *Age Diversity at Work: A Practical Guide for Business* (London: DWP).

DWP (2001b). *Ageism: The Attitudes and Experiences of Younger People* (London: HMSO).

DWP (2005). *Opportunity and Security Throughout Life: DWP 5-Year Strategy* (London: DWP).

Ebbinghaus, B. (2006). *Reforming Early Retirement and Social Partnership in Europe, Japan and the USA* (Oxford: Oxford University Press).

Employers Forum on Age (1999). *Report on a Survey of Senior Decision Makers in Small and Medium Enterprises,* (September, London: Employers Forum on Age).

EFA/Silcon (2000). *Employers Forum on Age/Silcon* (London: Employers Forum on Age/Silcon).

EFAD (2010). *Employers Forum on Age Discrimination, Age Discrimination,* EFAD).

Egri, C. and Ralston, D. (2004). 'Generation cohorts and personal values: A comparison of China and the United States', *Organization Science*, 15, 2, 210–20.

Elder, G. H., Jr. (1974). *Children of the Great Depression: Social Changes in Life Experience* (Chicago: University of Chicago Press).

Elder, G. H., Jr. and Giele, J. Z. (2009). *The Craft of Life Course Research.* (New York: Guilford Press).

Elliott, J. and Vaitilingam, R. (2008). *Now we are 50: Key Findings from the National Child Development Survey*, The Centre for Longitudinal Studies.

Elmuti, D. (1993). 'Managing diversity in the workplace: An immense challenge for both managers and workers', *Industrial Management*, 35, 4, 19–22.

Emmerson, C. and Tetlow, G. (2006). 'Labour market transitions', in J. Banks, E. Breeze, C. Lessof et al. (eds). *Retirement, health and relationships of the older population in England: The 2004 English longitudinal study of Ageing (Wave 2)* (London: Institute for Fiscal Studies).

Employers Forum on Age (2006). *Defining Ageism*, available at: http://www.efa.org.uk/publications/downloads/EFA-BandQ-Defining-Ageism.pdf.

Engel, L., Keifer, M. and Zahm, S. (2001). 'Comparison of a traditional questionnaire with an icon/calendar-based questionnaire to assess occupational history', *American Journal of Industrial Medicine*, 40, 502–11.

EQUALITY AND DIVERSITY: AGE MATTERS: Age Consultation 2003, by the Dti – it can be found at http://webarchive.nationalarchives.gov.uk/+/http://www.berr.gov.uk/files/file24331.pdf (retrieved 31 March 2010).

Eraut, M. (1997). 'Perspectives on defining The Learning Society', *Journal of Education Policy*, 12, 6, 551–58.

Eraut, M., Alderton, J., Cole, G. and Senker, P. (1999). 'The impact of the manager on learning in the workplace', in F. Coffield (e d.). *Speaking Truth to Power: Research and Policy on Lifelong Learning* (Bristol: Policy Press).

Erikson, E. (1950). *Childhood and Society* (New York: W. W. Norton & Company, Inc).

Eskilson, A. and Wiley, M. (1999). 'Solving for the X: Aspirations and expectations of college students', *Journal of Youth and Adolescence*, 28, 1, 51–70.

Esping-Andersen, G. (1990). *The Three Worlds of Welfare Capitalism* (Cambridge, UK: Polity Press).

Ettington, D. R. (1998). 'Successful career plateauing', *Journal of Vocational Behavior*, 52, 1, 72–88.

European Commission (2003). *Employment in Europe: Recent Trends and Prospects* (Luxembourg: Office for Official Publications of the European Communities).

European Commission (2004). *Increasing the Employment of Older workers and Delaying the Exit from the Labour Market*, available at: http://ec.europa.eu/employment_social/employment_analysis/docs/age_com_2004_146_en.pdf.

Evandrou, M. and Glaser, K. (2003). 'Combining work and family life: the pension penalty of caring', *Ageing and Society*, 23, 583–601.

Evans, D. A., Hebert, L. E., Beckett, L. A., Scherr, P. A., Albert, M. S., Chown, M. J., Pilgrim, D. M. and Taylor, J. O. (1997). 'Education and other measures of socioeconomic status and risk of incident Alzheimer's disease in a defined population of older persons', *Arch Neurol*, 54, 1399–405.

Eyerman, R. and Turner, B. (1998). 'Outline of a theory of generations', *European Journal of Social Theory*, 1, 1, 91–106.

Families and Work Institute (1950). *Generation & Gender in the Workplace* (MA: American Business Collaboration. Retrieved from http://familiesandwork.org/site/research/reports/genandgender.pdf (Watertown).

Farmer, E. and Soulsby, J. (2009). 'Making the most of experience – the East Midlands story' In: A. Chiva and J. Manthorpe (eds). *Older Workers in Europe,* (Maidenhead: Open University Press/McGraw Hill Education) pp. 142–53.

Feldman, D. C. (2007). 'Career mobility and career stability among older workers', in K. Shultz and G. Adams (eds). *Aging and Work in the 21st Century* (New Jersey, USA: Lawrence Erlbaum Associates).

Feldman, D. C. and Bolino, M. C. (1996). 'Careers within careers: Reconceptualizing the nature of career anchors and their consequences', *Human Resource Management Review,* 6, 2, 89–112.

Felstead, A., Jewson, N., Phizacklea, A. and Walters, S. (2000). 'A statistical portrait of working at home in the UK: Evidence from the Labour Force Survey', ESRC Future of Work Programme, Working Paper No 4, Leeds: University of Leeds.

Felstead, A., Fuller, A., Unwin, L., Ashton, D., Butler, P. and Lee, T. (2005). 'Surveying the scene: Learning metaphors, survey design and the workplace context', *Journal of Education and Work,* 18, 4, 359–83.

Felstead, A., Fuller, A., Jewson, N., Unwin, L. and Kakavelakis, K. (2007a). *Communities and Performance: Evidence from the 2007 Communities of Practice Survey* (Leicester: NIACE).

Felstead, A., Gallie, D., Green, F. and Zhou, Y. (2007b). *Skills at Work, 1986–2006* (Oxford: ESRC Research Centre on Skills, Knowledge and Organisational Performance).

Felstead, A. (2009). 'A disappearing divide? Age, skills and the experience of work in Britain', paper presented to the 30th Conference of the International Working Party on Labour Market Segmentation, 3–5 September 2009, University of Tampere, Finland.

Felstead, A., Fuller, A., Jewson, N. and Unwin, L. (2009). *Improving Working as Learning* (London: Routledge).

Ference, T. P., Stoner, J. A. F. and Warren, E. K. (1977). 'Managing the career plateau', *Academy of Management Review,* 2, 602–12.

Ferris, G. R. and King, T.R. (1992). 'The Politics of Age Discrimination in Organizations', *Journal of Business Ethics,* 11, 341–50.

Fevre, R., Gorad, S. and Rees, G. (2001). 'Necessary and unnecessary learning: The acquisition of knowledge and "skills" in and outside employment in South Wales in the 20th century', in F. Coffield (ed.). *The Necessity of Informal Learning* (Press: Policy).

Filipczak, B. (1994). 'It's just a job: Generation X at work', *Training,* 31, 4, 21–7.

Financial Times (21 October 2009a). 'Economists call for pensions at 70', *Financial Times.*

Financial Times (2009b). 'IoD backs retirement at 70', *Financial Times,* 20 October.

Fisk, E. and Warr, P. (1996). 'The role of perceptual speed, the central executive, and the phonological loop', *Psychology and Aging,* 11, 2, 316–23.

Fitzgerald, M. D., Tanaka, H., Tran, Z. V. and Seals, D. R. (1997). 'Age-related declines in maximal aerobic capacity in regularly exercising vs. sedentary women: a meta-analysis', *J Appl Physiol,* 83, 1, 160–5.

Flynn, M. and McNair, S. (2007). *Managing Age – A Guide to Good Employment Practice* (London: CIPD and TUC).

Fothergill, J., O'Driscoll, D. and Hashemi, K. (1995). 'The role of environmental factors in causing injury through falls in public places', *Ergonomics,* 38, 220–3.

Fouarge, D. and Schils. T. (2009). 'The effect of early retirement incentives on the training participation of older workers', *Labour*, 23 (Special Issue), 85–109.

Fourage, D. and Schils, T. (2009). 'Effect of Early Retirement Incentives on the Training Participation of Older Workers', *Labour*, 23, 85–109.

Fredman, F. M. (2003). 'The age of equality', in S. Fredman and S. Spencer (eds). *Age as an Equality Issue* (Oxford: Hart).

Fredman, S. 'The age of equality' in S. Fredman and S. Spencer (eds). *Age as an Equality Issue* (Oxford: Hart), 21–69.

Freeman, R. B. (2007). *Labor Market Institutions around the World,* Working Paper No. 13242, National Bureau of Economic Research. Retrieved October 26, 2009, (http://www.nber.org/papers/w13242).

Frerichs, F. and Naegele, G. (1997). 'Discrimination of older workers in Germany: Obstacles and options for the integration into employment', *Journal of Ageing and Social Policy*, 9, 1, 89–101.

Frerichs, F. and Sporket, M. (2007). *Employment and Labour Market Policies for an Ageing Workforce and Initiatives at the Workplace – National Overview Report: Germany*, available at: http://www.eurofound.europa.eu/publications/htmlfiles/ef07056.htm.

Frerichs, F. and Taylor, P. (2005). *Greying of the Labour Market: What can Britain and Germany Learn from Each Other?* (London: Anglo-German Foundation).

Freund, A. M. (1997). 'Individuating age salience: A psychological perspective on the salience of age in the life course', *Human Development*, 40, 5, 287–92.

Frone, M. R., Yardley, J. K. and Markel, K. S. (1997). 'Developing and testing an integrative model of the work-family interface', *Journal of Vocational Behavior*, 50, 145–67.

Froschauer, U. and Lueger, M. (2003). *Das qualitative Interview. Zur Praxis interpretativer Analyse sozialer Systeme* (Wien: UTB).

Fuller, A. and Unwin, L. (1999). 'A sense of belonging: The relationship between community and apprenticeship', in P. Ainley and H. Rainbird (eds). *Apprenticeship: Towards a New Paradigm of Learning* (London: Kogan Page).

Fuller, A. and Unwin, L. (2003). 'Learning as apprentices in the contemporary UK workplace: Creating and managing expansive and restrictive participation', *Journal of Education and Work*, 16, 4, 407–26.

Gates, J. (2009). 'Human capital investment in health: A measurement framework and estimates for the United States, 1952–78', *Review of Income and Wealth*, 30, 1, 39–52.

Gauchard, G., Chau, N., Mur, J. M. and Perrin, P. (2001). 'Falls and working individuals: Role of extrinsic and intrinsic factors', *Ergonomics*, 44, 14, 1330–9.

Geisler, E. (1999). 'Harnessing the value of experience in the knowledge-driven firm', *Business Horizon*, May–June, 18–26.

Genaidy, A., Rinder, M. and A-Rehi, A. (2008). 'The work compatibility improvement framework: an assessment of the worker–work environment interaction in the manufacturing sector', *Ergonomics*, 51, 8, 1195–218.

Genba, M. (2005). *Nenrei Sabetsu* [Age Discrimination at Work]. (Tokyo, Japan: Iwanami).

George, R. (2000). *Beschäftigung älterer Arbeitnehmer aus betrieblicher Sicht: Frühverrentung als Personalanpassungsstrategie in internen Arbeitsmärkten,* (München: Hampp).

Giancola, F. (2006). 'The generation gap: More myth than reality', *Human Resource Planning*, 29, 4, 32–7.

Gibbs, M., Hampton, S., Morgan, L. and Arendt, J. (2005). *Effect of Shift Schedule on Offshore Shiftworkers' Circadian Rhythms and Health*, HSE Research Report 318.

Giles, H. and Reid, S. (2005). 'Ageism across the lifespan: Towards a self-categorization model of aging', *Journal of Social Issues*, 61, 2, 389–404.

Gilleard, C. (2004). 'Cohorts and generations in the study of social change', *Social Theory and Health*, 2, 106–19.

Gluck, J. V., Olenick, A. and Hadler, N. M. (1998). 'Claim rates of compensable back injuries by age, gender, occupation, and industry: Do they relate to return-to-work experience?', *Occupational Health/Ergonomics Spine*, 23, 14, 1572–87.

Godin, I., Kittel, F., Coppieters, Y. and Siegrist, J. (2005). 'A prospective study of cumulative job stress in relation to mental health', *BMC Public Health*, 15, 5, 1–67.

Goffee, R. and Scase, R. (1992). 'Organisational change and the corporate career: The restructuring of managers' job aspirations', *Human Relations*, 45, 4, 363.

Goldberg, C. B., Finkelstein, L. M., Perry, E. L. and Konrad, A. M. (2004). 'Job and industry fit: The effects of age and gender matches on career progress outcomes', *Journal of Organizational Behavior*, 25, 7, 807–29.

Golden, L. (2008). 'Limited access: Disparities in flexible work schedules and work-at-home', *Journal of Family and Economic Issues*, 29, 1, 86–109.

Golsch, K., Haardt, D. and Jenkins, S. P. (2006). 'Late careers and career exits in Britain', in H. Blossfeld, S. Buchholz and D. Hofäcker (eds). *Globalization, Uncertainty and Late Careers in Society* (London: Routledge).

Gooderham, P. N. and Nordhaug, O. (2002). 'Are cultural differences in Europe on the decline?', *European Business Forum*, 2, 48–53.

Gooderham, P. N., Nordhaug, O. and Birkelund, G. (2004). 'Job values among future business leaders: The impact of gender and social background', *Scandinavian Journal of Management*, 20, 277–95.

Gordon, A. (1998). 'The Wages of Affluence: Labor and Management in Postwar Japan'. (Cambridge, Mass: Harvard University Press).

Gorman, E. H. and Kmec, J. A. (2007). 'We (Have to) Try Harder: Gender and Required Work Effort in Britain and the United States', *Gender & Society*, 21, 6, 828–56.

Gough, O. and Hick, R. (2009). 'Employee evaluations of occupational pensions', *Employee Relations*, 31, 158–67.

Government Equalities Office (2010). *Equality Bill: Making it Work* (London: GEO).

Granleese, J. and Sayer, G. (2006). 'Gendered ageism and "lookism": a triple jeopardy for female academics', *Women in Management Review*, 21, 6, 500–17.

Gravenstein, J., Cooper, J. and Orkin, F. (1990). 'Work and rest cycles in aanesthesia practice', *Anesthesiology*, 72, 4, 737–42.

Green, A., Eigel, L. M., James, J. B., Hartmann, D., and Malter, K. (in press). 'Multiple generations in the workplace: Understanding the research, influence of stereotypes and organizational applications'. In J. W. Hedge, & W. C. Borman (eds) *Work and aging handbook* (Oxford: Oxford University Press).

Greller, M. M. and Simpson, P. (1999). 'In search of late career: A review of contemporary social science research applicable to the understanding of late career', *Human Resource Management Review*, 9, 3, 309.

Greller, M. M. and Stroh, L. K. (2004). 'Making the most of 'late-career' for employers and workers themselves: Becoming elders not relics', *Organisational Dynamics*, 33, 2, 202–14.

Griffin, L. (2004). 'Generations and collective memory revisited: Race, religion and memory of civil rights', *American Sociological Review*, 6, 544–77.
Grimsley, R. (1973). *Kierkegaard: A biographical introduction* (London: Studio Vista).
Gunz, H. and Peiperl, M. (2007). *Handbook of Career Studies* (Los Angeles et al: Sage).
Gursoy, D., Maier, T. and Chi, C. (2008). 'Generational differences: An examination of the work values and generational gaps in the hospitality workforce', *International Journal of Hospitality Management*, 27, 448–58.
Hackett, R. D. (1990). 'Age, Tenure And Employee Absenteeism', *Human Relations*, 43, 601–19.
Haight, J. M. (2003). 'Human error and the challenges of an aging workforce', *Professional Safety*, December 2003, 18–24.
Hakim, C. (2007). 'Dancing with the devil? Essentialism and other feminist heresies', *The British Journal of Sociology*, 58, 1, 123–32.
Hakim, C. (2000). *Work-Lifestyle Choices in the 21st Century: Preference Theory*, (Oxford: Oxford University Press).
Hall, D. T. (1996). 'Protean careers of the 21st century', *Academy of Management Executive*, 10, 8–16.
Hall, D. T. (1987). 'Careers and socialization', *Journal of Management*, 13, 301–21.
Hall, D. T. (1976). *Careers in Organisations* (Glenview, IL: Scott, Foresman).
Hall, D. T. and Associates. (1996). *The Career is Dead; Long Live the Career: A Relational Approach to Career* (San Francisco, CA: Jossey-Bass).
Hall, D. T. and Mirvis, P. (1996). 'The new protean career: Psychological success and the path with a heart', in D. T. Hall (ed.). *The Career is Dead;Long Live the Career* (San Francisco: Jossey-Bass).
Hall, P. A. and Soskice, D. (2001). *Varieties of Capitalism: The Institutional Foundations of Comparative Advantage* (Oxford: Oxford University Press).
Hallett, M. (1997). 'Tap into the power of older workers', *Safety and Health*, 155, 2, 28–32.
Handy, J. and Davy, D. (2007). 'Gendered ageism: Older women's experiences of employment agency practices', *Asia Pacific Journal of Human Resources*, 45, 1, 85–99.
Hardy, M. A. (2006). 'Older workers', in R. H. Binstock and L. K. George (eds). *Handbook of Aging and the Social Sciences* (San Diego, CA: Academic Press).
Härmä, M. and Ilmarinen, J. (1999). 'Towards the 24-hour society – new approaches for aging shift workers?', *Scand J Work Environ Health*, 25, 6, 610–15.
Härmä, M., Tarjaa, H., Irjaa, K., Mikaela, S., Jussia, V., Anne, B. and Pertti, M. (2006). 'A controlled intervention study on the effects of a very rapidly forward rotating shift system on sleep-wakefulness and well-being among young and elderly shift workers', *International Journal of Psychophysiology*, 59, 1, 70–9.
Harper, S. and Leeson, G. (2006). *Future of Retirement* (London: HSBC).
Harper, S. and Ross, D. (2010). *The Relevance of Workability to the UK Oil and Gas Industry* OIA Working Paper.
Hartel, C. F., Y., Strybosch, V. E. and Fitzpatrick, K. (2009). *Human Resource Management: Transforming Theory into Innovative Practice* (NSW: Pearson Education).
Hartvigsen, J., Christensen, K. and Frederiksen, H. (2004). 'Back and neck pain exhibit many common features in old age: A population-based study of 4,486 Danish twins 70–102 years of age', *Spine*, 5, March 1, 576–80.

Hedge, J. (2008). 'Strategic human resource management and the older worker', *Journal of Workplace Behavioural Health*, 23, 1, 109.

Hellman, D. (2008). *When is Discrimination Wrong?* (Cambridge: Harvard University Press).

Hemingway, H., Shipley, M. J., Stansfeld, S. and Marmot, M. (1997). 'Sickness absence from back pain, psychosocial work characteristics and employment grade among office workers', *Scandinavian Journal of Work, Environment and Health*, 2, Apr 23, 121–9.

Hepple, B. (2003). *Age Discrimination in Employment* (Oxford: Hart).

Herbach, O., Mignonac, K., Vandenberghe, C. and Negrini, A. (2009). 'Perceived HRM Practices, Organizational Commitment and Voluntary Early Retirement Among Late-Career Managers', *Human Resource Management*, 48, 895–915.

Hermanns, H. (1991). 'Narratives Interview', in U. Flick, E. Kardorff von and H. Keupp (eds). *Handbuch Qualitative Sozialforschung* (München: Psychologie Verlags Union).

Herring, J. (2009). *Older People in Law and Society* (Oxford: OUP).

Herring, J. (2003). 'Children's rights for grown-ups', in S. Fredman and S. Spencer (eds). *Age as an Equality Issue* (Oxford: Hart).

Hertoghe, T. (2005). 'The "Multiple Hormone Deficiency" theory of aging: Is human senescence caused mainly by multiple hormone deficiencies?', *Ann NY Acad Sci*, 1057, 1, 448–65.

Herz, D. and Rones, P. (1989). 'Institutional barriers to the employment of older workers', *Monthly Labor Review*, 112, 4, 14–21.

Heslin, P. A. (2005). 'Conceptualizing and evaluating career success', *Journal of Organisational Behavior, Special Issue: Reconceptualizing Career Success*, 26, 2, 113–36.

Hewitt, S. (2008). 'Defusing the demographic time-bomb', *Human Resource Management International Digest*, 16, 7, 3–5.

Higo, M. (2006). 'Aging workforce in Japan: Three policy dilemmas', *Hallym International Journal of Aging*, 8, 2, 149–73.

Higo, M. and Atsuhiro, Y. (2009). *Japan: Public Policy*, Global Institute, Sloan Center on Aging & Work at Boston College, Global Policy Brief No 2. July 2009. Retrieved September 17, 2009 (http://agingandwork.bc.edu/documents/GPB02_Japan_2009-07-02.pdf).

Higo, M. and Yamada, A. (2009). 'Japan: Public policy'. Sloan Center on Aging & Work at Boston College, Global Policy Brief No 2. July 2009. Available at: http://agingandwork.bc.edu/documents/GPB02_Japan_2009-07-02.pdf. Retrived 12 March 2010.

HM Treasury (2006). *Prosperity for All in the Global Economy – World Class Skills, Final Report* (London: HM Treasury).

Ho, L. S., Wei, X.D. and Voon, J. P. (2000). 'Are Older Workers Disadvantaged in The Hong Kong Labour Market?', *Asian Economic Journal*, 14, 283–300.

Hodkinson, H. and Hodkinson, P. (2004). 'Rethinking the concept of community of practice in relation to schoolteachers' workplace learning', *International Journal of Training and Development*, 8, 1, 21–31.

Hofäcker, D. and Pollnerová, S. (2006). 'Late careers and career exits. An international comparison of trends and institutional background patterns', in H.-Blossfeld, S. Buchholz and Hofäcker. (eds). *Globalization, Uncertainty and Late Careers in Society* (London: Routledge).

Hofer, S. M. and Sliwinski, M. J. (2001). 'Understanding ageing', *Gerontology*, 47, 6, 341–52.

Holdbrook, M. B. and Schindler, R. M. (1989). 'Some exploratory findings on the development of musical tastes', *Journal of Consumer Research*, 16, 119–24.

Holdbrook, M. B. and Schindler, R. M. (1994). 'Age, sex and attitude toward the past as predictors of consumers' aesthetic tastes for cultural products', *Journal of Marketing Research*, 31, 412–22.

Holland, P., Berney, L., Blane, D. and Davey, G. (1999). 'The life grid method in health inequalities research', *Health Variations*, 3, 8–9.

Holliday, I. (2000). 'Productivist welfare capitalism: Social policy in East Asia', *Political Studies*, 48, 4, 706–23.

Hoogendoorn, W. E., Bongers, P. M., de Vet, H. C. W., Ariëns, G. A. M., van Mechelen, W. and Bouter, L. M. (2002). 'High physical work load and low job satisfaction increase the risk of sickness absence due to low back pain: Results of a prospective cohort study', *Occup Environ Med*, 59, 5, 323–8.

Hoogendoorn, W. E., van Poppel, M. N., Bongers, P. M., Koes, B. W. and Bouter, L. M. (2000). 'Systematic review of psychosocial factors at work and private life as risk factors for back pain', *Spine*, 25, 15, 2114–25.

Hoque, K. and Noon, M. (2004). 'Equal opportunities policy and practice in Britain: evaluating the "empty shell" hypothesis', *Work Employment and Society*, 18, 3, 481–506.

Hornstein, Z. (2001). *Age Discrimination Legislation* (York: Joseph Rowntree Foundation).

Horwitz, I. B. and McCall, B. P. (2004). 'The impact of shift work on the risk and severity of injuries for hospital employees: An analysis using Oregon workers' compensation data', *Occup Med Lond*, 54, 8, 556–3.

House of Commons (2004). *Welfare to Work: Tackling the Barriers to the Employment of Older People*, HC 1026 Session 2003–2004: 15 September 2004 (London: The Sationery Office).

Howell, S., Buttigieg, D. and Webber, W. W. (2006). 'Management attitudes to older workers in the retail sector', *Monash Business Review*, [Online], vol. 2, available at: http://publications.epress.monash.edu/loi/mbr.

HSE (Health and Safety Executive UK) (2005). *Noise at Work*, available at: http://www.hse.gov.uk/pubns/indg362.pdf.

Hui-Chun, Y. and Miller, P. (2005). 'Leadership style: The X Generation and Baby Boomers compared in different cultural contexts', *Leadership and Organisation Development*, 26, 1/2, 35–50.

Humphrey, A., Costigan, P., Pickering, K., Stratford, N. and Barnes, M. (2003). *Factors affecting the labour market participation of older workers* (Leeds: HMSO).

Hütter v Technische Universität Graz (2009). 3 C.M.L.R. 35.

Iellatchitch, A., Mayrhofer, W. and Meyer, M. (2003). 'Career fields: A small step towards a grand career theory?', *International Journal of Human Resource Management*, 14, 728–50.

Ilkmakunnas, S. (2005). 'Promoting employment among ageing workers; lessons from successful policy changes in Finland', *The Geneva Papers*, 30, 674–92.

Ilmarinen, J. (1995). ' Aging and work: The role of ergonomics for maintaining work ability during aging', in Bittner, A. C. Champney, P. C. (eds). *Advances in Industrial Ergonomics and Safety VII* (London and Bristol: Taylor and Francis).

Ilmarinen, J. (1998). *Workability Index* (Helsinki: Finnish Institute of Occupational Health).

Ilmarinen, J. (2001). 'Aging Workers', *Occup Environ Med*, 58, 8, 546–52.

Ilmarinen, J. (2002). 'Physical requirements associated with the work of aging workers in the European Union', *Experimental Aging Research*, 28, 1, 7–23.

Ilmarinen, J. (2005). *Toward a Longer Worklife! Ageing and the Quality of Worklife in the European Union* (Helsinki, Finland: Finnish Institute of Occupational Health).

Ilmarinen, J. and Rantanen, J. (1999). 'Promotion of work ability during ageing', *American Journal of Industrial Medicine*, 36, S1, 21–3.

Ilmarinen, J., Tuomi, K. and Klockars, M. (1997). 'Changes in the work ability of active employees as measured by the work ability index over an 11-year period', *Scandinavian Journal of Work, Environment and Health*, 23, Supp 1, 49–57.

ILO (2009). *LABORSTA Internet – Total Economically Active Population*, Retrieved August 24, 2009 (http://laborsta.ilo.org/).

ILO (2009). *Global Employment Trends-Update May* 2009 available at: http://www.ilo.org/wcmsp5/groups/public/—dgreports/—dcomm/documents/publication/wcms_106504.pdf.

IMF (2009). *World Economic Outlook October 2009: Sustaining the Recovery, 2009*, available at: http://www.imf.org/external/pubs/ft/weo/2009/02/pdf/text.pdf.

Inglehart, R. (1997). *Modernization and Postmodernization: Cultural, Economic, and Political Change in 43 Societies* (Princeton. N.J.: Princeton University Press).

Inglehart, R., Basáñez, M. and Menéndez Moreno, A. (1998). *Human Values and Beliefs: A Cross-Cultural Sourcebook: Political, Religious, Sexual, and Economic Norms in 43 Societies; Findings from the 1990–1993 World Value Survey* (Ann Arbor: University of Michigan Press).

Inkson, K. (2004). 'Images of career: Nine key metaphors', *Journal of Vocational Behavior*, 65, 96–111.

Inkson, K. (2006). *Understanding Careers: The Metaphors of Working Lives* (Thousand Oaks, CA: Sage).

Inouye, S. K., Albert, M. S., Mohs, R., Sun, K. and Berkman, L. F. (1993). 'Cognitive performance in a high-functioning community-dwelling elderly population', *Journals of Gerontology*, 48, 146–51.

Institute of Medicine (2001). *Musculoskeletal disorders and the workplace: Low back and upper extremities*, The National Academies Press.

Institute of Medicine (2004). *Keeping Patients Safe: Transforming the Work Environment of Nurses* (Washington, D.C.: National Academies Press).

Irving, P., Steels, J. and Hall, N. (2005). *Factors Affecting the Labour Market Participation of Older Workers*, Research Report No. 281, Department for Work and Pensions, (Leeds: HMSO).

Itzin, C. and Phillipson, C. (1995). 'Gendered ageism: a double jeopardy for women in organisations', in C. Itzin and J. Newman (eds). *Gender, Culture and Organizational Change: Putting Theory into Practice* (London: Routledge).

Ivancevich, J. M. and Gilbert, J. A. (2000). 'Diversity Management Time for a New Approach', *Public Personnel Management*, 29, 75–93.

IVR (2007). *Gives Time Now? Patterns of Participation in Volunteering* (London: Institute for Volunteering Research).

Jahoda, M. (1982). *Employment and Unemployment – A Social-Psychological Analysis* (Cambridge: Cambridge University Press).

James, J. A. (1994). 'Job tenure in the gilded age', in G. Grantham and M. MacKinnon (eds). *Labor Market Evolution: The Economic History of Market Integration, Wage Flexibility, and the Employment Relation* (New York: Routledge), pp. 185–204.

Japan Institute for Labour Policy and Training (2009). *Labor situation in Japan and analysis 2008/2009*. Tokyo, Japan: Japan Institute for Labor Policy and Training and Daitō Press.

Jennings, A. T. (2000). 'Hiring generation-X', *Journal of Accountancy*, 189, 55–9.

Jewson, N. and Mason, D. (1994). 'Race, employment and equal opportunities: Towards a political economy and an agenda for the 1990s', *Sociological Review*, 42, 4, 591–617.

Johnson, M. K. (2005). 'Family roles and work values: Processes of selection and change', *Journal of Marriage & Family*, 67, 2, 352–69.

Johnson, R. (2004). 'Job demands among older workers', *Monthly Labor Review*, 12, 7, 48–56.

Johnson, R. W. (2009). 'Family, Public policy, and Retirement Decisions: Introduction to the Special Issue', *Research on Aging*, 31, 2, 139–52.

Judge, T. A., Higgins, C. A., Thoresen, C. J. and Barrick, M. R. (1999). 'The big five personality traits, general mental ability, and career success across the life span', *Personnel Psychology*, 52, 3, 621–52.

Jurkiewicz, C. (2000). 'Generation X and the public employee'. *Public Personnel Management*, 29, 1, 55–74.

Jurkiewicz, C. E. and Brown, R. G. (1998). 'Gen Xers vs boomers vs matures: generational comparisons of public employee motivation', *Review of Public Personnel Administration*, 18, 18–36.

Jurkiewicz, C. E. (1998). 'Generation X and the public employee', *Public Personnel Management*, 29, 1, 55–74.

Shacklock, K. H., Fulop, L. and Hort, L. (2007). 'Managing older worker exit and re-entry practices – A revolving door?', *Asia Pacific Journal of Human Resources*, 45, 151–67.

Kan, M. Y. (2007). 'Work Orientation and Wives' Employment Careers: An Evaluation of Hakim's Preference Theory', *Work and Occupations*, 34, 4, 430–62.

Kanfer, R. and Ackerman, P. L. (2004). 'Aging, adult development, and work motivation', *Academy of Management Review*, 29, 3, 440–58.

Karasek, M. (2004). 'Melatonin, human aging, and age-related diseases', *Experimental Gerontology*, 39, 11/12, 1723–9.

Karp, D. A. (1987). 'Professionals beyond mid-life: Some observations on work satisfaction in the fifty-to-sixty year decade', *Journal of Aging Studies*, 1, 3, 209–23.

Karp, H., Sirias, D. and Arnold, K. (1999), 'Why generation X marks the spot', *Journal for Quality and Participation*, Jul/Aug 1999, 30–3.

Kastenbaum, R., Derbin, V., Sabatini, P. and Am, S. (1972). 'The ages of me: Toward personal and interpersonal definitions of functional age', *International Journal of Aging and Human Development*, 3, 197–212.

Kato, T. (2001). 'The end of lifetime employment in Japan?: Evidence from national surveys and field research', *Journal of the Japanese and International Economies*, 15, 4, 489–514.

Kemmlert, K. and Lundholm, L. (2001). 'Slips, trips and falls in different work groups – with reference to age and from a preventive perspective', *Applied Ergonomics*, 32, 2, 149–53.

Kerr, M. S., Frank, J. W., Shannon, H. S., Norman, R. W., Wells, R. P., Neumann, W. P., Bombardier, C. and Ontario Universities Back Pain Study Group (2001). 'Biomechanical and psychosocial risk factors for low back pain at work', *Am J Public Health*, 91, 7, 1069–75.

Kersley, B., Alpin, C., Forth, J., Bryson, A., Bewley, H., Dix, G. and Oxenbridge, S. (2005). *Inside the Workplace: First Findings from the 2004 Workplace Employment Relations Survey* Unpublished.

Keyserling, W. M. (2000a). 'Workplace risk factors and occupational musculosekeletal disorders, Part 1: A review of biomechanical and psychosocial research on risk factors associated with back pain', *AIHAJ*, 61, 1 Jan/Feb, 39–50.

Keyserling, W. M. (2000b). 'Workplace risk factors and occupational musculosekeletal disorders, Part 2: A review of biomechanical and psychophysical research on risk factors associated with upper extremity disorders', *AIHAJ*, 61, 2 Mar/May, 231–43.

Khan, K. (2009). 'Employment of the older generation', *Economic and Labour Market Review*, 3, 4, 30–6.

Kilpatrick, C. (2008). 'The New UK Retirement Regime', *Industrial Law Journal*, 37, 1–24.

King, H., Aubert, R. E. and Herman, W. H. (1998). 'Global burden of diabetes', *Diabetes Care*, 24, 9, 1414–31.

Kirkton, G. and Green, A. (2005). *The Dynamics of Managing Diversity: A Critical Approach*, 2nd edn (Oxford: Elsevier).

Köchling, A., Astor, M., Fröhner, K., Hartmann, E. A., Hitzblech, T., Jasper, G. and Reindl, J. (2000). *Innovation und Leistung mit älteren Belegschaften* (München und Mehring: Hampp Publishing).

Konrad, A. M. (1995). 'HRM structures: Coordinating equal employment opportunity or concealing organisational practices?', *Academy of Management Journal*, 38, 787–821.

Kooij, D., de Lang, A., Jansen, P. and Dikkers, J. (2007). 'Older workers' motivation to continue to work: five meanings of age', *Journal of Managerial Psychology*, 23, 4, 364–95.

Kooij, D., de Lange, A., Jansen, P. and Dikkers, J. (2008). 'Older workers' motivation to continue to work: Five meanings of age', *Journal of Managerial Psychology*, 23, 4, 364–93.

Kossek, E. E. and Lambert, S. J. (2005). *Work and Life Integration: Organizational, Cultural, and Individual Perspectives,* (Mahwah, New Jersey: Lawrence Erlbaum Associates).

Kovar, M. G. and LaCroix, A. Z. (1987). *Aging in the Eighties, Ability to Perform Work-Related Activities*, NCHS Advance Data 136: 1–12.

Kowalski-Trakofler, K., Steiner L. and Schwerha D. (2005). 'Safety considerations for the ageing workforce', *Safety Science,* 43, 10, 779–93.

Kragh, S. U. and Bislev, S. (2005). 'Universities and student values across nations', *Journal of Intercultural Communication*, http://www.immi.se/intercultural/.

Krekula, C. (2007). 'The Intersection of Age and Gender: Reworking Gender Theory and Social Gerontology', *Current Sociology*, 55, 2, 155–71.

Kubeck, J. E., Delp, N. D., Haslett, T. K. and McDaniel, M. A. (1996). 'Does job-related training performance decline with age?', *Psychology and Aging,* 11, 1, 92–107.

Kunreuther, F. (2003). 'The changing of the guard: What generational differences tell us about social-change organisations', *Nonprofit and Voluntary Sector Quarterly*, 32, 3, 450–7.

Kupperschmidt, B. (2000). 'Multigenerational employees: strategies for effective management', *The Health Care Manager*, 19, 1, 65–76.

Labour Force Survey (2009). Office of National Statistics. Available at: www.statistics.gov.uk (retrieved 31 March 2010).

Lamping, W. and and Rüb, F. W. (2004). 'From the conservative welfare state to an "Uncertain something else": German pension politics in comparative perspective', *Policy and Politics*, 32, 2, 169–91.

Landrigan, C. P., Rothschild, J. M., Cronin, J. W., Kaushal, R., Burdick, E., Katz, J. T., Lilly, C. M., Stone, P. H., Lockley, S. W., Bates, D. W. and Czeisler, C. W. (2004). 'Effect of reducing interns' work hours on serious medical errors in intensive care units', *N Engl J Med*, 351, 18, 1838–48.

Lange, A. H., de, T., T. W., Jansen, P. G. W., Smulders, P., Houtman, I. L. D. and Kompier, M. A. J. (2006). 'Age as a factor in the relation between work and mental health: Results from the longitudinal TAS study', in J. Houdmont and S. McIntyre (eds). *Occupational Health Psychology: European Perspectives on Research, Education and Practice* (Maia, Portugal: ISMAI Publications), pp. 21–45.

Lankard, B. (1995). *New Ways of Learning in the Workplace. ERIC Digest. Clearing House on Adult Career and Vocational Education* (Columbus, Ohio: Educational Resources Information Centre).

Latham, G. P. and Pinder, C. C. (2005). 'Work motivation theory and research at the dawn of the twenty-first century', *Annual Review of Psychology*, 56, 1, 485–516.

Lave, J. and Wenger, E. (1991). *Situated Learning: Legitimate Peripheral Participation* (New York: Cambridge University Press).

Lawrence, B. S. (1988). 'New wrinkles in the theory of age: Demography, norms and performance ratings', *Academy of Management Journal*, 31, 2, 84–95.

Lazear, E. P. (1979). 'Why is there mandatory retirement?', *Journal of Political Economy*, 87, 6, 1261–84.

Leibold, M. and Voelpel, S. (2006). *Managing the Aging Workforce. Challenges and Solutions* (Erlangen: Publicis and Wiley).

Leman, S. (2003). 'Participating in adult learning: Comparing the sources and applying the results', in N. Sargant and F. Aldridge (eds). *Adult Learning and Social Division: A Persistent Pattern, Volume 2* (Leicester: Institute of Adult Continuing Education).

Levinson, D. J., Darrow, C. N. and Klein, E. B. (1978). *The Seasons of a Man's Life,* (New York: Random House).

Levtak, S. (2005). 'Health and safety of older nurses', *Nursing Outlook*, 53, 2.

Lewis, J. (2002). 'Individualisation, assumptions about the existence of an adult worker model and the shift towards contractualism', in A. Carling, S. Duncan and R. Edwards (eds). *Analysing Families, Morality and Rationality in Policy and Practice* (London: Routledge).

Liff, S. (1999). 'Diversity and equal opportunities: room for a constructive compromise?', *Human Resource Management Journal*, 9, 1, 65–75.

Lincoln, J. R., Gerlach, M. L. and Ahmadjian, C. L. (1996). '*Keiretsu* networks and corporate performance in Japan', *American Sociological Review*, 61, 1, 67–88.

Lindley, R. and Duell, N. (2006). *Ageing and Employment: Identification of Good Practice to Increase Job Opportunities and Maintain Older Workers in Employment.*

Available at: http://www.diversityatwork.net/EN/Docs/Ageing%20and%20 Employment.pdf.

Lindsay, C. and McQuaid, R. (2004). 'Avoiding the "McJobs": Unemployed job seekers and attitudes to service work', *Employment and Society*, 18, 297–319.

Lippman, S. (2008). 'Rethinking risk in the new economy: Age and cohort effects on unemployment and re-employment', *Human Relations*, 1259–92.

Lippmann, S. (2008). 'Rethinking risk in the new economy: Age and cohort effects on unemployment and re-employment', *Human Relations*, 61, 1259–92.

Lissenburg, S. and Smeaton, D. (2003). *Employment Transitions of Older Workers: The Role of Flexible Employment in Maintaining Labour Market Participation and Promoting Job Quality* (Bristol: Policy Press).

Litvin, D. R. (1997). 'The discourse of diversity: from biology to management', *Organization*, 4, 2, 187–209.

Lloyd-Sherlock, P. (2010). *Population Ageing and International Development: From Generalization to Evidence* (Bristol, UK: Polity Press).

Locke, E. A. and Latham, G. P. (2004). 'What should we do about motivation theory? Six recommendations for the twenty-first century', *Academy of Management Review*, 29, 3, 388–403.

London, M. (1993). 'Relationship between career motivation, empowerment and support for career development', *Journal of Occupational and Organisational Psychology*, 66, 1, 55–69.

London, M. (1990). 'Enhancing career motivation in late career', *Journal of Organisational Change Management*, 3, 2, 58–71.

London, M. and Greller, M. M. (1991). 'Demographic trends and vocational behavior: A twenty year retrospective and agenda for the 1990s', *Journal of Vocational Behavior*, 38, 2, 125–64.

Longhi, S. and Platt, L. (2008). *Pay Gaps across Equalities Areas*, Research report, No. 9 (Manchester: Equality and Human Rights Commission).

Lorbiecki, A. and Jack, G. (2000). 'Critical turns in the evolution of diversity management', *British Journal of Management*, 11, supplement 1, S17–S31.

Lord, R. L. and Farrington, P. A. (2006). 'Age-related differences in the motivation of knowledge workers', *Engineering Management Journal*, 18, 20–6.

Loretto, W. (2006). 'Employers' Attitudes, practices And policies towards older workers', *Human Resource Management Journal*, 16, 313–30.

Loretto, W., Duncan, C. and White, P. (2000). 'Ageism and employment: controversies, ambiguities and younger people's perceptions', *Ageing and Society*, 20, 3, 279–302.

Loretto, W., Vickerstaff, S. and White, P. (2007). 'Flexible work and older workers', in W. Loretto, S. Vickerstaff and P. White (eds). *The Future for Older Workers, New Perspectives* (Bristol: Policy Press), pp. 139–60.

Loretto, W., Vickerstaff, S. and White, P. (2007). *The Future for Older Workers – New Perspectives* (Bristol: Polity Press).

Loretto, W., Vickerstaff, S. and White, P. (2006). 'Introduction Themed Section: What do older workers want?', *Social Policy and Society*, 5, 4, 479–83.

Loretto, W., Vickerstaff, S. and White, P. (2005). *White Older Workers and the Options for Flexible Work*, Working Paper Series, No. 31 (London: Equal Opportunities Commission).

Loretto, W. and White, P. (2006a). 'Employers' attitudes, practices and policies towards older workers', *Human Resource Management Journal*, 16, 3, 313–30.

Loretto, W. and White, P. (2006b). 'Work, More Work and Retirement: Older Workers' Perspectives', *Social Policy and Society*, 5, 495–506.

Low Pay Commission (2004). *Protecting Younger Workers* (Norwich: HMSO).

Loxley v BAE Systems (2008). ICR 1348.

Lucas, R. E. (2009). *Address to the Public Policy Forum 'Australian Immigration: Responding To A Changing Global Environment*, available at: http://www.immi.gov.au/about/speeches-pres/_pdf/2009-06-15-public-policy-forum.pdf.

Lucas, R. E. (1993). 'Ageism and the UK Hospitality Industry', *Employee Relations*, 15, 33–42.

Lundberg, D. and Marshallsay, Z. (2007). *Older Workers' Perspectives on Training and Retention of Older Workers* (Adelaide: National Centre for Vocational Education Research: National Vocational Education and Training Research and Evaluation Program Report).

Lutz, W. (2008), *European Demographic Datasheet 2008*, available at: http://www.oeaw.ac.at/vid/datasheet/download/European_Demographic_Data_Sheet_2008.pdf,

Lyon, P., Hallier, J. and Glover, I. (1998). 'Divestment or investment? The contradictions of HRM in relation to older employees', *Human Resource Management Journal*, 8, 1, 56–66.

Lyon, P. and Pollard, D. (1997). 'Perceptions of the older employee: Is anything really changing?', *Personnel Review*, 26, 4, 245–57.

Lyons, S., Duxbury, L. and Higgins, C. (2007). 'An empirical assessment of generational differences in basic human values', *Psychological Reports*, 101, 339–52.

Mabey, C. (2004). 'Development in Europe: Implications for research and practice', *Advances in Developing Human Resources*, 6, 4, 504–13.

Maccoby, M. (1988). *Why Work? Leading the New Generation* (New York: Simon and Schuster).

Machin, S. and Wilkinson, D. (1995). *Employee Training: Unequal Access and Economic Performance* (London: Institute for Public Policy Research).

Mackey, D. C. and Robinovitch, S. N. (2006). 'Mechanisms underlying age-related differences in ability to recover balance with the ankle strategy', *Gait & Posture*, 23, 1, 59–68.

Macky K., Gardner, D. and Forsyth, S. (2008). 'Generational differences at work: Introduction and overview', *Journal of Managerial Psychology*, 23 8, 857–61.

Macnicol, J. (2008). 'Older men and work in the twenty-first century: What can the history of retirement tell us?', *Journal of Social Policy*, 37, 4, 579–95.

MacNicol, J. (2006). *Age Discrimination: An Historical and Contemporary Analysis* (Cambridge: Cambridge University Press).

Mahoney, J. (1976). 'Age and values: The generation non-gap', *Psychological Reports*, 39, 62.

Mai, W. (2008). 'Competence development for ageing employees in Siemens. The Compass process from the point of view of the works council', in B. Nyhan and T. Tikkanen (eds). *Innovative Learning Measures for Older Workers* (Luxembourg: Office for Official Publications of the European Communities), pp. 14–28.

Mainiero, L. A. and Sullivan, S. E. (2005). 'Kaleidoscope careers: An alternate explanation for the "opt-out" revolution', *The Academy of Management Executive*, 19, 1, 106–23.

Mallon, M. and Cohen, L. (2001). 'Time for a change? Women's accounts of the move from organizational careers to self-employment', *British Journal of Management*, 12, 217–30.

Maltby, T. (2007). 'The employability of older workers: What works?', in W. Loretto, S. Vickerstaff and P. White (eds). *The Future for Older Workers – New Perspectives* (Bristol: Polity Press).

Maltby, T., de Vroom, B., Mirabile, M. and Overbye, E. (2003). *Ageing and the Transition to Retirement. A Comparative Analysis of European Welfare States* (Alderstot: Ashgate).

Mannheim, K. (1952). 'The problem of generations', in P. Kecskemeti (ed.). *Essays on the Sociology of Knowledge* (London: Routledge and Kegan).

Mason, W. H. and Wolfinger, N. H. (2001). *Cohort Analysis*. (California Centre for Population Research, University of California – Los Angeles), CCPR-005-01.

Marshall, V. W., Clarke, P. and Ballantyne, P. J. (2001). 'Instability in the retirement transition: Effects on health and well-being in a Canadian study', *Research on Aging*, 23, 379–409.

Marszalek, A. (2000). 'Thirst and work capacity of older people in a hot environment', *Int J Occup Saf Ergon*. Spec No. pp. 135–42.

Martyn, K. and Belli, R. (1997). 'Retrospective data collection using event history calendars', *Nursing Research*, 51, 4, 270–4.

Maurer, A., Oszustowicz, B. and Stocki, R. (1994). 'Gender and attitudes toward work', *International Journal for the Advancement of Counselling*, 17, 35–46.

Maurer, T. J. (2001). 'Career-relevant learning and development, worker age, and beliefs about self-efficacy for development', *Journal of Management*, 27, 2, 123.

Maurer, T. J., Weiss, E. M. and Barbeite, F. G. (2003). 'A model of involvement in work-related learning and development activity: The effects of individual, situational, motivational, and age variables', *The Journal of Applied Psychology*, 88, 4, 707–24.

Mayhew, K., Elliott, M. and Rijkers, B. (2008). 'Upskilling older workers', *Ageing Horizons*, 8, 13–21.

Mayrhofer, W., Meyer, M. and Steyrer, J (eds). (2005). *macht?erfolg?reich?glücklich? Einflussfaktoren auf Karrieren (power? success? richness? happiness? Factors influencing careers)*. (Wien: Linde).

Mayrhofer, W., Nordhaug, O. and Obeso, C. (2009). 'Career and job preferences among elite business students', *Beta. Scandinavian Journal of Business Research*, 22, 38–64.

Mayring, P. (2003). *Qualitative Inhaltsanalyse* (Weinheim und Base: Beltz Verlag).

McCormick, B. (1997). 'Regional unemployment and labour mobility in the UK', *European Economic Review*, 41, 581–9.

McCoy v James McGregor and Sons (2007). 00237/07IT.

McCrarey, S. (2005). 'Motivating the workforce with a positive culture: Recognition that works', *Franchising World*, 37, 3, 54–8.

McCrudden, C. and Kountouros, H. H. (2006). *Human Rights and European Equality Law*, Oxford Legal Studies Research Paper No. 8/2006.

McEvoy, G. M. and Cascio, W. F. (1989). 'Cumulative evidence of the relationship between employee age and job performance', *Journal of Applied Psychology*, 74, 1, 11–17.

McGregor, J. and Gary, L. (2002). 'Stereotypes and older workers: The New Zealand experience', *Social Policy Journal of New Zealand*, 18 June, 163–77.

McHarg, A. and Nicolson, D. (2006). 'Justifying Affirmative Action: Perception and Reality', *Journal of Law and Society*, 33, 1–41.

McKinsey & Company (2007). 'Acting on global trends: A McKinsey global survey', *The McKinsey Quarterly*. Retrieved from http://www.mckinseyquarterly.com/Acting_on_global_trends_A_McKinsey_Global_Survey_1998.

McMullin, J., Comeau, T. and Jovic, E. (2007). 'Generational affinities and discourses of difference: A case study of highly skilled information technology workers', *British Journal of Sociology*, 58, 2, 297–316.

McNair, S. (2006). 'How different is the older labour market? Attitudes to work and retirement among older people in Britain', *Social Policy and Society*, 5, 4, 485–95.

McNair, S. (2009). *Demography and Lifelong Learning, NIACE Inquiry into the Future of Lifelong Learning Thematic Paper 1* (Leicester: National Institute of Adult Continuing Education).

McNair, S., Flynn, M. and Dutton, Y. (2007). *Employer Responses to an Ageing Workforce: A Qualitative Study* (London: DWP).

McNair, S., Flynn, M., Owen, L., Humphreys, C. and Woodfield, S. (2004). *Changing Work in Later life: A Study of Job Transitions* (University of Surrey: Centre for Research into the Older Workforce).

McVittie, C., McKinlay, A. and Widdicombe, S. (2003). 'Committed to (Un)equal Opportunities?: "New ageism" and the Older Worker', *British Journal of Social Psychology*, 42, 595–612.

Mead, G. H. (1934). *Mind, Self, and Society.* (Chicago: University of Chicago Press).

Meadows, P. (2004). *The Economic Contribution of Older People*, for Age Concern England (London: Volterra Consulting and Age Concern).

Melamed, T. (1995). 'Career success: The moderating effect of gender', *Journal of Vocational Behavior*, 47, 35–60.

Metcalf, H. (2009). *Pay Gaps across the Equality Strands: A Review*, Research report, No. 14 (Manchester: Equality and Human Rights Commission).

Metcalf, H. and Meadows, P. (2006). *Survey of Employers Policies, Practices and Preferences Relating to Age* (London: DWP/DTI).

Metcalf, H. and Thompson, M. (1990). *Older Workers: Employers' Attitudes and Practices*, IMS Report no. 194 (Brighton: Institute of Manpower Studies).

Meyer, J. P., Becker, T. E. and Van Dick, R. R. (2006). 'Social Identities and Commitments at Work: Toward an Integrative Model', *Journal of Organizational Behavior*, 27, 665–83.

Ministry of Health, Labor, and Welfare (2008). *White Paper on Aging Society*, 2008 (Tokyo, Japan: Office of Government Public Relations).

Ministry of Health, Labour, and Welfare (MHLW) (2009). *20 Nenban Rōdōkeizai no Bunseki [Analysis of Labor Economy, 2008 edition]* (Tokyo, Japan: Office of Government Public Relations.).

Ministry of Justice (2009). *Employment Tribunal and EAT Statistics (GB) April 2009 to 31 March 2009* (London: Tribunals Service/Ministry of Justice).

Mirvis, P. H. and Hall, D. T. (1994). 'Psychological success and the boundaryless career', *Journal of Organisational Behavior (1986–1998)*, 15, 4, 365–81.

Mitchell, T. R., Holtom, B. C., Lee, T. W., Sablynski, C. J. and Erez, M. (2001). 'Why people stay: Using job embeddedness to predict voluntary turnover', *Academy of Management Journal*, 44, 1102–21.

Mollica, K. A. (2003). 'The influence of diversity context on white men's and racial minorities' reactions to disproportionate group harm', *The Journal of Social Psychology*, 143, 415–25.

Monk, T. H. (2005). 'Aging human circadian rhythms: Conventional wisdom may not always be right', *J Biol Rhythms*, 20, 4, 366–74.

Moore, S. (2009). 'No matter what I did I would still end up in the same position', *Work, Employment and Society*, 23, 4, 655–71.

Mor Barak, M. E. and Levin, A. (2002). 'Outside of the corporate mainstream and excluded from the work community: A study of diversity, job satisfaction and well-being', *Community, Work & Family*, 5, 2, 133–57.

Morrow-Howell, N., Gao, J., Zou, L. and Xie, Y. (2009, Summer). *Productive Aging Conference report,* CSD Report 09-51 (St. Louis, MO: Center for Social Development, George Warren Brown School of Social Work, Washington University).

Morschhäuser, M. (2006). *Reife Leistung: Personal- und Qualifizierungspolitik für die künftige Altersstruktur* (Berlin: Sigma).

Muller, M. (1999). 'Unitarism, pluralism and human resource management in Germany', *Management International Review*, 39, Special Issue 3, 125–44.

Muller-Camen, M., Croucher, R., Flynn, M. and Schroder, H. (2010). 'National institutions and employers' Age management practices in Britain and Germany: "Path dependence" and option creation', *Human Relations*, forthcoming.

Muller-Camen, M., Tempel, A., Almond, P., Edwards, T., Ferner, A., Peters, R. and Wächter, H. (2004). *Human Resource Management in US Multinationals in Germany and the UK* (London: Anglo-German Foundation).

Munnell, A. H. and Sass, S. (2008). *Working Longer: The Solution to the Retirement Income Challenge* (Washington, DC: Brookings Institution Press).

Muntaner, C., Van Dussen, D. J., Li, Y., Zimmerman, S., Chung, H. and Benach, J. 'Work organization, economic inequality, and depression among nursing assistants: A multilevel modeling approach', *Psychol Rep*, 98, 2, 585–601.

Murphy, E. F., Gordon, J. D., and Anderson, T. L. (2004). 'Cross-cultural, cross-cultural age and cross-cultural generational differences in values between the United States and Japan', *Journal of Applied Management and Entrepreneurship*, 9, 1, 21–47.

Naegele, G. A. and Walker, A. (2006). *A Guide to Good Practice in Age Management* (Luxembourg: European Foundation for the Improvement of Living and Working Conditions).

Naegele, and Krämer, K. (2001). 'Recent developments in the employment and retirement of older workers in Germany', *Journal of Aging and Social Policy*, 13, 1, 69–82.

National Academy on an Aging Society (2004). *Diabetes: A Drain on US Resources*, available at: http://www.agingsociety.org/agingsociety/pdf/diabetes.pdf.

National Institute of Population and Social Security Research (2007). *Annual Report on Social Security Statistics* (Tokyo, Japan: Office of Government Public Relations).

National Silver Human Resource Center (NSHRC) (2008). *Active Ageing – National Statistics*. Retrieved 4 September 2009 (http://www.zsjc.or.jp/rhx/upload/Statistics/2.pdf).

Near, J. P. (1984). 'Reactions to the career plateau', *Business Horizons*, 27, 4, 75–9.

Nelson, T. D. (2004). *Ageism: Stereotyping and Prejudice against Older Persons*, (Cambridge, MA: MIT Press).

Nestle (2008). *Code of Business Conduct* (Geneva: Nestle).

Neumark, D. (2009). 'Age Discrimination in Employment Act and the Challenge of Population Aging', *Research on Aging*, 31, 41.

Ng, T. W. H., Eby, L. T., Sorensen, K. L. and Feldman, D. C. (2005). 'Predictors of objective and subjective career success: A meta-analysis', *Personnel Psychology*, 58, 367–408.

Ni Léime, A. (2009), 'Getting on or getting out? The impact of gender on promotion decision-making among older workers in Ireland', Paper presented at the 9th Conference of the European Sociological Association 'European Society or European Societies? 2–5 September 2009, Lisbon.

Nicholson, P. J. and D'Auria, D. A. (1999). 'Shift work, health, the working time regulations and health assessments', *Occup Med Lond*, 49, 3, 127–37.

Nikandroua, I., Aposporia, E., Panayotopouloua, L., Stavroub, E. and Papalexandrisa, N. (2008). 'Training and firm performance in Europe: The impact of national and organisational characteristics', *The International Journal of Human Resource Management*, 19, 11, 2057–78.

Noble, S. M. and Schewe, C. D. (2003). 'Cohort segmentation: An exploration of its validity' *Journal of Business Research,* 56, 979–87.

Nordhaug, O., Gooderham, P., Zhang, X. and Birkelund, G. (2010). Elite business students in China and Norway: Job related values and preferences. *Scandinavian Journal of Educational Research*, 54 (2), 109–23.

Nusbaum, N. J. (1999). 'Aging and sensory senescence', *South Med J*, 92, 3, 267–75.

Nyhan, B. and Tikkanen, T. (2008). *Innovative Learning Measures for Older Workers* (Luxembourg: Office for Official Publications of the European Communities).

O'Bannon, G. (2001). 'Managing our future: The generation X factor', *Public Personnel Management*, 35, 95–109.

O'Rand, A. M. and Campbell, R. T. (1999). 'On reestablishing the phenomenon and specifying ignorance: Theory development and research design in aging', in V. L. Bengtson and K. W. Schaie (eds). *Handbook of Theories of Aging* (New York: Springer Publishing Company), pp. 59–78.

O'Brien-Pallas, L., Shamian, J., Thomson, D., Alksnis, C., Koehoorn, M., Kerr, M. and Bruce, S. (2004). 'Work-related disability in Canadian nurses', *Journal of Nursing Scholarship*, 36, 4, 352–7.

OECD (1997). *Manual for Better Training Statistics: Conceptual, Measurement and Survey Issues* (Paris: Organisation for Economic Co-operation and Development).

OECD (2004). *Ageing and Employment Practices – UK,* Organisation for Economic Cooperation and Development).

OECD (2006). *Live Longer, Work Longer,* Organisation for Economic Cooperation and Development.

OECD (2010). *OECD StatExtract,* available at: stats.oecd.org/Index.aspx?DatasetCode=ALFS_SUMTAB.

Office for National Statistics (2009). *Pension Trends. Chapter 4: The Labour Market and Retirement*, available at: http://www.statistics.gov.uk/downloads/theme_compendia/pensiontrends/Pension_Trends_ch04.pdf.

Office of National Statistics (2009). Available at: www.statistics.gov.uk (retrieved 31 March 2010).

Office for National Statistics (2009). *http://www.statistics.gov.uk* (accessed 29 August 2009).

Ohio Bureau of Workers' Compensation (BWC) (2001). *Older Workers Safety Tips*, available at: http://www.ohiobwc.com/employer/brochureware/olderworkers/safetytips.asp.

Ohio Bureau of Workers' Compensation (2005). *Employing Older Workers and Controlling Workers*, available at: http://www.ohiobwc.com/employer/brochureware/olderworkers/default.asp.

Ohio Job and Family Services (2007). *Identifying Regional Skill Shortages Dayton Metropolitan Statistical Area*, available at: http://lmi.state.oh.us/Research/skill/DaytonSummary.pdf.

Oklahoma Nurses Association (ONA) (2005). 'House of Delegates resolution: Implications of fatigue on patient safety', *Okla Nurse*, 50, 4, 7–8.

O'Neil, D. and Bilimoria, D. (2005). 'Women's career development phases: Idealism, endurance, and reinvention', *Career Development International*, 10, 3, 168–89.

Ono, H. (2007). *Lifetime Employment in Japan: Concepts and Measurements*, SSE/EFI Working Paper Series in Economics No. 624, Stockholm School of Economics. Retrieved June 12, 2009 (http://paa2007.princeton.edu/download.aspx?submissionId=7223).

Organization for Economic Co-Operations and Development (2007). *Pensions at a Glance 2007* (Paris, France: OECD Publishing).

Organization of Economic Co-operation and Development (2008). *Employment Outlook 2007* (Paris, France: OECD Publishing).

Organization for Economic Co-Operation and Development (2009a). *OECD: Factbook 2009: Economic, Environmental and Social Statistics*. Retrieved October 15, 2009 (http://www.oecd.org/document/62/0,3343,en_21571361_34374092_34420734_1_1_1_1,00.html).

Organization for Economic Co-operations and Development (2009b). *OECD in Figures 2009* (Paris, France: OECD Publishing).

Oxley, H. (2009). *OECD Health Working Papers no. 42: Policies for Healthy Ageing: An Overview*, available at: http://www.olis.oecd.org/olis/2009doc.nsf/linkto/DELSA-HEA-WD-HWP(2009)1.

Ozanne, E. (2001). 'Lifelong career development', in W. Patton and M. McMahon (eds). *Career Development Programmes: Preparation for Lifelong Career Decision Making* (Victoria, Australia: Acer Press).

Palacios de la Villa v Cortefiel Servicios (2007). C-411/05 ECJ October 16 2007.

Palfrey, J. and Gasser, U. (2008). *Born Digital: Understanding the First Generation of Digital Natives* (New York: New York Basic Books).

Palmer, K. T., Griffin, M. J., Syddall, H. E., Davis, A., Pannett, B. and Coggon, D. (2002). 'Occupational exposure to noise and the attributable burden of hearing difficulties in Great Britain', *Occup Environ Med*, 59, 9, 634.

Parker, B. and Chusmir, L. (1990). 'A generational and sex-based view of managerial work values', *Psychological Reports*, 66, 947–50.

Parkes, K. R. and Swash, S. (2000). *Injuries in Offshore Oil and Gas Installations; An Analysis of Temporal and Occupational Factors*, Technology Report:OTO199-097 HSE).

Parry, E. and Tyson, S. (2009). 'Organizational reactions to UK age discrimination legislation', *Employee Relations*, 31, 5, 471–88.

Parry, E. and Tyson, S. (2006). 'Organisations strategies for approaching age discrimination at work', *Presented at the British Academy of Management (HR Division) Conference*, 2006, Kings College, London.

Parry, E. and Urwin, P. (2009). *Tapping into Talent: The Age Factor and Generation Issues* (London: CIPD).

Parry, E. and Urwin, P. (2010 forthcoming). 'Generational differences in work values: A review of theory and evidence', *International Journal of Management Reviews.*

Patrickson, M. and Ranzijn, R. (2006). 'Workforce ageing: The challenges for 21st Century Management', *International Journal of Organisational Behaviour,* 10, 4, 729.

Patrickson, M. and Ranzijn, R. (2004). 'Bounded choices in work and retirement in Australia', *Employee Relations,* 26, 422–32.

Performance and Innovation Unit (2000). *Winning the Generation Game* (London: The Stationary Office).

Petersen, A. and Willig, R. (2004). 'Work and recognition, reviewing new forms of pathological developments', *Acta Sociologica,* 47, 4, 338–50.

Peterson, S. and Spiker, B. (2005). 'Establishing the positive contributory value of older workers: A positive psychology perspective', *Organizational Dynamics,* 34, 2, 153–67.

Petru, R., Wittmann, M., Nowak, D., Birkholz, B. and Angerer, P. (2005). 'Effects of working permanent night shifts and two shifts on cognitive and psychomotor performance', *International Archives of Occupational and Environmental Health,* 78, 2, 109–16.

Pfeffer, J. (1983). 'Organizational demography', *Research in Organizational Behavior,* 5, 299–357.

Phillipson, C. and Smith, A. (2005). *Extending working life: A review of the research literature,* Department for Work and Pensions research Report No.299 (Leeds: DWP).

Pienta, A. M., Burr, J. A. and Mutchler, J. E. (1994). 'Women's Labor Force Participation in Later life: The Effects of Early Work and Family Experiences', *Journal of Gerontology: Social Sciences,* 49, 5, S231–S239.

Pikhart, H., Bobak, M., Pajak, A., Malyutina, S., Kubinova, R., Topo, R., Sebakova, H., Nikitin, Y. and Marmot, M. (2004). 'Psychosocial factors at work and depression in three countries of Central and Eastern Europe', *Social Science & Medicine,* 58, 8, 1475–82.

Pillay, H., Boulton-Lewis, G., Wilss, L. and Lankshear, C. (2003). 'Conceptions of work and learning at work: Impressions from older workers', *Studies in Continuing Education,* 25, 1, 95–111.

Pirkl, J. (1995). 'Transgenerational design: Prolonging the American dream', *Generations,* 19, 1, 32–6.

Pitt-Catsouphes, M., Matz-Costa, C. and Besen, E. (2009, April). *Age & Generations: Understanding experiences at the workplace* (Research Highlight 06). (Chestnut Hill, MA: Sloan Center on Aging and Work at Boston College).

Platman, K. (2004). 'Flexible employment in later life: Public policy panaceas in the search for mechanisms to extend working lives', *Social Policy and Society,* 3, 2, 181–88.

PMSEIC (n.d.). *Promoting Healthy Ageing In Australia,* available at: http://www2.fhs.usyd.edu.au/arow/a/Kendig-Healthy%20Ageing.pdf.

Porcellato, L., Carmichael, F., Hulme, C., Ingha, B. and Prashar, A. (2010). 'Giving older workers a voice; constraints on employment', *Work Employment and Society,* 25, 1, forthcoming.

Porter, N. B. (2003). 'Sex Plus Age Discrimination: Protecting Older Women Workers', *Denver University Law Review,* 81, 79.

Powell, G. N., Butterfield, A. and Parent, J. D. (2002). 'Gender and managerial stereotypes: Have the times changed?', *Journal of Management*, 28, 177–93.

Powell, G. N. and L. A. Mainiero (1992). 'Cross-currents in the river of time: Conceptualizing the complexities of women's careers', *Journal of Management*, 18, 2, 215–37.

PPHSA (Pulp and Paper Health and Safety Association) (2006). *Slips Trips and Falls – Can they be Prevented?*, available at: http://www.pphsa.on.ca/OccHealth/STF/stf.htm.

Prasad, P., Mills, A. J., Elmes, M. and Prasad, A. (1995). *Managing the Organizational Melting Pot. Dilemmas of Workplace Diversity* (London: Sage).

Prime Minister of Australia (2009). *Education Revolution*, available at: http://www.pm.gov.au/topics/education.cfm.

Pulham v Barking LBC (2008). UKEAT/0516/08/RN.

Punakallio, A. (2003). 'Balance abilities of different-aged workers in physically demanding jobs', *Journal of Occupational Rehabilitation*, 13, 1, 33–43.

Quaranta, A., Assennato, G. and Sallustio, V. (1996). 'Epidemiology of hearing problems among adults in Italy', *Scand Audiol Suppl*, 42, 9–13.

Rabasca, L. (2000). 'Book notes: Growing old, staying spry', *APA Monitor on Psychology*, 31, 8.

Rabbit, P. and Lowe, C. (2000). 'Patterns of cognitive ageing', *Psychological Research*, 63, 3/4, 308–16.

Ralston, D. A., Egri, C. P., Stewart, S., Terpstra, R. H. and Kaicheng, Y. (1999). 'Doing business in the 21st century with the new generation of Chinese managers: A study of generational shifts in work values in China', *Journal of International Business Studies*, 30, 2, 415–27.

Randstad (2008). *2008 World of Work* (New York: Rochester).

Redman, T. and Snape, E (2002). 'Ageism in teaching: Stereotypical beliefs and discriminatory attitudes towards the over 50s', *Work, Employment and Society*, 16, 355–71.

Reitman F. and Schneer, J. A. (2003). 'The promised path: A longitudinal study of managerial careers', *Journal of Managerial Psychology*, 18, 1/2, 60–75.

Remery, C., Henkens, K., Schippers, J. and Ekamper, P. (2003). 'Managing an Aging Workforce and a Tight Labour Market: Views Held By Dutch Employers', *Population Research and Policy Review*, 22, 21–40.

Rennie, S. (1993). 'Equal opportunities as an ethical issue', *Equal Opportunities Review*, 51, Sep/Oct, 7.

Rhodes, S. (1983). 'Age-related differences in work-attitudes and behaviour: A review and conceptual analysis', *Capitalizing on a Generation Gap*, 93, 2, 415–27.

Riach, K. (2009). 'Managing difference: Understanding age diversity in practice', *Human Resource Management Journal*, 19, 3, 319–35.

Riach, K. (2007). 'Othering' older worker identity in recruitment', *Human Relations*, 60, 11, 1701–26.

Rix, S. E. (2004). 'Public policy and the aging workforce in the United States', *Social Policy & Society*, 3, 2, 171–9.

Roberts, B. W. and Friend, W. (1998). 'Career momentum in midlife women: Life context, identity, and personality correlates', *Journal of Occupational Health Psychology*, 3, 3, 195–208.

Roberts, I. (2006). 'Taking age out of the workplace: Putting older workers back in?', *Work, Employment and Society*, 20, 1, 67–86.

Robson, S. M. and Hansson, R. O. (2007). 'Strategic self-development for successful aging at work', *International Journal of Aging & Human Development,* 64, 4, 331–59.

Rodrigues, V. F., Fischer, F. M. and Brito, M. J. (2001). 'Shift work at a modern offshore drilling rig', *J Hum Ergol (Tokyo),* 30, 1/2, 167–72.

Rogers, W. A. (1996). 'Assessing age-related differences in the long-term retentionof skills', in W. A. Rogers, A. D. Fisk, N. Walker et al. (eds). *Aging and SKilled Performance* (Mahwah, N.J.: Erlbaum).

Rolls Royce plc v Unite (2008). EWHC 2420 (QB).

Ross, D. and Harper, S. (2009). *Assessing the Work Ability of an Ageing Workforce: Evidence from the UK Offshore Oil and Gas Industry,* Presentation to ISA, 2009.

Rouch, I., Wild. P., Ansiau, D. and Marquié, J. C. (2005). 'Shiftwork experience, age and cognitive performance', *Ergonomics,* 48, 10, 1282–93.

Rousseau, D. B. and Schalk, R. (2000). *Psychological Contracts in Employment: Cross-National Perspectives* (Thousand Oaks, CA.: Sage).

Rousseau, D. M. (1995). *Psychological Contracts in Organizations: Understanding Written and Unwritten Agreements* (Thousand Oaks: Sage).

Rousseau, D. M. (2001). 'Schema, promise and mutuality: The building blocks of the psychological contract', *Journal of Occupational and Organizational Psychology,* 74, 511–841.

Rump, J. (2003). *'Alter und Altern: Die Berücksichtigung der Intergenerativität und der Lebensphasenorientierung'*, in H. Wächter, G. Vedder and M. Führing (eds). *Personelle Vielfalt in Organisationen* (München: Hampp).

Russell, C. (2007). 'What Do Older Women and Men Want? Gender Differences in the "Lived Experience" of Ageing', 55, 2, 173–92.

Rutherford (No. 2) v. Secretary of State for Trade and Industry (2006). UKHL 19 para 71.

Ryder, N. (1965). 'The cohort as a concept in the study of social change', *American Sociological Review,* 30, 6, 843–61.

Rynes, S. L. and Gerhart, B. (2000). *Compensation in Organizations* (San Francisco: Jossey-bass).

Salter, T. (2004). 'Retirement Age: Economic Outcome Or Social Choice? Pension Flexibility And Retirement Choice', *Pension,* 9, 256–74.

Salthouse, T. A. (1991a). *Theoretical Perspectives on Cognitive Aging* (Hillsdale, N.J.: Erlbaum).

Salthouse, T. A. (1991). 'Mediation of adult age differences in cognition by reductions in working memory and speed of processing', *Psychological Science,* 2, 3, 179–83.

Salthouse, T. A. (2004). 'What and when of cognitive aging', *Current Directions in Psychological Science,* 13, 4, 140–4.

Sanders, G. and Tuschke, A. (2007). 'The adoption of institutionally contested organisational practices: The emergence of stock option pay in Germany', *Academy of Management Journal,* 50, 1, 33–56.

Sargeant, M. (2005). 'Age discrimination: Equal treatment with exceptions', *International Journal of Discrimination and the Law,* 6, 251–66.

Schaeffer, J. (2000). *Kemper Reports* (Chicago, IL: Kemper Distributors).

Schein, E. H. (1996). 'Career anchors revisited: Implications for career development in the 21st century', *Executive-ADA,* 10, 80–8.

Schein, E. H. (1984). 'Organizational socialization and the profession of management', in D. A. Kolb, I. M. Rubin and J. M. McIntyre (eds). *Organizational Psychology* (Englewood Cliffs, N.J.: Prentice-Hall).

Schizaz, C. (1999). 'Capitalizing on a generation gap', *Management Review*, 88, 6, 62–8.

Schmid, G. and Hartlapp, M. (2008). 'Aktives Altern in Europa', *Aus Politik und Zeitgeschichte*, 18/19, 6–14.

Schmidt, M. (2008). 'Age discrimination under the German AGG 2006', in M. Sargeant (ed.). *The Law on Age Discrimination in the EU* (Aspen: Kluwer Law International).

Schneck, M. E. and Heagerstrom-Portnoy, G. (2003). 'Practical assessment of vision in the elderly', *Ophthalmology Clinics of North America*, 16, 2, 269–87.

Schneider, B. A., Daneman, M. and Murphy, D. R. (2005). 'Speech comprehension difficulties in older adults: Cognitive slowing or age-related changes in hearing?', *Psychology and Aging*, 20, 2, 261–71.

Schooler, C. (1987). 'Psychological effects of complex environments during the life-span: A review and theory', in C. Schooler and W. Scheue (eds). *Cognitive structure and social functioning over the life course* (Norwood, NJ: Ablex).

Schooler, C., Mulatu, M. S. and Oates, G. (1999). 'The continuing effects of substantively complex work on the intellectual functioning of older workers', *Psychology and Aging*, 14, 483–506.

Schroder, H., Hofacker, D. and Muller-Camen, M. (2008). 'HRM and the employment of older workers', *International Journal of Human Resource Development and Management*, 9, 2/3, 162–79.

Schuller, T. and Watson, D. (2009). *Learning Through Life: Inquiry into the Future for Lifelong Learning* (Leicester: National Institute of Adult Continuing Education).

Schulz, J. H. and Binstock, R. H. (2008). *Nation: The Economics and Politics of Growing Older in America* (Baltimore, MD: Johns Hopkins University Press).

Schuman, H. and Rogers, W. (2004). 'Cohorts, chronology and collective memories', *Public Opinion Quarterly*, 68, 217–54.

Schuman, H. and Scott, J. (1989). 'Generations and collective memories', *American Sociological Review*, 54, 359–81.

Schumann, M. and Sartain, L. (2006). *Brand for Talent. Eight Essentials to Make Your Talent as Famous as Your Brand* (San Francisco: Jossey-Bass).

Schwartz, S. H. (1994). 'Beyond individualism/collectivism: new dimensions of values'. In U. Kim, H. C. Triandis, C. Kagitçibasi, S. C. Choi, & G. Yoon (eds). *Individualism and Collectivism: Theory application and methods* (Newbury Park, CA: Sage).

Schwartz, D. and Kleiner, B. (1999). 'Relationship between age and employment opportunities', *Equal Opportunities International*, 18, 5/6, 105–10.

Scott, L. D., Rogers, A., Hwang, W. and Zhang, Y. (2006). 'Effects of critical care nurses' work hours on vigilance and patients' safety', *Am J Crit Care*, 15, 1, 30–7.

Scottish Executive (2005). *Healthy Working Lives – A Plan For Action*, available at: http://www.scotland.gov.uk/library5/health/hwls-04.asp.

Segal, U. A. (1992). 'Values, personality and career choice', *The Journal of Applied Social Sciences*, 16, 143–59.

Segers, J., Inceoglu, I., Vloeberghs, B. B. D. and Henderickx, E. (2008). 'Protean and boundaryless careers: A study on potential motivators', *Journal of Vocational Behavior*, 73, 212–30.

Seidler, A., Nienhaus, A., Bernhardt, T., Kauppinen, T., Elo, A. L. and Frölich, L. (2004). 'Psychosocial work factors and dementia', *Occup Environ Med*, 61, 962–71.

Seifert, H. (2008). 'Alternsgerechte Arbeitszeiten', *Aus Politik und Zeitgeschichte*, 19, 23–30.

Seike, A. and Yamada, A. (2004). *Kōreisha Shūrou no Keizaigaku [The Economics of Older Worker Labor Force Participation]* (Tokyo, Japan: Nihon Keizai Shinbunsha).

Senior Community Service Employment Program (SCSEP) (2007). *U.S. Department of Labor Employment & Training Administration*, FY 2004 Performance Results Summary. Retrieved 25 August 2009 (http://www.doleta.gov/Seniors/html_docs/GranteePerf.cfm).

Sessa, V., Kabacoff, R., Deal, J. and Brown, H. (2007). 'Generational differences in leader values and leadership behaviours', *The Psychologist-Manager Journal*, 10, 1, 47–74.

Sfard, A. (1998). 'On two metaphors for learning and the dangers of choosing just one', *Educational Researcher*, 27, 2, 4–13.

Shephard, R. J. (1999). 'Age and physical work capacity', *Experimental Aging Research*, 25, 4, 331–43.

Shephard, R. J. (2000). 'Aging and productivity: Some physiological issues', *Aging and Productivity: Some Physiological Issues*, 25, 5, 535–45.

Sheridan, A. and Conway, L. (2001). 'Workplace flexibility: reconciling the needs of employers and employees', *Women in Management Review*, 18, 1, 5–11.

Sherman, S. R. (1994). 'Changes in age identity: Self-perceptions in middle and late life', *Journal of Aging Studies*, 8, 4, 397–412.

Shinar, D. and Schieber, F. (1991). 'Visual requirements for safety and mobility of older drivers', *Human Factors*, 14, 1 Feb, 135–52.

Siebert, S. and Heywood, J. S. (2009). 'Understanding the labour market for older workers', *Economic Affairs*.

Simpson, R., Sturges, J., Woods, A. and Altman, Y. (2005). 'Gender, Age, and the MBA: An Analysis of Extrinsic and Intrinsic Career Benefits', *Journal of Management Education*, 29, 2, 218–47.

Sit, R. A. and Fisk, A. D. (1999). 'Age-related performance in a multiple-task environment', *Journal of the Human Factors and Ergonomics Society*, 41, 1, 26–34.

Skidmore, P. (2004). 'The European employment strategy and labour law: A German case study', *European Law Review*, 29, 52–73.

Skillclear (2009). *Government-Approved Shortage Occupation Lists for Tier 2 of the Points-Based System 15 June 2009*, available at: http://www.skillclear.co.uk/Skills-Shortage-Occupation-List.pdf.

Skule, S. (2004). 'Learning conditions at work: A framework to understand and assess informal learning in the workplace', *International Journal of Training and Development*, 8, 1, 8–17.

Smeaton, D., Vegeris, S. and Melahat, S. (2009). *Older Workers: Employment Preferences, Barriers and Solutions*, Manchester: Equality and Human Rights Commission Research Report No. 43.

Smith, G. A. and Brewer, N. (1995). 'Slowness and age: Speed-accuracy mechanisms', *Psychology and Aging*, 10, 2, 238–47.

Smith, J. (2008). *Welcoming Workplace. Designing Office Space for an Ageing Workforce in the 21st Century Knowledge Economy* (London: Helen Hamlyn Centre).

Smola, K. W. and Sutton, C. D. (2002). 'Generational differences: Revisiting generational work values for the new millennium', *Journal of Organizational Behavior*, 23, 363–82.

Smola, K. W. and Sutton, C. D. (2002). 'Generational differences: revisiting generational work values for the new millennium', *Journal of Organizational Behavior*, 73, 212–30.

Snape, E. and Redman, T. (2003). 'Too old or too young? The impact of perceived age discrimination', *Human Resource Management Journal*, 13, 1, 78–89.

Spirduso, W. W. and Asplund, L. A. (1995). 'Physical activity and cognitive function in the elderly', *Quest*, 47, 395–410.

Standard Life (2009). *The Death of Retirement*, available at: http://www.standardlife.com/media/business_reports.html. (accessed 10 August 2009).

Steers, R. M., Mowday, R. T. and Shapiro, D. L. (2004). 'Introduction to special topic forum: The future of work motivation theory', *Academy of Management Review*, 29, 3, 379–87.

Sterns, H. L. and Doverspike, D. (1989). 'Aging and the retraining and learning process in organizations', in I. Goldstein and R. Katze (eds). *Training and Development in Work Organizations* (San Francisco, CA: Jossey-Bass), pp. 299–332.

Sterns, H. L. and Miklos, S. M. (1995). 'The aging worker in a changing environment: Organisational and individual issues', *Journal of Vocational Behavior*, 47, 3, 248–68.

Stoney, C. and Roberts, M. (2003), *The Case for Older Workers at TESCO: An Examination of Attitudes, Assumptions and Attributes*. Working Paper 53, School of Public Policy and Administration, Carlton University.

Strauss, W. and Howe, N. (1991). *Generations: The History of America's Future 1584–2069*, (New York: William Morrow and Company, Inc).

Stroh, L. K., Brett, J. F. and Reilly, A. H. (1992). 'All the right stuff: A comparison of female and male managers' career progression', *Journal of Applied Psychology*, 16, 143–59.

Sturges, J. (1999). 'What it means to succeed: Personal conceptions of career success held by male and female managers at different ages', *British Journal of Management*, 10, 239–52.

Sturges, J. (2004). 'The individualization of the career and its implications for leadership and management development', in J. Storey (ed.). *Leadership in Organizations: Current Issues and Key Trends* (UK: Routledge).

Sullivan, S. E. and Arthur, M. (1992). 'The evolution of the boundaryless career concept: Examining physical and psychological mobility', *Journal of Vocational Behavior*, 77, 251–60.

Sullivan, S. E. and Arthur, M. B. (2006). 'The evolution of the boundaryless career concept: Examining physical and psychological mobility', *Journal of Vocational Behavior*, 69, 1, 19–29.

Super, D. E. (1990). 'A life-span, life-space approach to career development', in D. Brown and L. Brooks (eds). *Career Choice and Development: Applying Contemporary Theories to Practice* (San Francisco, CA: Jossey-Bass), pp. 197–261.

Super, D. E. (1957). *The Psychology of Careers* (New York: Harper).

Suzuki, K., Ohida, T., Kaneita, Y., Yokoyama, E. and Uchiyama, M. (2005). 'Daytime sleepiness, sleep habits and occupational accidents among hospital nurses', *Journal of Advanced Nursing*, 52, 4, 445–53.

Svejenova, S. (2005). 'The path with the heart: Creating the authentic career', *Journal of Management Studies*, 42, 947–74.

Sweet, S. and Moen, P. (2006). 'Advancing a career focus on work and the family: Insights from the life course perspective'. In M. Pitt-Catsouphes, E. E. Kossek & S. Sweet (eds). *The Work and Family Handbook: Multi-Disciplinary Perspectives and Approaches* (Mahwah, NJ: Lawrence Erlbaum Associates), pp. 189–208.

Sweet. S. (2009). *When is a Person Too Young or Too Old to Work? Cultural Variations in Europe*. Issue Brief No. 2. (Chestnut Hill, MA: Sloan Center on Aging & Work. Retrieved on January 1, 2010 from: http://agingandwork.bc.edu/documents/GIB02_TooYoung-Old_ToWork_2009-02-18.pdf).

Swift, J. (2006). 'Justifying Age Discrimination', *Industrial Law Journal*, 35, 228–42.

Szinovacz, M. (1989). 'Retirement, Couples, and Household Work', in S. J. Bahr and E. T. Peterson (eds). *Aging and the Family* (MA: Lexington Books).

TAEN (2009). *Survey of Jobseekers Aged 50+* (London: The Age and Employment Network).

Tajfel, H. and Turner, J. C. (1986). 'The social identity theory of intergroup behavior', in S. Worchel and W. G. Austing (eds). *Psychology of Intergroup Relation* (Chicargo: Nelson Hall).

Takayama, N. (2002). *Nihon Teki Jinzaikanri no Arikata [Transitions in Human Resource Managements in Japanese Firms]* (Tokyo, Japan: Iwanami).

Tapscott, D. (2006). *Grown Up Digital: How the Net Generation is Changing Your World* (York et al: McGraw-Hill).

Tate and Lyle. (2008). *Company Code of Conduct*, available at: http://www.tateandlyle.com/TateAndLyle/social_responsibility/code_of_conduct/default.htm.

Taylor, P. (2002). *'Improving Employment Opportunities for Older Workers: Developing a Policy Framework*. Summary of EU Expert presentation on Getting the Policy Framework Right at the Ninth EU-Japan Symposium Improving Employment Opportunities for older workers, 21–2 March 2002, Brussels.

Taylor, P. (2004). 'Age and Work: International Perspectives', *Social Policy and Society*, 32, 163–70.

Taylor, P. (2008). 'Sing if you're glad to be grey: Working towards a happier older age in the United Kingdom', in P. Taylor (ed.). *Ageing Labour Forces: Promises and Prospects* (Cheltenham: Edward Elgar).

Taylor, P. and Urwin, P. (2001). 'Age and participation in vocational education and training', *Work, Employment and Society*, 15, 4, 763–79.

Taylor, P. and Walker, A. (1994). 'The ageing workforce: Employers attitudes towards older people' *Work, Employment and Society*, 8, 4, 569–91.

Taylor, P. and Walker, A. (1998). 'Employers and older workers: Attitudes and employment practices', *Ageing and Society*, 18, 641–58.

Taylor, P. and Walker, A. (2003). 'Age discrimination in the labour market and policy responses: The situation in the United Kingdom', *The Geneva Papers on Risk and Insurance*, 28, 4, 612–24.

Taylor, P. and Walker, A. (1998). 'Policies and practices towards older workers: A framework for comparative research', *Human Resource Management Journal*, 8, 3, 61–76.

Terjesen, S., Vinnicombe, S. and Freeman, C. (2007). 'Attracting generation Y graduates: Organisational attributes, likelihood to apply and sex differences', *Career Development International*, 12, 6, 504–22.

Tharenou, P. (1999). 'Gender differences in advancing to the top', *International Journal Management Reviews*, 1, 111–32.

The Incorporated Trustees of the National Council on Ageing (Age Concern England) v Secretary of State for Business, Enterprise and Regulatory Reform (2009). IRLR 373 (ECJ).

Thomas R. (1996). *Redefining Diversity* (New York: American Management Ass.).

Toomingas, A., Theorell, T., Michélsen, H. and Nordemar, R. (1997). 'Associations between self-rated psychosocial work conditions and musculoskeletal symptoms and signs'. Stockholm MUSIC I Study Group', *Scand J Work Environ Health*, 23, 2, 130–9.

Towers Perrin (2009). *Towers Perrin 2010 Health Care Cost Survey*, Retrieved September 26, 2009 (http://www.towersperrin.com/hcg/hcc/TPHCCS2010srvycharts.pdf).

Trade Union Congress (2005). *Ready, Willing and Able: Employment Opportunities for Older People* (London: TUC).

Trades Union Congress (2003). *Fairness throughout Working Life: TUC Response to Age Matters* (London, UK: TUC).

Trampusch, C. (2003). 'Institutional resettlement: The case of early retirement in Germany', in W. Streeck and K. Thelen (eds). *Beyond Continuity: Institutional Change in Advance Political Economies* (Oxford: Oxford University Press).

Tremblay, M., Roger, A. and J. Toulouse (1995). 'Career plateau and work attitudes: An empirical study of managers', *Human Relations*, 48, 3, 221–37.

Tsui, A., Egan, T. D. and O'Reilly, C. A. III (1992). 'Being Different: Relational Demography and Organizational Attachment', *Administrative Science Quarterly*, 37, 549–79.

TUC (2006). *Health and Safety*, available at: http://www.tuc.org.uk/h_and_s/index.cfm.

Tulgan, B. (1997). 'Generation X: Slackers? Or the workforce of the future?', *Employment Relations Today*, 24, 2, 55–64.

Tulving, E. and Craik, F. (2000). *The Oxford Handbook of Memory* (New York: OUP).

Turner, B. (2002). 'Strategic generations: Historical change, literary expression and generational politics', in J. Edmunds and B. Turner (eds). *Generational Consciousness, Narrative and Politics* (Maryland: Rowman and Littlefield).

Turner, B. (1998). 'Ageing and generational conflicts: A reply to Sarah Irwin', *British Journal of Sociology*, 49, 2, 299–304.

Twenge, J. M. and Campbell, S. M. (2008). 'Generational differences in psychological traits and their impact on the workplace', *Journal of Managerial Psychology*, 23, 8, 862–77.

US Census Bureau (2009). *United States Census 2009*, Retrieved 19 October 2009 (http://www.census.gov/).

U.S. Department of Labor (2008). 'Unemployed persons by marital status, race, Hispanic or Latino ethnicity, age, and sex'. Available at: http://www.bls.gov/cps/cpsaat24.pdf. Retrieved 23 December 2009.

US Equal Employment Opportunity Commission (2008). *The Age Discrimination in Employment Act of 1967*, Retrieved 22 September 2009 (http://www.eeoc.gov/policy/adea.html).

US Office of Management and Budget (2008). *Detailed Information on the Senior Community Service Employment Program Assessment.* Retrieved 2 October 2009 (http://www.whitehouse.gov/OMB/expectmore/detail/10000328.2003.html).

United Nations (2008). *Unemployed Persons by Marital Status, Race, Hispanic or Latino Ethnicity, Age, and Sex,* Retrieved October 23, 2009, http://www.bls.gov/cps/cpsaat24.pdf).

United Nations (2009). *World Population 2008.* (New York: United Nations, Department of Economic and Social Affairs).

Urwin, P. (2004). *Age Matters: A Review of Existing Survey Evidence,* Department of Trade and Industry Employment Relations Research Series No 24 (London: DTI).

van Maanen, J. and Schein, E. H. (1979). 'Toward a theory of organizational socialization', *Research in Organizational Behavior,* 1, 209–64.

Vansteenkiste, M., Duriez, B., Simons, J. and Soenens, B. (2006). 'Materialistic values and well-being among business students: Further evidence of their detrimental effect' *Journal of Applied Social Psychology,* 36, 2892–908.

Vickerstaff, S., Loretto, W., Billings, J., Brown, P., Mitton, L., Parkin, T. and White, P. (2008). *Encouraging labour market activity among 60–64 year olds,* Department for Work and Pensions Research Report No 531.

Villosio, C. (2008). *Working Conditions of an Ageing Workforce* (Dublin: European Foundation for the Improvement of Living and Working Conditions).

Vogler-Ludwig, K. (2005). *Ageing and Employment: Identification of Good Practice,* Project Report (München: Economix).

Vroom, V. (1964). *Work and Motivation* (New York: Wiley).

Wagner, D. (2007, Summer). 'Managing an age-diverse workforce', *MIT Sloan Management Review,* 48, 4, 9.

Waldman, D. A. and Avolio, B. J. (1986). 'A meta-analysis of age differences in job performance', *Journal of Applied Psychology,* 71, 1, 33–8.

Walker, A. (1999). *Combating Age Barriers in Employment – A Guide to Good Practice* (Dublin: European Foundation).

Walker, A. (2005). *Understanding Quality of Life in Old Age* (New York: Open University Press).

Walker, N., Fain, W. B., Fisk, A. D. and McGuire, C. L. (1997). 'Aging and decision making: driving-related problem solving', *Human Factors: Journal of the Human Factors and Ergonomics Society,* 39, 3, 438–44.

Walker-Bone, K. and Cooper, C. (2005). 'Hard work never hurt anyone: Or did it? A review of occupational associations with soft tissue musculoskeletal disorders of the neck and upper limb', *Ann Rheum Dis,* 64, 10, 1391–6.

Walker, H., Grant, D., Meadows, M. and Cook, I. (2007). 'Women's Experiences and Perceptions of Age Discrimination in Employment: Implications for Research', *Social Policy and Society,* 6, 37–48.

Walker, E. A. and Webster, B. J. (2007). 'Gender, age and self-employment: some things change, some things stay the same', *Women in Management Review,* 22, 2.

Wang, M., Adams, G., Beehr, T. and Schultz, K. (2009). 'Bridge employment and retirement: Issues and opportunities during the latter part of one's career', in S. G. Baugh and S. E. Sullivan (eds). *Maintaining Focus, Energy and Options over the Career* (Charlotte, North Carolina: Information Age Publishing).

Warhurst, C. and Nickson, D. (2007). 'Employee experience of aesthetic labour in retail and hospitality', *Work, Employment and Society,* 21, 103–20.

Warr, P. (2001). 'Age and work behaviour: Physical attributes, cognitive abilities, knowledge, personality traits and motives', *International Review of Industrial and Organizational Psychology, Volume,* 16, 1–36.

Warr, P. and Fay, D. (2001). 'Age and personal initiative at work', *European Journal of Work and Organisational Psychology*, 10, 3, 343–53.

Warr, P. and Pennington, J. (1993). 'Views about age discrimination and older workers', in P. Taylor, A. Walker, B. Casey et al. (eds). *Age and Employment: Policies, Attitudes and Practices* (London: Institute of Personnel Management).

Waters, T. R. (2004). 'National efforts to identify research issues related to prevention of work-related musculosekeletal disorders', *Journal of Electromyography and Kinesiology*, 14, 7–12.

Weber, Max (1904/1949). 'Objectivity in social science and social policy', *in Max Weber on* The Methodology of the Social Sciences (eds/trans. E. A. Shils and H. A. Finch) (Glencoe, Illinois, Free Press), pp. 49–112.

Weckerle, J. R. and Shultz, K.S. (1999). 'Influences on the Bridge Employment Decision among Older USA Workers', *Journal of Occupational and Organizational Psychology*, 72, 317–29.

Welzel, C. and Inglehart, R. (2005). *Modernization, Cultural Change, and Democracy* (York: Cambridge University Press).

Wenger, E. (1998). *Communities of Practice: Learning, Meaning, and Identity* (Cambridge: Cambridge University Press).

Westerholm, P. and Kilborn, A. (1997). 'Aging and work: The occupational health services' perspective', *Occupational end Environmental Medicine*, 54, 11, 777–80.

Weyers, S., Peter, R., Boggild, H., Jeppesen, H. J. and Siegrist, J. (2006). 'Psychosocial work stress is associated with poor self-rated health in Danish nurses: A test of the effort-reward imbalance model', *Scandinavian Journal of Caring Sciences*, 20, 1, 26–34.

Whiteoak, J. W., Crawford, N. G. and Mapstone, R. H. (2006). 'Impact of gender and generational differences in work values and attitudes in an Arab culture', *Thunderbird International Business Review*, 48, 1, 77–91.

Whitley, R. (2005). 'How national are business systems?', in G. Morgan, R. Whitley and E. Moen (eds). *Changing Capitalisms? Internationalisation, Institutional Change and Systems of Economic Organisation* (Oxford: Oxford University Press).

Whitley, R. (1999). *Divergent Capitalisms: The Social Structuring and Change of Business Systems* (Oxford: Oxford University Press).

Wilde, O. (1894). 'Phrases and philosophies for the use of the young'. *The Chameleon, December* 1894.

Williamson, J. B. and Higo, M. (2009). 'Why Japanese workers remain in the labor force so Long: Lessons for the United States?', *Journal of Cross-Cultural Gerontology*, 24, 4, 321–37.

Wilson, F. (2004). *Organizational Behaviour and Work, A Critical Introduction* (Oxford: Oxford University Press).

Wilson, T. and Davies, G. (1999). 'The changing career strategies of managers', *Career Development International*, 4, 2, 101–7.

Winn, F. and Bittner, A. (2005). 'Extended framework for older worker competence: Effects of cognitive complexity on performance', *International Congress Series*, 1280, 35–40.

Wise, S. (2003). *Older Nurses and Working Hours: Some Indicative Findings from the Work-Life Balance and Careers in NHS Nursing and Midwifery Project* (Edinburgh: Napier University).

M. Wong, E. Gardiner, W. Lang and L. Couon (2008). 'Generational differences in personality and motivation: Do they exist and what are the implications for the workplace?', *Journal of Managerial Psychology*, 23, 8, 878–90.

Woods, R. H. and Sciarini, M. P. (1995). 'Diversity programs in chain restaurants', *Cornell Hotel & Restaurant Administration Quarterly*, 36, 18–24.

Wright, P., Ferris, S. P., Hiller, J. S. and Kroll, M. (1995). 'Competitiveness through Management of Diversity: Effects on Stock Price Valuation', *Academy of Management Journal*, 38, 272–88.

Zanoni, P. and Janssens, J. M. (2003). 'Deconstructing difference: The rhetoric of human resource managers' diversity discourses', *Organization Studies*, 25, 1, 55–74.

Zemke, R., Raines, C. and Filipczak, B. (2000). *Generations at Work: Managing the Clash of Veterans, Boomers, Xers and Nexters in your Workplace* (New York: Amacom).

# Index